S0-BWU-752

The Future of Social Security

Studies in Social Economics
TITLES PUBLISHED

STUDIES IN SOCIAL ECONOMICS

Alicia H. Munnell

The Future of Social Security

THE BROOKINGS INSTITUTION
Washington, D.C.

Library of Congress Cataloging in Publication Data:

Munnell, Alicia Haydock.
  The future of social security.

  (Studies in social economics)
  Includes bibliographical references and index.
  1. Social security—United States.   I. Title.
II. Series.
HD7125.M75   368.4'00973   76-51883
ISBN 0-8157-5896-0
ISBN 0-8157-5895-2 pbk.

9 8 7 6 5 4 3 2 1

THE BROOKINGS INSTITUTION is an independent organization devoted to nonpartisan research, education, and publication in economics, government, foreign policy, and the social sciences generally. Its principal purposes are to aid in the development of sound public policies and to promote public understanding of issues of national importance.

The Institution was founded on December 8, 1927, to merge the activities of the Institute for Government Research, founded in 1916, the Institute of Economics, founded in 1922, and the Robert Brookings Graduate School of Economics and Government, founded in 1924.

The Board of Trustees is responsible for the general administration of the Institution, while the immediate direction of the policies, program, and staff is vested in the President, assisted by an advisory committee of the officers and staff. The bylaws of the Institution state: "It is the function of the Trustees to make possible the conduct of scientific research, and publication, under the most favorable conditions, and to safeguard the independence of the research staff in the pursuit of their studies and in the publication of the results of such studies. It is not a part of their function to determine, control, or influence the conduct of particular investigations or the conclusions reached."

The President bears final responsibility for the decision to publish a manuscript as a Brookings book. In reaching his judgment on the competence, accuracy, and objectivity of each study, the President is advised by the director of the appropriate research program and weighs the views of a panel of expert outside readers who report to him in confidence on the quality of the work. Publication of a work signifies that it is deemed a competent treatment worthy of public consideration but does not imply endorsement of conclusions or recommendations.

The Institution maintains its position of neutrality on issues of public policy in order to safeguard the intellectual freedom of the staff. Hence interpretations or conclusions in Brookings publications should be understood to be solely those of the authors and should not be attributed to the Institution, to its trustees, officers, or other staff members, or to the organizations that support its research.

Foreword

Social security, the largest and probably least controversial of the federal government's social and economic programs, continues to enjoy broad public support as it has since 1935. However, recent projections of a dramatic increase in costs are eroding confidence in its success in the future.

Alicia Munnell's study delineates the issues facing social security today and explores various options for reform intended to ensure that it will remain financially stable. Its financial stability is now threatened by the growing number of aged persons as a proportion of the working population and a benefit formula that, for those still working, adjusts for inflation twice, once in the computation of benefits and again in the computation of the taxable wage base. Both threats can be overcome, in the author's view, as can various inequities in the system. She concludes that the system is in no danger of collapse and that the difficulty lies in choosing among solutions. She regards the crisis as an opportunity for wide-ranging reform and for more rationally integrating the social security system with other retirement income programs.

A draft of the manuscript of this book was made available as a background paper for a conference of experts on social security held at the Brookings Institution in June 1976. Chapter 8 is a summary of the conference discussion.

Alicia H. Munnell, an assistant vice president and economist for the Federal Reserve Bank of Boston, wrote this book as a member of the Brookings associated staff. She is grateful for the support of the bank's president, Frank E. Morris, and its director of research, Robert W. Eisenmenger, and for the assistance of Julie O'Connor, Teresa Amott, and Ann Connolly of the bank's staff.

The author is also grateful to all those who read and commented on parts of the manuscript, among them Henry J. Aaron, Carolyn Shaw Bell,

Michael Boskin, John A. Brittain, John J. Carroll, Peter Diamond, Milton Glanz, William Hsiao, Richard A. Musgrave, John L. Palmer, Joseph A. Pechman, Michael K. Taussig, and Larry Thompson, and the participants in the 1976 conference of experts. The author is indebted to Evelyn Fisher, who purged the manuscript of numerous errors; to Claire Goldman and Anna Estle, who typed the manuscript; to Diane Iredell, who edited it; and to Florence Robinson, who prepared the index.

This is the thirteenth publication in the Brookings series of Studies in Social Economics, a program of research on selected problems in the fields of health, education, social security, and welfare.

The views expressed here are the author's alone and should not be ascribed to the officers, trustees, and staff members of the Brookings Institution, to the Federal Reserve Bank of Boston, to the Social Security Administration, or to any of those who were consulted or who commented on the manuscript.

GILBERT Y. STEINER
Acting President

January 1977
Washington, D.C.

Contents

ix

xi

Appendix Tables

Figures

chapter one *Introduction*

Today's social security program covers over 90 percent of the working population and pays more than $83 billion annually in benefits to the retired, the disabled, their dependents and survivors. Current members of the system, both working and retired, have been promised future benefits exceeding $4 trillion. A program of this size demands close scrutiny of its expansion and careful analysis of its potential economic impact.

The growth of the social security program in recent years has been unprecedented. Between 1966 and 1976 total benefit payments ballooned from over $20 billion to over $80 billion—a fourfold increase. Even after adjustment for inflation, benefit payments doubled in the decade. During the last five years of the decade, real benefits rose 50 percent while real gross national product rose only 13 percent.[1]

To finance the rise in benefits, social security taxes have significantly increased. In 1965, employers and employees paid a combined tax of 7.25 percent on the first $4,800 of wages; by 1975, the combined tax had increased to 11.7 percent of the first $14,100. By 1977, the maximum taxable wage had increased to $16,500. In the twelve-year period the maximum tax levied on a covered worker has climbed from $348 to $1,930, more than a fivefold increase.

Recently, the social security system has come under considerable criticism as opponents and supporters alike question its long-run financial viability in the face of dramatic demographic shifts and an indexed benefit formula that overcompensates future retirees for cost-of-living increases. The large forecast deficits are a legitimate cause for concern, and without modification of the existing program, social security will require extraor-

---

1. The figures refer to fiscal years and include health insurance benefits as well as old age, survivors, and disability benefits.

dinarily high tax rates after the turn of the century. If social security is to be successful, it must adapt to a changing economic, social, and institutional environment.

These changes and their implications for social security are the subject of this book. Since the primary emphasis is on the old age and survivors portion (OASI) of the old age, survivors, disability, and health insurance (OASDHI) program, little attention is given to the disability program and none to health insurance. (Table 1-1 compares the size and importance of OASI with the health and disability portions of the program.)

Organization of the Volume

Traditionally, social security has combined the goals of earnings replacement and income maintenance. In 1939 the simple wage-replacement role of social security was supplemented by a welfare role with the implementation of the minimum benefit, dependents' benefits, and a steeply progressive benefit formula. A stress on social adequacy was appropriate to a social insurance program that provided the major portion of retirement income to the country's aged. However, the income maintenance role of social security is now duplicated by the supplemental security income (SSI) program, which provides needs-related benefits to the low-income elderly. Furthermore, the wage-replacement role of social security is often duplicated by private pension programs, which were considerably strengthened by the Employee Retirement Income Security Act of 1974. The success of both this program and SSI has implications for the desirable limits of social security benefits. These implications are discussed in chapter 2.

Chapter 3 examines the overindexing of the benefit structure through the overadjustment for inflation and outlines the issues that must be resolved to correct this error. It explores in detail the existing benefit system and the possibility of moving toward a proportional benefit structure. The minimum benefit in light of the introduction of SSI and the dependents' benefits in light of the greater number of women in the labor force are also discussed.

Chapter 4 focuses on recent evidence that social security provisions affect retirement behavior. The retirement test and the availability of benefits at the age of sixty-two encourage withdrawal from the labor force. In view of the improved health and longevity of the elderly it is difficult to justify these provisions. Furthermore, the costs of the social security sys-

Table 1-1. Distribution of OASDHI Benefits, by Program and Type of Beneficiary, Fiscal Year 1976

Program and type of beneficiary	Benefits (billions of dollars)	Percent of benefits
Old age and survivors insurance	61.8	74.2
Retired workers	40.5	48.7
Dependents and survivors	21.1	25.3
Special, 72 and over	0.2	0.2
Disability insurance	9.2	11.1
Health insurance	12.3	14.7
Total	83.3	100.0

Source: Social Security Administration, Office of Research and Statistics.

tem are extremely sensitive to the ratio of retirees to workers. Both the projected imbalance between the number of workers and number of retired and the improved health and life expectancy of the elderly argue not only for reversing the trend toward early retirement but for extending the retirement age. The chapter concludes with alternative measures to encourage work force participation by the elderly.

Chapter 5 deals with both the form and the adequacy of social security financing. The first section evaluates the appropriateness of relying on the payroll tax as the primary source of revenue. The choice of financing, by payroll tax or general revenue, depends on the nature of the system; as long as social security pursues the dual objectives of income maintenance and earnings replacement, there is an argument for instituting general revenue financing. However, if the welfare role of OASI declined and benefits were proportional to contributions, the payroll tax (with exemptions for low-income workers) would be the appropriate tax. (Welfare support for the aged would be provided through the SSI program, financed by general revenues.)

The second part of chapter 5 examines both the short- and long-run financing problems of social security. The current shortage of funds, attributable primarily to a prolonged recession and the subsequent downward shift in the trend growth of real wages, will require increased revenues within the next few years. Consideration is given to the alternatives of raising the tax rate, increasing the limit on maximum taxable earnings, transferring health insurance revenues to OASDI, and depending on general revenue financing. A projection of nearly a 30 percent combined employer-employee OASDI tax rate by the year 2050 has brought into question the long-run viability of the program. Almost half of the increase can be attributed to the rising ratio of benefits to preretirement earnings because of an overadjustment of benefits for inflation. The remainder of the increase comes from the changing ratio of the aged to the working population—there are now over thirty beneficiaries for every hundred workers, but it is estimated that by the year 2050 there will be fifty-one beneficiaries for every hundred workers. The increase in costs caused by demographic change is inevitable. However, that caused by overindexing is unnecessary, and the impact of this irrational provision on the costs of the system makes the need for immediate remedial action urgent.

Chapter 6 discusses the potentially important effect of social security on the way people save and the effect of that on capital accumulation. If individuals view their social security contributions as saving, they tend not to accumulate other saving. However, their social security contributions are not accumulated in a fund as are private savings, but are paid out in benefits to the currently retired. Therefore, reduction of individual private saving in response to social security reduces the economy's total saving and its rate of capital accumulation. Empirical evidence seems to indicate that social security contributions have had a negative impact on saving, although in the past the net impact on the economy has been mitigated by an increase in saving effort resulting from a constant lowering of the retirement age. The advantages and disadvantages of accumulating reserves in the social security trust fund are discussed in the context of forecast capital needs and the limited investment opportunities for fund assets.

Chapter 7 presents options for modifying the social security program. Chapter 8 summarizes the discussions at a conference held at the Brookings Institution in June 1976, to discuss the basic issues raised in the earlier chapters and to evaluate the options for the future of social security in the United States.

chapter two **The Role of Social Security**

The social security system has undergone many changes in role and scope since Congress passed the Social Security Act in 1935. Over the same period other provisions for retirement income, in both the public and the private sectors, have also seen significant development (see table 2-1). We now have a three-tiered system of retirement income maintenance: (1) welfare programs, which provide a minimum guaranteed income to the needy elderly; (2) compulsory public contributory programs; and (3) private provisions for retirement comprised of private pensions and individual saving.

Programs in these three levels dispense billions of dollars in benefits every year, but coordination of the programs has been haphazard. If the overall system is to operate properly, each level should play a specific role, distinct from but integrated rationally with the other two. At present, however, there are costly overlaps, and in many cases the tiers work at cross-purposes.

Individual Equity and Social Adequacy

The 1935 Social Security Act set up a system that bore a much stronger resemblance to a private insurance plan than to social security as we know it today. At that time, the accumulation of trust funds was planned and the principle of a fair rate of return to each worker was stressed.[1] The concept that each worker should receive at least as much in benefits as he had contributed was considered crucial to public acceptance of a compulsory program and has since come to be known as the individual equity goal of social insurance. Individual equity is naturally the major criterion by which

1. Joseph A. Pechman, Henry J. Aaron, and Michael K. Taussig, *Social Security: Perspectives for Reform* (Brookings Institution, 1968), pp. 32–33.

5

Table 2-1. Retirement Beneficiaries under Major Types of Programs, Selected Years, 1940–74

Thousands

	Public plans						Private plans
		Federal government			State and local government	Total[b]	
Year	OASDI	Railroad retirement	Civil service	Other federal[a]			
1940	77.2	102.0	47.4	67.2	113.0	406.8	160
1945	591.8	129.1	62.5	99.0	155.0	1,037.4	310
1950	1,918.1	174.8	111.0	127.4	222.0	2,553.3	450
1955	5,443.2	329.2	164.9	166.0	335.0	6,438.3	980
1960	10,309.7	440.0	263.3	212.1	535.0	11,760.1	1,780
1965	13,918.2	498.4	359.4	401.9	725.0	15,902.9	2,750
1970	16,869.6	552.5	477.1	645.4	1,085.0	19,629.6	4,740
1971	17,402.5	557.9	515.6	696.9	1,165.0	20,337.9	5,180
1972	17,953.3	560.1	553.1	750.4	1,241.0	21,057.9	5,550
1973	18,685.7	558.8	623.7	802.6	1,320.0	21,990.8	6,080
1974	19,408.9	554.0	700.1	857.2	1,395.0	22,915.2	6,390

Sources: Public plans, Social Security Administration, *Social Security Bulletin, Annual Statistical Supplement*, various issues; private plans, Alfred M. Skolnik, "Private Pension Plans, 1950–74," *Social Security Bulletin*, vol. 39 (June 1976), p. 4.

a. Includes beneficiaries under veterans' programs.

b. These figures overstate the number of beneficiaries under public programs because, as some people are covered under more than one plan, there is duplication between categories.

a private plan is judged, since workers would not choose to participate in a plan that failed to recompense them fairly for their contributions.

In a social insurance plan, however, where universal and compulsory protection is the goal, individual equity can be deemphasized and social adequacy substituted. Social adequacy is essentially a welfare criterion, which measures benefits not against lifetime contributions but rather against a standard of living beneath which society feels no one should fall. In cases where an individual's contributions do not entitle him to the socially desired level of benefits, individual equity and social adequacy conflict.

The 1939 amendments to the Social Security Act resolved the conflict in favor of social adequacy, because the needs of millions of the elderly were not being met by the states' old age assistance programs.[2] At that time, the 1935 guarantee of a fair rate of return was eliminated and benefits were based on average earnings during a shorter period of coverage than

2. Although the 1935 Social Security Act addressed the issue of social adequacy by weighting the benefit formula in favor of low earners, it was in the 1939 amendments that the social adequacy goal was emphasized.

the original base of lifetime contributions. The principle of individual equity was further weakened by the 1939 provision for dependents' benefits.

Over the years since 1939, the minimum benefit, then a purely administrative technicality, has been justified on grounds of social adequacy and is now very high relative to minimum contributions. In addition, dependents' benefits have grown and a progressive benefit structure has been instituted. As a result, today's benefit structure is heavily weighted in favor of those low-earnings workers who contribute the least to the system.

The prevalence of these social adequacy components has caused some economists to view the system as an annual income transfer from the working population to the aged. Within this framework, the tax and the benefits are evaluated separately, with the inevitable conclusion that the payroll tax is extremely regressive and imposes a heavy financial burden on the working poor. The major policy implication in this evaluation is that income for the aged should not be financed by a payroll tax whose regressivity weakens the effectiveness of the transfer but should be financed through general revenues by the more progressive income tax.

On the other hand, many would argue that it is difficult to rationalize the design of the present social security program from a perspective of an annual transfer program.[3] The goal of an annual transfer scheme is to channel funds to relatively poor people and not to award benefits on the basis of contributions. Since most of the elderly are poor, a social security pension could accomplish the transfer, but there would be no rationale for higher benefits for those who contributed more. A purely redistributive goal would be achieved most efficiently through an expanded means-tested program such as the supplemental security income program instituted in 1974.

Individual Equity vs. Social adequacy

Many observers find it more useful to view social security as primarily a compulsory saving mechanism with certain insurance attributes rather than an annual transfer from workers to retirees. The rationale for such a program is twofold: paternalism and market failure. People's failure to provide adequately for their retirement needs can often be attributed to a myopic view of the trade-off between present and future consumption. In addition, many people simply lack the information and investment channels to help them accumulate and protect their savings for retirement.

In a completely laissez-faire world, there would be no reason to interfere with anyone's saving decisions. Those who did not save enough dur-

3. This is based upon notes prepared by Peter A. Diamond, as part of his work for the Consultant Panel on Social Security, 1975–76.

ing their working years or who invested unwisely could simply be made to pay the consequences by suffering in poverty during their retirement. However, since our society has certain humanitarian values, the burden of support for those who have not provided for themselves falls on friends, relatives, or society as a whole. Social security can be seen as a way of forcing workers to set aside a certain amount of income for retirement consumption and ensuring that such provisions will be adequate, thus preventing the burden of support from falling on others.

Low-income workers who cannot save enough of their meager earnings present a special problem. It is not feasible to argue that those who cannot satisfy even their basic needs of food, clothing, and shelter should be forced to save some of their income for retirement. Fortunately, mechanisms are now available outside the social security program, on both the tax and benefit sides, to alleviate the burden on the poor. The earned income credit, introduced in 1975 under the individual income tax, offsets the payroll tax for some low-income families, and the supplemental security income program augments social security benefits for the low-income aged. With these special provisions for the poor, social security could function as a compulsory saving program with emphasis on individual equity and play the central role in the three-tiered system of retirement income.

The Three-Tiered System

Since earnings from work represent the major source of income for most Americans, the cessation of those earnings upon retirement from the labor force imposes an economic hardship, which society has tried to lessen through a variety of public and private programs. This network of programs is composed of three tiers: needs-related programs for the poorest retirees; compulsory earnings-related social insurance, which replaces wages for the largest segment of the retired population; and private provisions for retirement through pension plans, savings, and insurance.

The first tier of retirement benefits is designed to ensure an adequate minimum income to retirees falling below a certain standard of living. It is composed of the federal supplemental security income program and the state public assistance programs, which in many cases supplement the federal minimum income guarantee. In the second tier of retirement benefits are the federal social security programs (OASDI) and various other federal pension plans such as the civil service retirement system, the railroad retirement system, and military pensions.[4] Benefits in each of these programs bear a relation to earnings and length of service in covered employment and are free of the means test imposed in the first tier. The third tier, individual efforts to ensure adequate income in the retirement years, is made up of a variety of private plans, supported by public policies that regulate and promote them.

The First Tier: Welfare Programs

Before 1974, most states provided for the needy aged, disabled, and blind through their federally supported public assistance programs. Although the federal government shared in the costs through grants-in-aid, the programs were administered at the state or local level. Each state set its own benefit levels and eligibility requirements; therefore the amount of support furnished these groups varied widely among states. Since state public assistance programs were largely independent of federal policy, their existence did not lessen the perceived burden of the income adequacy principle of social security. In fact, the growth of social security held down the number of old age assistance recipients, since social security provided enough income to raise its beneficiaries above the need threshold (see table 2-2).

Today, however, the welfare system has been greatly strengthened by the enactment in 1972 of the supplemental security income (SSI) program, which replaces the old network of state systems with a single, federally financed and operated program of cash payments to the elderly, blind, and disabled. Under SSI, which is administered by the Social Security Administration and fully financed from general revenues, benefit levels, eligibility conditions, and means tests are uniform nationwide. States have the option of supplementing SSI payments and are required to do so for those current recipients who would receive less under SSI than under the former federal-state-local system.

Since SSI is a welfare program, applicants must prove need by conforming to certain income and asset limitations. There is no requirement of employment in covered industry, and the program pays no survivors' bene-

4. Military retired pay is based solely on length of service and earnings and thus belongs in the second tier. Other military programs, such as those based on degree of disability or those that incorporate income and asset limitations, may more appropriately belong in the first tier.

Table 2-2. Percent of Aged Population Receiving Social Security Benefits and Public Old Age Assistance, Selected Years, 1940–74

Year	OASDHI	OAA or SSI[a]	OASDHI and OAA or SSI[a]	Percent of OAA or SSI recipients receiving OASDHI[a]
1940	0.7	21.7	n.a.	n.a.
1945	6.2	19.4	n.a.	n.a.
1950	16.4	22.4	2.2	9.8
1955	39.4	17.9	3.4	19.2
1960	61.6	14.1	4.1	28.5
1965	75.2	11.7	5.2	44.7
1970	85.5	10.4	6.3	60.4
1971	84.9	10.2	6.2	61.4
1972	85.6	9.6	6.1	63.3
1973	86.7	8.9	5.6	62.5
1974	88.3	9.6	6.8	70.8

Source: *Social Security Bulletin, Annual Statistical Supplement, 1974* (GPO, n.d.), p. 54.
n.a. Not available.
a. Old age assistance was succeeded by supplemental security income in 1974.

fits, so dependents of recipients must meet SSI requirements in their own right. As of July 1976, SSI guarantees income of $167.80 a month for one recipient and $251.80 a month for an eligible couple. The first $20 of additional monthly income does not affect the benefit. However, any un-earned income (with the exception of the $20) in excess of the monthly guarantee reduces the benefit dollar for dollar, and monthly wages over $65 reduce it by 50 cents for each dollar of earned income.

Supplemental security income also imposes a limit on the asset holdings of recipients. Briefly, eligibility is confined to those whose nonexcluded assets do not exceed $1,500 ($2,250 for couples). Excluded assets include homes (recent law eliminates value limitation), household goods, personal effects, and automobiles with a market value under $1,200. Life insurance policies whose face value is less than $1,500 are also excluded. (The rules governing countable income and asset holdings are generally quite complex and unwieldy; this description is not intended to be comprehensive.)[5]

The SSI program must be viewed as more than a logical and equitable revamping of the existing public assistance programs. In 1973, the year

5. For a more detailed discussion of SSI provisions see Robert M. Ball, "Social Security Amendments of 1972: Summary and Legislative History," *Social Security Bulletin*, vol. 36 (March 1973), pp. 23–25.

before SSI became effective, there were 1.8 million aged covered by the states' old age assistance programs. Original estimates projected that the number of aged eligible for the new SSI benefits in January 1974 would increase to 4.9 million, or 23 percent of the population aged sixty-five and over.[6] The actual experience was somewhat less dramatic but did show a significant 36 percent increase in beneficiaries to 2.5 million (see table 2-3). In addition to the increase in beneficiaries the average payment level increased 15 percent, these two factors resulting in a 45 percent growth in expenditures on welfare to the aged with the introduction of SSI.

The existence of this federal minimum income guarantee promises to have a profound impact on the future role of social security. Since SSI was designed as a floor beneath which no elderly person's income could fall, it can be argued that it weakens the rationale for the welfare or social adequacy role of social security, freeing the program to restructure benefits along less progressive lines. That 70 percent of aged SSI recipients have some income from social security suggests that SSI and social security are trying to fulfill the same objective for the same target population.[7] However, SSI is a more efficient vehicle for meeting this welfare criterion than social security, because a means test ensures that funds actually go to those with a demonstrable need. Progressive social security benefits distort the contributions-to-benefits ratio in the interest of social adequacy but actually augment the income of many elderly people who are relatively well off because of unearned income or a second pension. In effect, many who should be ineligible receive welfare through a social security program.

Moreover, lack of proper coordination between SSI and social security creates serious distortions and inequities in the income maintenance system for the aged. Low-wage retirees currently receive negligible returns from their lifetime of payroll tax payments. For example, consider a couple entitled to social security benefits of $252 a month. (This benefit is considerably above the minimum monthly benefit of $162 for a couple.) If they had no other sources of income and few assets other than their own income, they would receive a $20 supplement from SSI,[8] bringing their total monthly income to $272. If they had never contributed to social security, SSI alone would guarantee them $252 a month. An additional

6. Thomas G. Staples, "Supplemental Security Income: The Aged Eligible," *Social Security Bulletin*, vol. 36 (July 1973), p. 33.

7. *Social Security Bulletin*, vol. 39 (June 1976), p. 80.

8. Their benefit is calculated by subtracting from the monthly guarantee of $252 all social security benefits in excess of the $20 exception. Therefore, their benefit is equal to $252 − ($252 − $20) = $20.

Table 2-3. Comparison of Benefits under Old Age Assistance in 1973 and
Supplemental Security Income in 1974

Program and date	Recipients (thousands)	Average monthly benefit (dollars)	Yearly payments (millions of dollars)
State OAA, December 1973[a]	1,820	76.15	1,743
Federal SSI and state supplements, December 1974[a]	2,478	87.84	2,525
Federally administered	2,286	92.32[b]	2,436
State administered	192	34.60	89

Sources: James C. Callison, "Early Experience under the Supplemental Security Income Program," *Social Security Bulletin*, vol. 37 (June 1974), table 1; Robert J. Myers, *Social Security* (Irwin for McCahan Foundation, 1975); and *Social Security Bulletin*, various issues.

a. The federally administered average benefit reflects the basic SSI payment and federally administered state supplements. The state administered average benefit reflects state administered supplements to those who had received old age assistance but did not qualify for SSI—states are required to provide supplements so that no decrease in payments occurs. Thus, total number of recipients is the sum of the recipients of the federally administered and state administered programs, and total average benefit is a weighted average of the federally administered and state administered figures.

b. October 1974 through December 1974.

$20 a month is all they would receive from a lifetime of payroll tax payments.

The flaw in coordination arises because all unearned income in excess of $20 a month is deducted dollar for dollar from the basic SSI benefit. This is equivalent to a 100 percent marginal tax rate.[9] The inequity would be alleviated if the tax rate were reduced to 50 percent.[10] Every low-income beneficiary would then be better off in retirement as a result of social security contributions. For instance, the couple in the example would forfeit only 50 cents of SSI for each dollar of social security income above the $20 allowance and therefore could retain $136[11] of its SSI guarantee, ending up with a total monthly retirement income of $388 ($252 from social security and $136 from SSI).

One further important difficulty exists in coordinating SSI with social security. The minimum age for SSI benefits is currently sixty-five, which means that there is no supplemental support for the millions of OASDI recipients who elect early retirement benefits. Lowering SSI eligibility to the age of sixty-two, in line with the social security early retirement option, would solve the problem but would increase the use of SSI payments to

9. From the standpoint of efficiency, use of a high marginal tax rate is not a flaw. Taxing all other income at as high a rate as possible (subject to work incentive considerations) ensures that limited welfare funds are funneled to those most in need.

10. Lowering the implicit tax on social security benefits has been suggested by Michael K. Taussig, "The Social Security Retirement Program and Welfare Reform," *Studies in Public Welfare*, paper 7, prepared for the Subcommittee on Fiscal Policy of the Joint Economic Committee, 93:1 (GPO, 1973), pp. 14–39.

11. With a 50 percent tax on social security benefits in excess of $20, the couple's benefit would be calculated as $252 − 0.5 ($252 − $20) = $136.

offset the actuarial reduction of benefits for early retirees and would thus introduce further inequities.

There has been concern that SSI might grow into a huge guaranteed income program covering much broader categories of need than it does at present, and it has been suggested that SSI threatens to replace social security entirely.[12] However, as long as it remains a noncompulsory, noncontributory welfare program subject to a means test, it is difficult to imagine how it could serve as a public pension plan—particularly if the present area of overlap was eliminated.

The Second Tier: Compulsory Public Pension Plans

The major public pension plan is, of course, the old age, survivors, and disability insurance, which now covers 90 percent of the work force and which will probably continue to provide the major portion of retirement income for most of the aged. The 1968 Social Security Survey of the Aged revealed that 77 percent of all aged beneficiary units (a unit being one person or a couple) received only social security benefits, whereas 19 percent received other public or private pensions in addition to social security and 4 percent received other public pension benefits only.[13] The other public pension plans can be divided into two groups: those that are essentially independent of social security, in particular the civil service retirement system; and those designed to build on social security income, such as military retired pay or railroad retirement. State and local government pensions fall into either of the two groups.

During 1975, 100 million people worked in OASDI-covered employment and the system paid out over $55 billion in retirement benefits.[14] Taken as an aggregate, the state and local government systems were the next largest public pension program, with approximately 9 million contributors and $5.7 billion in recurring benefit payments.[15] The civil service

12. Robert J. Myers, "With SSI, Who Needs Social Security?" *Challenge*, vol. 16 (November–December 1973), p. 59.

13. Social Security Administration, Office of Research and Statistics, *Demographic and Economic Characteristics of the Aged: 1968 Social Security Survey*, Research Report 45 (GPO, 1975), p. 71.

14. Social Security Administration, Office of Research and Statistics, unpublished data; and *Social Security Bulletin*, vol. 39 (June 1976), p. 36.

15. Benefit and contributor data refer to 1974. See Bureau of the Census, *Finances of Employee-Retirement Systems of State and Local Governments in 1973–74*, GF 74 no. 2 (Department of Commerce, 1975), p. 3 for benefit amount, and table 4, from which contributors were estimated.

retirement system numbered 2.7 million contributors and paid out roughly $7 billion in retirement benefits. The armed forces retirement program, which is noncontributory, supported $6 billion in retirement benefits. Finally, the railroad retirement system's 550,000 contributors provided over $3 billion in retirement benefit payments in 1975.[16] Each of these programs are briefly described below. The main issue in the coordination of social security and the other public pension plans is the incidence of dual beneficiaries, people who are eligible to collect benefits under more than one system. If social security benefits were tied strictly to contributions, collection of simultaneous benefits would not introduce any inequities into the overall system. Under the present progressive benefit structure, however, dual beneficiaries can receive much more retirement income than the beneficiaries of a single pension plan.

CIVIL SERVICE RETIREMENT. Most civilians who work for the federal government are covered under the Civil Service Retirement Act rather than under social security. The employee contributes to the federal civil service system through a mandatory 7 percent deduction from salary. The government contributes through appropriations from general revenues and matching contributions from the employee's agency.

Civil service benefits are computed on the basis of length of service and "high-three" average salary, an average based on the three consecutive years of highest earnings. Child survivors of employees are entitled to benefits and a retiree can provide for other dependent survivors by accepting a reduced annuity.[17] Automatic cost-of-living adjustments are made biannually in accordance with increases in the consumer price index. Until October 1976, current benefits were increased by the amount of the CPI increase plus one bonus percentage point. This additional 1 percent was originally defended as a compensation for the lag in the adjustment process. However, such an offset would logically be required only once for each worker rather than each time benefits were increased. The procedure was then justified on the grounds that beneficiaries should share in any increased productivity after retirement. The bonus was finally eliminated in the fall of 1976.

---

16. The statistics on the civil service, armed forces, and railroad retirement systems were provided by the Social Security Administration and the offices of the various systems.

17. The reduction is so small—2.5 percent of the first $300 of monthly benefits and 10 percent above $300—that most of those eligible elect survivors' coverage at the time of retirement.

Many government employees also work in OASDI-covered employment at some time in their careers, attaining insured status under social security. This practice is quite common, because only five years of government service are required for full vesting under the civil service plan and only ten years of covered employment are required for fully insured status under social security. As a result of social security's minimum benefit provision and progressive benefit formula—really welfare provisions—the combined income from the two pensions can be quite high. A federal employee who works forty quarters in employment covered by social security qualifies for a monthly payment of $107.90 (the minimum benefit effective June 1976) in addition to a civil service pension. It has been estimated that 40 percent of all civil service pensioners receive cash benefits from social security.[18]

Using social security funds in such an inefficient way increases tax rates and lowers benefits for other recipients, most of whom have paid payroll taxes for many years and have no other pension. The most obvious method of resolving the dual beneficiary inequity is coverage of federal employees under social security. However, extending social security coverage to these workers may be difficult, since the civil service retirement system is intended to correspond to a private pension plan and has a broad and politically influential base of support. Elimination of the minimum benefit would solve the inequity of dual coverage. A short period of work in covered employment would then be recompensed under the stricter wage replacement criterion proposed here for the social security benefit structure.

STATE–LOCAL GOVERNMENT PENSION PLANS. Approximately three-quarters of all state and local government employees are covered under pension plans administered by their employers.[19] These plans have experienced explosive growth since 1942, as detailed in table 2-4. Between 1962 and 1974, membership expanded at an even faster pace than employment, and assets more than tripled.

Before 1951, state and local government employees were not eligible to participate in the federal social security program. Since then, various amendments to the Social Security Act have authorized state and local governments to elect coverage under OASDI for some or all of their em-

18. James R. Storey, "Public Income Transfer Programs: The Incidence of Multiple Benefits and the Issues Raised by Their Receipt," in *Studies in Public Welfare*, paper 1, prepared for the Subcommittee on Fiscal Policy of the Joint Economic Committee, 92:2 (GPO, 1972), p. 26.

19. Bureau of the Census, *Census of Governments, 1972*, vol. 6, no. 1, *Employee Retirement Systems of State and Local Governments* (GPO, 1973), pp. 1, 9.

**Table 2-4. Growth of State and Local Government Retirement Systems,
Selected Years, 1942–74**

Year	Member- ship (millions)	Current contributors (millions)	Bene- ficiaries (thousands)	Monthly payment (millions of dollars)	Average monthly payment (dollars)	End of year assets (millions of dollars)
1942	1.5	n.a.	158	11.4	72	1,865
1957	4.0	3.7	522	60.4	116	12,834
1962	5.4	5.0	739	101.4	137	23,294
1967	7.1	6.5	1,030	166.7	162	39,265
1972	9.1	8.4	1,463	326.4	223	68,760
1974	9.7	n.a.	1,627	413.1	254	87,488

Sources: Bureau of the Census, *Census of Governments, 1967*, vol. 6, no. 2, *Employee Retirement Systems of State and Local Governments* (GPO, 1968), pp. 1, 4; *Census of Governments, 1972*, vol. 6, no. 1, *Employee Retirement Systems of State and Local Governments* (GPO, 1973), p. 10; Bureau of the Census, *Finances of Employee Retirement Systems of State and Local Governments in 1973–74*, GF 74 no. 2 (GPO, 1975), tables 1, 4. All figures except those for end-of-year financial assets refer to the last months of the fiscal year.
n.a. Not available.

ployees. Since most state plans and numerous local plans now provide at least some of their membership with this coverage, the incidence of dual beneficiaries has risen and can be expected to continue to rise. In 1976, about 60 percent of state and local retirement system members were concurrently covered under social security.[20]

Dual coverage arising from integration with social security does not pose a problem for the social security system, since those workers contribute to the system just as workers in private employment and their benefits from state and local governments are generally designed as supplements to OASDI. However, employees whose systems are not integrated with social security are a cost problem for the system, since they may qualify by working the minimum amount of time in covered employment. These dual beneficiaries, like those who collect both federal civil service retirement benefits and social security, would be affected by the elimination of the minimum benefit. Their combined benefits would then more closely and equitably reflect their earnings histories.

THE RAILROAD RETIREMENT SYSTEM. The railroad retirement system, which covered 550,000 workers and had over a million beneficiaries in 1975, is a relatively small, mature pension plan whose relation to social security has grown increasingly complex over its forty-year history. The Railroad Retirement Act of 1974 was a major effort to coordinate the railroad pension plan with social security. It was estimated at the time of its

20. Social Security Administration, Office of Program Evaluation and Planning.

adoption that 40 percent of the beneficiaries on the railroad rolls were also receiving benefits under OASDHI.[21]

The problem of dual beneficiaries under railroad retirement and social security was made more acute because of the nature of the financial interchange instituted in the 1951 amendments to the Railroad Retirement Act. Under that interchange, the railroad trust fund was reimbursed each year by an amount that placed the social security program in the same financial position it would have been in if railroad employment were covered under social security.

Transfers from the OASDI trust funds to the railroad fund totaled over $9 billion at the end of 1975.[22] Nonetheless, the railroad trust fund was in a perilous financial position in the early 1970s because the amount transferred to the railroad fund on behalf of a dual beneficiary was often far less than the amount transferred for a single beneficiary. In some cases it was even less than the payroll taxes credited to the social security system.

Under the Railroad Retirement Act of 1974, railroad workers receive a two-tier benefit: the first tier, computed under the social security benefit formula, is based on the employee's combined railroad and social security service. However, any actual social security benefit the employee is entitled to as a result of work in covered employment is subtracted from that amount, thus preventing a dual payment for the same employment. The second tier, based on only railroad service and earnings, is the sum of several components, each of which reflects the different methods of treating service before and after January 1, 1975, the changeover date established by the act.

In addition, to protect beneficiaries who are eligible for dual benefits on the basis of service before 1975, a windfall benefit is paid. This payment represents the amount by which the sum of benefits arrived at by calculating benefits *separately* for railroad service and for social security credits exceeds the benefits that accrue as a result of the combined earnings.

The railroad retirement amendments were also intended to correct the overadjustment for rising prices and money wages, which has distorted the social security cost-of-living adjustment scheme. Under a decoupling plan, which applies only to tier-two benefits, automatic increases in the maxi-

21. Alfred M. Skolnik, "Restructuring the Railroad Retirement System," *Social Security Bulletin*, vol. 38 (April 1975), p. 26.
22. *Social Security Bulletin, Annual Statistical Supplement, 1974*, pp. 62, 63; *1976 Annual Report of the Board of Trustees of the Federal Old Age and Survivors Insurance and Disability Insurance Trust Funds*, H. Doc. 94-505, 94:2 (GPO, 1976), pp. 31, 33.

mum earnings base are deducted before the CPI cost-of-living factor is applied to benefits. Thus, duplicate corrections for price rises and wage increases are avoided in the tier-two benefit structure. Since the tier-one structure is corrected in the same manner as social security benefits, it will continue to be subject to the same overindexing until social security is decoupled. (See chapter 3 for a discussion of overindexing in the social security benefit structure.)

As a result of the 1974 amendments, the railroad retirement system now coordinates quite well with social security, providing an adequate level of benefits in an equitable manner. Elimination of the minimum social security benefit would not disturb this relation between the two programs.

VETERANS' PENSIONS. Since 1957, members of the armed forces have been regular contributing members of the social security system; before that time, various special provisions provided for gratuitous wage credits that entitled them to benefits and, in particular cases, entitled their survivors to survivors' benefits. Current members of the armed forces pay regular payroll taxes on earnings and, in addition, are given noncontributory wage credits of $300 for each quarter of military employment after 1956. These credits, in effect, raise the average monthly earnings used in the computation of monthly and lump-sum retirement payments by taking into account remuneration in kind.

Career soldiers earn, in addition to social security credits, simultaneous credits toward a military pension. These pensions are noncontributory and are financed from general revenues. There are no vesting provisions in this program for those with insufficient years of service to qualify for pensions (thirty years of service, or twenty years with the consent of government) so only career soldiers collect the benefits ("retired pay"). Survivors' benefits are payable in a manner analogous to that of the civil service retirement system (except that they are reduced by the amount of the spouse's social security benefit to eliminate dual survivors' benefits). Benefits are automatically adjusted for changes in the cost of living. Until 1963 the adjustment process was coupled to changes in the wage level, but the system was then decoupled and now operates much like the civil service adjustment.

For those veterans with insufficient years of service to collect retired pay, a separate program administered by the Veterans Administration pays benefits under two circumstances: payments for service-related disabilities, which are considered an earned right of disabled veterans, their dependents, and their survivors; and needs-related payments when the disability is not connected to military service (but, for example, to age).[23] Those veterans who do not qualify for retired pay or for VA pensions are considered compensated by their social security coverage. Thus, the basic retirement income for all veterans is supplied by social security, supplemented by retired pay and, in cases of need or disability, by a VA pension. In a three-tiered system, needs-related VA pensions function like SSI in fulfilling the social adequacy goal; social security provides universal, guaranteed benefits; and retired pay provides supplementary income, similar to a private pension.

The Third Tier: Private Retirement Income

Private provisions to ensure adequate retirement income take three major forms: private pension plans for employees of firms offering this benefit, individual tax-free retirement savings plans for the self-employed and for employees of firms not offering private plans, and private saving.

It is estimated that, in 1974, 29.8 million wage earners and salaried workers were covered under private employer-financed retirement plans. Coverage under private plans doubled between 1950 and 1974, from 22 percent of the private labor force to 44 percent.[24] Annual contributions to private pensions increased more than twelvefold, from $2 billion in 1950 to $25 billion in 1974. The 1974 contribution was over half of the $48 billion payroll tax payment to the OASI trust fund for the same year. Federal tax policy has encouraged the growth of pensions in several ways. Up to certain limits, employer contributions to qualified plans are tax deductible by the employer, earnings and capital gains on plan assets are tax exempt, and the employee contributions and income from such plans are not taxable to the employee until the actual distribution takes place.

By 1974, 6.4 million retirees and survivors were receiving benefits from private pension plans (table 2-5), compared to 19.7 million beneficiaries of old age and survivors insurance.[25] These beneficiaries were paid a total

23. Veterans with nonservice-connected disabilities are subject to an income and assets test. The pension is slowly phased out as income (all except 10 percent of any other retirement benefits plus the larger of the spouse's earned income or up to $1,200 of her total income) rises to $2,700, or $3,900 if the veteran has a dependent.

24. Alfred M. Skolnik, "Private Pension Plans, 1950–74," *Social Security Bulletin*, vol. 39 (June 1976), p. 4.

25. Beneficiaries of old age and survivors insurance are from *Social Security Bulletin*, vol. 39 (January 1976), p. 48.

Table 2-5. Growth of Private Pensions, Selected Years, 1950–74

	Contributions (millions of dollars)			Benefits		Reserves, end of year (billions of dollars)
Year	Total	Employer	Employee	Number of bene-ficiaries (thousands)	Amount of payments (millions of dollars)	
1950	2,080	1,750	330	450	370	12.1
1955	3,840	3,280	560	980	850	27.5
1960	5,490	4,710	780	1,780	1,720	52.0
1965	8,360	7,370	990	2,750	3,520	86.5
1970	14,000	12,580	1,420	4,740	7,360	137.1
1973	21,100	19,390	1,710	6,080	11,220	180.2
1974	25,020	23,020	2,000	6,390	12,930	191.7

Source: Alfred M. Skolnik, "Private Pension Plans, 1950–74," *Social Security Bulletin*, vol. 39 (June 1976), p. 4.

of $12.9 billion, which averages slightly more than $2,000 per recipient. Generally, men retiring in 1974 received about 37 percent of preretirement earnings in private pension benefits. An earlier sample survey of pension beneficiaries provides some information on the distribution of benefits among various recipients. Figure 2-1 shows that whereas about half of the men retiring during the year ending at mid-1970 received annual benefits between $1,000 and $3,000, 20 percent received less than $1,000 and 32 percent received over $3,000.

In spite of the rapid growth in pensions, congressional investigations in the late 1960s and early 1970s found that many plans were seriously underfunded or mismanaged and that the vesting provisions of some plans were so stringent as to deprive many employees of the retirement income upon which they had based their financial planning. In addition, it was found that many employees lost all rights to a pension when they changed employers or when their firms went bankrupt, were reorganized, or merged with others. As a result of these abuses, the third tier of retirement benefits has failed to provide many retirees with needed income security.

After many years of study, Congress passed the Employee Retirement Income Security Act of 1974, which set minimum vesting and portability standards for private plans and created the Pension Benefit Guaranty Corporation, which operates much like the Federal Deposit Insurance Corporation. The PBGC, which is financed by contributions from covered plans, is empowered to pay as much as $750 monthly to a retiree whose

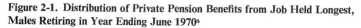

Figure 2-1. Distribution of Private Pension Benefits from Job Held Longest, Males Retiring in Year Ending June 1970ᵃ

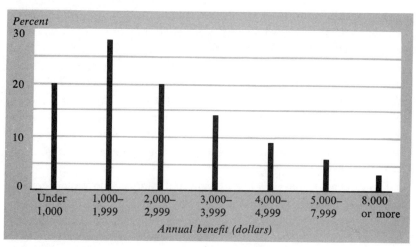

Source: Walter W. Kolodrubetz, "Private Retirement Benefits and Relationship to Earnings: Survey of New Beneficiaries," *Social Security Bulletin*, vol. 36 (May 1973), p. 19.
a. Includes only retirees who were entitled to OASDI benefits as well as private pensions.

pension plan fails to meet its obligations.[26] The act also set financial and fiduciary standards for pension plans, thus ensuring actuarially sound bases and responsible and prudent management. Enforcement is supported by the reporting and disclosure provisions in the act and is entrusted to the Department of Labor.

The act also introduced individual retirement accounts (IRAs) for workers not covered by a company or union plan. Under this scheme, a worker may set aside for retirement up to 15 percent of annual income or $1,500, whichever is less. Both contributions to and earnings from the account are tax exempt until retirement. Under the act, the worker is required to invest these funds in a special Treasury bond, in annuities that do not begin to pay out until the holder has reached retirement age, or in a trust administered by a bank or by a responsible person. The self-employed are also given more liberal tax treatment by the act, as they are now allowed to take tax deductions of as much as $7,500 (the previous limit was $2,500) for contributions toward retirement funds. The earnings on these

26. Upon termination of a plan, insured retirement benefits not covered by plan assets are paid from the PBGC insurance fund. However, the employer is liable to PBGC for reimbursement up to 30 percent of his net worth.

funds are not taxed until they are withdrawn after the worker reaches sixty-five.

As a result of the 1974 legislation, middle- and high-income workers can supplement their social security benefits through either private pension plans or IRAs. A man retiring in June 1976 who had earned in all years the maximum earnings taxable for social security received a social security benefit equivalent to 31 percent of preretirement (1975) earnings.[27] According to a study by the Bankers Trust Company, a male worker received an average additional 37 percent of previous earnings in private pension benefits. Therefore, workers with private pension coverage as well as social security are insured against a serious decline in income upon retirement.[28]

The problem is that only half of wage and salary employees are covered by private pension plans, and many will not have full benefits upon reaching retirement age because of job changes and other factors. Pension coverage is also highly correlated with income, as high-wage workers are more likely to be covered by a private pension than low-wage workers. The 1974 law provides a partial solution, since noncovered workers who are able to save have recourse to an individual retirement account. However, low-wage workers who have no private pension and who cannot save on their own must rely on government programs. How much of their retirement income should be provided by social security and how much through the supplemental security income program is discussed in chapter 3.

A second problem with the private pension system is that some low- and middle-income workers are effectively denied pension benefits because their plans are integrated with social security. Those workers whose earnings fall below the social security wage base are most affected by this integration provision. A 1974 study found that 60 percent of the 412,376 active corporate-type pension plans were integrated, but integration affects only about 25 to 30 percent of the 30 million participants covered by private pensions. The discrepancy arises because small plans (with fewer than twenty-six participants) are more than twice as likely to be integrated with social security than are large plans. An estimated 64 percent of small plans were integrated but only 29 percent of plans with twenty-six or more workers.[29]

27. See table 3-2.
28. See Skolnik, "Private Pension Plans," pp. 13–14.
29. Raymond Schmitt, "Integration of Private Pension Plans With Social Security," *Studies in Public Welfare,* paper 18, prepared for the Subcommittee on Fiscal Policy of the Joint Economic Committee, 93:2 (GPO, 1974), pp. 174–75.

Table 2-6. Monthly Private Pension Benefits under Excess and Offset Methods of Integration with Social Security, Four Workers in 1976[a]

Earnings in year before retirement (dollars)		Social security benefit (dollars)	Benefit, excess method[b]		Benefit, offset method[c]	
Annual	Monthly		Dollars	Percent of earnings	Dollars	Percent of earnings
3,000	250	185	0[b]	0.0	0	0.0
6,000	500	260	0	0.0	0	0.0
12,000	1,000	360	75	7.5	66	6.6
24,000	2,000	387	375	18.8	348	17.4

Source: Based on examples in Raymond Schmitt, "Integration of Private Pension Plans with Social Security," *Studies in Public Welfare*, paper 18, prepared for the Subcommittee on Fiscal Policy of the Joint Economic Committee, 93:2 (GPO, 1974).

a. Assumes worker retired in 1976 with thirty years of covered earnings.

b. Formula: 30 percent of annual earnings over $9,000.

c. Formula: 30 percent of monthly earnings minus 65 percent of social security primary benefit

Two of the most popular integration schemes are the excess method and the offset method. The following examples demonstrate how integration discriminates against the low-wage worker. The excess method, in which benefits are provided only on the basis of earnings in excess of some level set by the plan, is the most typical method. The basic earnings level is related to the average social security taxable wage in effect during the worker's life. For instance, an excess plan might have an integration level of $9,000 and provide annual benefits upon retirement at sixty-five of 30 percent of average earnings in excess of $9,000 (see table 2-6).

Under the offset plan, the private pension provided by the employer is reduced by a certain percentage of the primary social security benefit. This percentage can be as high as 83.3 percent but typically is somewhat lower. For example, a formula might provide a participant with a monthly pension of 1 percent of average pay for each year of service reduced by 65 percent of the social security primary benefit. Table 2-6 presents benefits using this formula for four wage earners with thirty years of service, retiring at sixty-five in 1976.

Although integration is based on the logical notion that public and private retirement programs should function as a unified system, integration in practice tends to deny private pension benefits to workers whose earnings fall below the social security wage base. In fact, integration is based on the principle that, since the social security program is weighted in favor of low-income workers, the private pension system should favor high-income workers, so that all workers will have the same rate of earnings replacement when they retire. Disallowing integration would significantly raise the cost of this type of private pension plan. Nevertheless, if social security is to function as a retirement income base, supplemented by private plans, provisions must be made to ensure private pension benefits to low- and middle-income workers. Adequate retirement income for low-wage workers must now come from a combination of social security and supplemental security income.

Middle- and high-income workers, however, can supplement their social security benefits through either private pension plans or individual retirement accounts. It is important to recognize that the availability of these private resources places a ceiling on the desirable level of compulsory public protection. Large public benefits for middle- and high-income retirees are unnecessary and may interfere with private saving initiatives.

Summary

Developments over the last forty years in provisions for retirement income have refined the role that social security can effectively play in the future. Social adequacy is most efficiently achieved in the supplemental security income program, which bases payments on demonstrable need and not on covered employment. Transferring this objective entirely to SSI would leave to social security a still gargantuan task—providing the major portion of retirement income for virtually the entire work force. The strengthening of private pension plans, which has been achieved by favorable tax treatment and stringent regulation, will increase the number of retired who receive supplementary pension benefits, while the introduction of individual retirement accounts will encourage saving for retirement. For the future, then, social security should view its role as bounded from below by SSI and from above by private provisions for retirement income.

chapter three **The Benefit Structure**

Since 1939, the simple wage replacement role of social security has been supplemented by welfare considerations such as a minimum benefit, dependents' benefits, and a progressive benefit formula. The policy of favoring low-income workers was established in the Great Depression, a time when no adequate income maintenance programs were available for the aged. During the last four decades, the country's economic life and social programs have changed markedly, yet there has been little reevaluation of the social security benefit structure.

Furthermore, the benefit structure requires immediate attention because the automatic price adjustments introduced in the 1972 legislation contain a technical flaw. The adjustments not only overcompensate workers for inflation, but make replacement rates (the ratio of benefits to preretirement earnings) highly dependent on the interaction of price and wage increases.[1] The instability of the replacement rates is reflected in the alarming estimated future costs of the social security program, a large portion of which are unnecessary and simply due to this unintended feature of the 1972 legislation.

In the process of correcting the overindexing error, Congress will be

1. Throughout this book, replacement rates have been calculated as the ratio of benefits to earnings in the year before retirement. Using only that year as a measure of preretirement earnings and living standard is usually not justified because it has been found that those earnings can differ significantly from a worker's normal income level. A better measure of the extent to which benefits replace earnings is the ratio of benefits to average earnings over a number of years, say the ten preceding retirement. The Consultant Panel on Social Security recommends that replacement rates be calculated using seven of the last ten years before retirement, ignoring the year of highest earnings and the two years of lowest earnings. (*Report of the Consultant Panel on Social Security to the Congressional Research Service*, 94:2 [GPO, 1976], p. 15.) However, throughout this book, replacement rates have been based on simulated earnings histories, which show no unusual fluctuations in earnings in the year before retirement, and for the purposes of this book, are acceptable.

Table 3-1. Replacement Rates and Family Benefit as a Percent of Primary Insurance Amount, by Type of Beneficiary, June 1976[a]

Type of beneficiary	Family benefit as percent of PIA	Replacement rates[b] for three earnings levels		
		Low[c] ($3,439 in 1975)	Median[d] ($8,255 in 1975)	Maximum[e] ($14,100 in 1975)
Male worker				
Aged 65	100.0	0.663	0.462	0.330
Aged 62	80.0	0.530	0.369	0.264
Male worker aged 65 with wife				
Aged 65	150.0	0.994	0.693	0.495
Aged 62	137.5	0.911	0.635	0.453
Male worker aged 62 with wife				
Aged 65	130.0	0.862	0.600	0.429
Aged 62	117.5	0.779	0.543	0.387
Widow aged 65; spouse retired at				
Age 65	100.0	0.663	0.462	0.330
Age 62	82.5	0.547	0.381	0.272
Widow aged 62; spouse retired at				
Age 65	82.9	0.549	0.383	0.273
Age 62	82.5	0.547	0.381	0.272
Widow aged 60	71.5	0.474	0.330	0.236

Source: Social Security Administration, Office of the Actuary.

a. Assumes worker retired January 1, 1976.

b. The ratio of the PIA at award (June of year) to monthly taxable earnings in the year just before retirement. The wage and price assumptions are the same as the intermediate assumptions used in the *1976 Annual Report of the Board of Trustees of the Federal Old Age and Survivors Insurance and Disability Insurance Trust Funds*, H. Doc. 94-505, 94:2 (GPO, 1976), 4 percent annual increase in prices and 5.75 percent annual increase in wages.

c. Assumes wages before 1975 followed the trend of the median wage in past years.

d. Assumes taxable earnings equal to the median in each year.

e. Assumes income equal to the maximum taxable amount each year.

required to make decisions either implicitly or explicitly about fundamental characteristics of the social security program: the appropriate ratio of benefits to wages, how this ratio should vary over time, how to distinguish among workers with widely differing wage histories, and how the benefits of low-wage workers should compare with those of high-wage workers.

The Structure Today

Each individual's social security benefit is determined by a two-stage process. First, the wage earner's primary insurance amount (PIA) is computed. Second, the relation of the wage earner to the individual drawing the benefit and the age he is when claiming the benefit are figured in. The

ratio of benefits to preretirement earnings for various earnings histories
and family status are presented in table 3-1. Below are some details of the
benefit calculation. (More information is provided in the appendix.)

The primary insurance amount itself is computed in two stages. The
first stage is the calculation of the worker's average monthly earnings
(AME) in the period before retirement, disability, or death. The AME
is then used to compute the PIA through the application of an eight-
bracket formula.

The calculation of AME is based on wages in covered employment up
to the maximum taxable amount for the years after 1950 or the age of
twenty-one and before the year the worker dies, is disabled, or reaches
sixty-two.[2] Five years of lowest earnings and all years of disability may be
excluded from the calculation, and years of higher earnings after sixty-two
can be substituted for years of lower earnings before sixty-two.

For example, for a man retiring at sixty-five in 1976 the calculation of
AME would include earnings in the years 1951–74 (after 1950 and before
sixty-two or 1975, whichever is later.)[3] Excluding five years of low earn-

2. Currently, the period used in the calculation of the AME for men is in a state
of transition, as the ending year is being changed from sixty-five to sixty-two to
coincide with that used for women. For a man, the period is measured to the year
he reaches sixty-two or the year 1975, whichever is later; for a woman, the period is
measured to the year she reaches sixty-two.

3. Men reaching sixty-five before 1978 have a longer averaging period than
women for calculation of AME, because before the 1972 amendments computation
at age sixty-five was applicable to men, while sixty-two was used for women. Therefore, men reaching sixty-five in 1972 had to use sixteen years for a computation
period, while women used thirteen years. This discrepancy was eliminated by the
1972 legislation, and sixty-two was adopted as the computation age for both sexes.
The transition was accomplished by freezing the computation period at nineteen years
for men aged sixty-five during the years 1975–78. Thereafter, the AME is to be calculated from 1950 (or the age of twenty-one) to the age of sixty-two for both sexes.
The periods for computing AMEs for those aged sixty-five during the years 1971–79
are as follows:

Year of attainment	Years in computation of AME	
	Men	Women
1971	15	12
1972	16	13
1973	17	14
1974	18	15
1975	19	16
1976	19	17
1977	19	18
1978	19	19
1979	20	20

ings and substituting a year of higher earnings after 1974 for a year of lower earnings included in the averaging period would result in an AME based on nineteen years of earnings from 1957 through 1975, less any years excluded as a period of disability. Thus, a worker who had always earned the maximum taxable amount would have an AME of $133,500 (sum of creditable earnings from 1957 to 1975) divided by 228 (nineteen years times twelve months), or $585.[4]

The AME is then used as the basis for the worker's PIA, the benefit amount payable to a fully insured worker retiring at sixty-five. For workers with very low AMEs there is a minimum benefit ($107.90 in 1976), and there is also a special minimum benefit for workers with a long history of low wages. For most workers, however, benefits are calculated on the basis of the PIA computational formula. In 1976, the PIA formula consisted of eight brackets as follows:[5]

> 137.77 percent of the first $110 of AME
> + 50.11 percent of the next $290 of AME
> + 46.83 percent of the next $150 of AME
> + 55.04 percent of the next $100 of AME
> + 30.61 percent of the next $100 of AME
> + 25.51 percent of the next $250 of AME
> + 22.98 percent of the next $175 of AME
> + 21.28 percent of the next $100 of AME.

Applying the PIA formula to a wage earner with an AME of $585 yields a primary benefit of $387.30,[6] the amount a fully insured worker retiring at sixty-five would receive. A worker with a wife, dependent husband, child, or dependent grandchild will receive an additional 50 percent of the

4. This figure is considerably below the 1976 maximum monthly covered earnings amount of $1,275 under the 1976 $15,300 ceiling, because lower levels of covered earnings were in effect during most of the worker's earning history.

5. The formula that follows in the text is designed to accommodate a taxable earnings ceiling of $15,300 or monthly earnings of $1,275, even though monthly earnings are generally substantially lower because of lower covered earnings in effect throughout most of the worker's earnings history. A worker earning the maximum taxable amount in all years would have average monthly earnings of $585, while a worker who dies or is disabled at the age of twenty-four after working in 1975 and 1976 can have average monthly earnings based on only two years of covered employment, giving an AME of $1,225 ([$15,300 + $14,100]/24). Thus, whenever the maximum is raised in response to an increase in the level of average wages, the formula is adjusted to reflect the full increase.

6. Actually, benefit amounts are determined from a benefit table that gives AME intervals and the corresponding PIA. The PIA computational formula approximates this table. Thus, the formula yields a PIA of $386.40, while the actual PIA from the benefit table is $387.30.

PIA. A widow or dependent widower receives 100 percent of the worker's PIA, while a surviving child or grandchild receives 75 percent. There is a ceiling, however, on total family benefits payable on the basis of one earnings history. If the insured worker's AME is $627 or less, the maximum family benefit is approximately 134.7 percent of the first $436 of AME plus 67.4 percent of the next $191. If the AME is greater than $627, the maximum family benefit is approximately 175 percent of the worker's PIA.

If a fully insured worker retires at sixty-five, the monthly benefit equals the PIA. However, a worker can retire as early as sixty-two with an actuarial reduction in benefits of $5/9$ percent for each month before the age of sixty-five. If retirement is delayed past sixty-five, benefits are increased by $1/12$ percent for every month after sixty-five and before retirement, up to seventy-two. Certain dependents and survivors can also claim reduced benefits earlier than sixty-five. Wives, divorced wives, and dependent husbands are eligible for permanently reduced benefits at sixty-two. Widows, divorced widows, and dependent widowers can receive permanently reduced benefits as early as sixty.

Since social security payments are meant to replace earnings lost because of retirement, disability, or death, there is a limit to the amount of earned income a person can receive while collecting social security benefits. This limit, discussed in greater detail in chapter 4, is known as the retirement test, or earnings test. For 1976, a beneficiary could earn up to $2,760 annually or $230 monthly with no reduction in benefits. However, a dollar of benefits is withheld for each $2 of earnings over $2,760. Although the test is applied on an annual basis, benefits are payable in any month in which the worker earns $230 or less. Thus, seasonal workers can receive well over $2,760 and still retain eligibility for benefits during most of the year. In addition, beneficiaries aged seventy-two or older are exempt from the earnings test.

Social security benefits have been exempt from the personal income tax from the beginning of the program. The reasoning behind this favorable tax treatment was twofold. First, the worker's contribution toward his retirement benefit was subject to tax when earned. Second, the aged were presumed to be needy. The tax exemption of social security benefits reduces the effective progressivity of the program, since those with high incomes facing high marginal rates receive a larger tax break than low-income retirees. In addition, such favorable treatment is not given benefits from other pension plans, in which all income in excess of the worker's contribution is subject to tax.

Revising the tax treatment of social security benefits may be desirable on several counts. First, the double personal exemption available to people sixty-five and over precludes the necessity of providing favorable tax treatment to the elderly through exemption of social security benefits. Second, taxing social security benefits would help ensure that the benefit structure aids the needy and not those reaping windfalls because their social security benefit is a second pension. Finally, if social security benefits were taxed, the resulting revenue could be directed back to the old age, survivors, and disability trust funds, allowing the system to pay higher benefits or to reduce long-run costs.

Benefits and Inflation

The 1972 amendments introduced into the Social Security Act a mechanism whereby the benefit formula is adjusted automatically in response to changes in the cost of living. Unfortunately, this desirable adjustment is marred by a serious technical flaw, which overcompensates workers for inflation and makes replacement rates (ratio of benefit to workers' final wage) highly dependent on the exact pattern of future wage and price increases. The wage and price assumptions incorporated in the 1976 projections of the Board of Trustees (wage growth of 5.75 percent and consumer price index growth of 4 percent) would result in benefit protection rising 55 percent over the assumed increase in wages during the next century.[7] As shown in table 3-2, many future retirees would get benefits higher than any wages they had earned.

Inflation Adjustment Procedure

The current procedure for making cost-of-living adjustments is to change the factors in the PIA computational formula. In January 1976 the formula set an earner's primary insurance amount equal to roughly 129 percent of the first $110 of average monthly earnings, 47 percent of the next $290, 44 percent of the next $150, and so on through five more brackets. Since inflation during the past year averaged 6.4 percent, the formula automatically changed in June 1976, to 138 percent (1.064 of 129.5 percent) of the first $110, plus 50 percent (1.064 of 47 percent)

7. Social Security Administration, Office of the Actuary.

Table 3-2. Replacement Rates[a] for Three Earnings Levels for Males Retiring at the Age of Sixty-five in Selected Years, 1975–2050

	Replacement rates for three earnings levels[a]		
Year	Low earnings[b] ($3,439 in 1975)	Median earnings ($8,255 in 1975)	Maximum earnings ($14,100 in 1975)
1975[c]	0.623	0.434	0.310
1980	0.636	0.468	0.348
1985	0.650	0.496	0.340
1990	0.676	0.516	0.348
1995	0.716	0.522	0.358
2000	0.797	0.551	0.378
2005	0.896	0.576	0.397
2010	0.941	0.600	0.412
2015	0.988	0.622	0.424
2020	1.027	0.642	0.434
2025	1.066	0.659	0.444
2030	1.102	0.676	0.452
2035	1.136	0.690	0.460
2040	1.167	0.704	0.467
2045	1.196	0.717	0.474
2050	1.221	0.728	0.480

Source: Social Security Administration, Office of the Actuary.
a. The ratio of the PIA at award (June of year) to monthly taxable earnings in the year just before retirement. The wage and price assumptions are the same as the intermediate assumptions used in the *1976 Annual Report of the Board of Trustees of the Federal Old Age and Survivors Insurance and Disability Insurance Trust Funds*, H. Doc. 94-505, 94:2 (GPO, 1976), 4 percent annual increase in prices and 5.75 percent annual increase in wages.
b. Represents a person who has worked steadily at slightly below the minimum wage.
c. Rates for 1975 are actual.

of the next $290, and so forth for all the brackets in the formula. This adjustment causes each worker's PIA to increase by the same percentage as the increase in the CPI.

When benefits are increased as a result of the automatic adjustment provision, the earnings base that determines the maximum amount of earnings creditable for benefit purposes and the exempt amount under the earnings test are also increased. This adjustment is based on changes in average covered wages and not, as for benefits, on changes in the CPI. For the 1976 adjustment, the average taxable wage of all covered employees for the first quarter of 1975 was compared with a similar figure for 1974.[8]

8. As a result of legislative action in January 1976, future-earnings base adjustments will be calculated from annual rather than quarterly earnings data. Annual reporting is scheduled to begin in 1978. Since earnings data for the entire year are not available until the following year, the new method requires shifting the measuring period back one year. Thus, the taxable base and exempt amount for 1981—to be

The actual increase of 7.47 percent was applied to the $14,100 base effective in 1975, and the result of $15,154 was rounded to the nearest $300 to yield the $15,300 applicable for 1976.

Overadjustment for Inflation

The inflation adjustment works well for those beneficiaries of the social security system who are already retired. For them, monthly benefits increase by the same amount as the cost of living, thus maintaining the purchasing power of their benefits at its original level. At the same time, however, the procedure introduces an unintended overadjustment into the future benefit levels of those who are still working.[9]

This side effect arises because the same PIA conversion formula is used both for currently retired workers and for future retirees, creating what is known as a "coupled" system.[10] For the currently retired, inflation has no effect on the average monthly wage used in the PIA formula; their AMEs remain fixed at the actual level of their past earnings. However, those still in the labor force will, over the long run, get wage increases to compensate for the effects of inflation, and the taxable wage base will be increased automatically in line with the growth in average wages. As a result of the inflation-induced wage increases, these workers will have higher AMEs when it comes time for them to retire and will therefore be entitled to higher social security benefits.

In this way, the present adjustment mechanism gives future retirees a double increase in benefits every time there is an increase in the cost of

determined in 1980—will be based on the increase in annual covered earnings from 1978 to 1979. Although annual reporting is to begin in 1978, the measuring period has been shifted back for 1977. Thus, the wage base and exempt amount for 1977 are calculated on the basis of the increase in earnings from the first quarter of 1974 to the first quarter of 1975.

9. The following discussion is based on an analysis of the dynamics of the benefit formula by Lawrence H. Thompson in two papers, "An Analysis of the Factors Currently Determining Benefit Level Adjustments in the Social Security Retirement Program" and "An Analysis of the Issues Involved in Securing Constant Replacement Rates in the Social Security OASDI Program," Technical Analysis papers 1 and 5 (Social Security Administration, Office of Income Security Policy, 1974 and 1975).

10. This was the procedure followed by Congress for all ad hoc benefit increases legislated between 1950 and 1972. The coupling procedure has the advantages of simplicity and a smooth transition for those on the roll at the time of the increase and those coming on the roll shortly thereafter. It also produces consistent and equitable results for recomputation of benefit amounts for those who work beyond the minimum retirement age at high earnings levels.

living, first from the adjustment of the benefit formula and second from the higher taxable wage base owing to higher earnings. In fact, if inflation rates were constant and there were no offsetting downward effects of rising wages and a lengthening computational period, future retirees would be compensated exactly twice for inflation, and replacement rates would rise by the rate of the price increase.

In reality, the impact of the inflation overadjustment is not as great as that because there are two other features of the procedure that exert downward pressure on the replacement rates over time. One of these is the effect on benefits of the progressive PIA formula and the other is the legislatively mandated increase in the computation period for calculating average monthly earnings.

THE OFFSETTING EFFECT OF RISING WAGES. The current PIA computational formula is progressive in the sense that high-wage workers have a lower replacement rate than low-wage workers. This inverse relation between replacement rates and a worker's preretirement wages is derived directly from the PIA benefit formula in which (with one exception) the percentage applied to the AME declines in each successive bracket.

As the average level of wages rises over time, each successive group of newly retired workers earning the average for their group will find themselves in higher brackets of the PIA formula, having smaller percentages of their AME replaced by retirement benefits. As an illustration, in a long period of zero inflation the benefit formula would never change, since the conversion factors are adjusted only in response to increases in prices. As wages rose, the average worker would have successively smaller percentages applied to the increases in his AME and the benefit would grow at a slower rate than the AME. Eventually, most of the average monthly earnings would fall into the highest bracket, which implies a lower replacement rate.

In the absence of the inflation adjustments, then, replacement rates tend to decline over time as wages rise, because of the progressivity of the benefit formula. The tendency of inflation to increase replacement rates and of rising wages to depress them has caused replacement rates to be very sensitive to the interplay of wage and price increases.

LENGTHENING THE CALCULATION PERIOD FOR AME. There is an additional factor that influences the future path of replacement rates—the lengthening of the calculation period for AME. For a person retiring at sixty-five in 1976, average monthly wages were based on the annual earnings in covered employment in the nineteen years of highest earnings (seventeen for a female) of the twenty-four-year computation period. Present legislation provides that in the future the number of years on which the AME is based will be increased by one year each calendar year until the averaging period reaches thirty-five years in 1994.[11] This provision simply ensures that a new entrant's entire working life after the age of twenty-one is included in the computation period.

In a period when wages are rising, any lengthening of the years included in the computation of AME will exert a downward influence on replacement rates, other things being equal. Replacement rates decline because benefits are lower, since they are based on a lower AME. The AME is lower because the extra year included in the computation is the year of relatively lowest earnings. The lengthening of the averaging period means that two workers with exactly the same earnings histories but who reach the age of sixty-two in different years will have different benefits. The worker who reaches sixty-two earlier, computing AME over a shorter period and thereby excluding early years of low earnings, will have a higher AME and a higher benefit.

While lengthening the computation period does exert a downward pressure on replacement rates, its impact differs from the other adjustments in that the downward trend ends in 1994. Once the computation period reaches thirty-five years in 1994, this particular factor will have no further effect on replacement rates.

NET IMPACT OF PRICES, WAGES, AND CALCULATION PERIOD. Overadjustment for inflation causes replacement rates to rise whenever prices increase; the progressivity of the benefit formula causes replacement rates to fall whenever wages rise. The net impact of these two factors on replacement rates depends on whether the wage effect or the price effect is dominant. Table 3-3 presents replacement rates for a seventy-five-year period under alternative assumptions about the rate of increase in wages and prices. These data can be used to demonstrate the impact of inflation, rising wages, and the lengthening computation period.

The depressing effect of rising wages on replacement rates can be seen by comparing two series with the same rate of price increase but different rates of wage growth. Series A and B have the same 4 percent inflation

11. Until 1978, a man retiring at sixty-five would use the higher of two figures— the number of years from 1950 to the age of sixty-two, or the years 1951 through 1974—less five years of low earnings. After 1978, the number of years increases by one each year until 1994 when, for all workers retiring at sixty-five, the number of years between the ages of twenty-one and sixty-two, less five years of low earnings, reaches a maximum of thirty-five years. See note 3.

Table 3-3. Replacement Rates[a] under Four Wage and Price Assumptions for Males
with Average Taxable Earnings in All Years, Retiring at Sixty-five,
Selected Years, 1975–2050

	Annual increases			
Year	Series A: real wages 1%; prices 4%	Series B: real wages 2%; prices 4%	Series C: real wages 2%; prices 3%	Series D: real wages 2%; prices 2%
1975[b]	0.434	0.434	0.434	0.434
1980	0.472	0.468	0.468	0.464
1985	0.514	0.495	0.490	0.478
1990	0.548	0.508	0.500	0.482
1995	0.570	0.510	0.494	0.473
2000	0.617	0.533	0.510	0.478
2005	0.661	0.553	0.522	0.482
2010	0.704	0.572	0.530	0.480
2015	0.746	0.589	0.536	0.477
2020	0.785	0.603	0.541	0.473
2025	0.822	0.616	0.545	0.470
2030	0.858	0.628	0.549	0.466
2035	0.891	0.639	0.553	0.463
2040	0.923	0.649	0.556	0.460
2045	0.954	0.658	0.559	0.458
2050	0.983	0.667	0.562	0.456

Source: Social Security Administration, Office of the Actuary.
a. The ratio of the primary insurance amount at award (June of year) to monthly taxable earnings in the year just before retirement.
b. Rates for 1975 are actual (see table 3-2).

assumption, but series A assumes annual real wage growth of 1 percent, while in series B real wages rise 2 percent a year. This 1 percentage point difference in the rate of wage growth results in significantly lower replacement rates under series B by the year 2050, when the replacement rate with the higher wage growth will be 0.667 compared to 0.983 under the low wage-growth assumption—a difference of 47 percent.

Comparing replacement rates under series B and C illuminates the effect of the overadjustment for inflation. Both series assume that real wages grow at 2 percent, but the inflation rate is 1 percentage point higher in B than C. The higher rate of inflation causes the replacement rate to climb to 0.667 by the year 2050 compared to 0.562 under the lower inflation assumption.

The impact of the lengthening computation period can be seen by comparing within any series the behavior of replacement rates over the period 1985–95 (years in which lengthening occurs) to their behavior over the period 1995–2005 (years when the lengthening is complete). For example, series C, in which real wages grow at 2 percent and prices increase 3 percent, shows the replacement rate rising only 0.008 percent between 1985 and 1995. However, during the second ten-year period, 1995–2005, replacement rates rise by 0.057 percent, seven times the earlier increase. The same behavior is also true for the other three series.

Table 3-3 illustrates still another interesting pattern. When the rate of real wage growth is equal to the rate of price increase, the two effects eventually offset one another, and replacement rates become relatively stable. If real wages and prices rise at 2 percent, as they did during the late fifties and throughout the sixties, the replacement rates stabilize around the initial values (see series D). Thus, the legislated inflation adjustments to the percentages in the benefit formula during this period did not destabilize replacement rates, which explains why the procedure caused little concern when it was introduced as an automatic feature in the 1972 legislation.

For the cases in which wages and prices rise at different rates, the enormous variation in replacement rates becomes a serious defect. Replacement rates should be set by deliberate policy rather than as an accidental result of the benefit calculation formula. This is necessary both for intergenerational equity and for accurate actuarial analysis of future costs. Therefore, it is essential that the current inflation adjustment procedure be modified to yield replacement rates that are predictable over time to avoid excessive increases in long-run costs.

The Issues in Decoupling

To correct the current overindexing of benefits introduced in the 1972 legislation, the system must be decoupled so that benefits in payment and potential benefits are adjusted separately. Benefits for retired workers would continue to be adjusted by the CPI as under the present law, but benefits for future retirees would use a new indexing mechanism to avoid the present overadjustment.

For those still in the work force, two alternative decoupling schemes have been suggested. The 1975 Social Security Advisory Council suggested indexing earnings histories by wages to calculate an average monthly *indexed* earnings (AMIE) and then adjusting the benefit formula for changes in the cost of living by increasing the break points in line with the increase in average wages while keeping the percentage factors constant.[12] The result of this indexing procedure would be a decoupled system with stable replacement rates. In 1975, President Ford proposed such a wage indexing scheme combined with the following three-factor benefit formula that would closely duplicate current replacement rates:

91% of the first $175 of AMIE
+ 33% of the next $875 of AMIE
+ 17% of AMIE in excess of $1,050.

Once the initial benefit amount for an individual were determined, subsequent increases in the monthly benefit would depend on increases in the CPI, as in the present law.

An alternative decoupling scheme, proposed by the Consultant Panel on Social Security, would index the earnings histories by the CPI and make cost-of-living adjustments by increasing the break points in the benefit formula in line with the increase in prices rather than average wages. The benefit formula proposed by the consultant panel also consists of three brackets:

80% of the first $200 of AMIE
+ 35% of the next $400 of AMIE
+ 25% of AMIE in excess of $600.[13]

Indexing earnings histories by prices rather than wages would produce adjusted wages that reflect the real purchasing power of previous earnings rather than the relative earning position of the worker. More important, indexing the break points by the CPI would produce slowly declining replacement rates, a result that may be desirable to ease future financial burdens of the system.

Creating any decoupled system will inevitably alter the pattern of benefits paid to future retirees.[14] Therefore, the selection of a particular benefit computation procedure requires resolution (either implicitly or explicitly) of the following fundamental issues about the structure of the social security system:

Vertical equity. How should benefits be related to covered earnings?

12. *Reports of the Quadrennial Advisory Council on Social Security,* H. Doc. 94-75, 94:1 (GPO, 1975), pp. 106–08.
13. *Report of the Consultant Panel on Social Security to Congressional Research Service,* p. 17.
14. The framework discussed below was proposed by John Palmer. The discussion also benefited from the work of Jane L. Ross, Lawrence Thompson, and Paul Van de Water.

Decisions must be made concerning the optimal progressivity of the benefit formula and the need for a minimum benefit and dependents' benefits.

Horizontal equity. How do we distinguish among workers with widely divergent wage histories? This touches on questions of indexing past wages to provide an equitable adjusted basis for calculating benefits, the determination of the optimal period for averaging, and the possibility of length-of-service credits.

Intertemporal equity. How should replacement rates behave over time?

The present benefit structure is not the product of deliberate policy decisions but rather the result of ad hoc adjustments over the last forty years. Therefore, the process of decoupling should be seized as an opportunity to explicitly resolve each of the issues raised above and to design a rational program.

Vertical Equity: Relation of Benefits to Average Monthly Earnings

The existing benefit structure, in which replacement rates vary according to wage level and family status, reflects what has been viewed as the necessary trade-off between social adequacy and individual equity. Although the progressive benefit formula, the minimum benefit, and dependents' benefits were once necessary and have done much to alleviate poverty among the aged, they have produced inequities that can and should be corrected. The progressive benefit formula and the statutory minimum benefit have produced very high replacement rates for low-wage workers and surprisingly low replacement rates for people earning the maximum taxable amount. Because of dependents' benefits, replacement rates for workers with dependents are well above those for other workers.[15] Similarly, replacement rates for two-earner families are significantly lower than those for one-earner families because of the additional benefits given workers with nonworking wives.

PROGRESSIVITY OF THE BENEFIT FORMULA. As discussed earlier, the present benefit formula consists of eight brackets. In all but one of the

15. Some experts justify the provision of dependents' benefits as equalizing the retirement living standards of single workers and workers with families, assuming that it is easier for single workers to build up private retirement savings than it is for families with the same income. If this argument is accepted, the equivalence of retirement living standards is still distorted in favor of married workers, because the existing 50 percent of wife's benefit and 75 percent surviving child's benefit exceed the actual costs of supporting such dependents. Reducing these benefits to 30 percent (the estimated cost of support for an additional household member) would equalize living standards between single and married retirees.

brackets the percentage of earnings replaced decreases as average earnings increase. The formula is structured so that the benefits of low-wage workers are a higher proportion of their preretirement earnings than those of high-wage workers. Viewed in a lifetime framework, progressivity implies a disproportionately high rate of return on the contributions of low-income workers. As part of a decoupling scheme, it would be possible to design a benefit formula that closely duplicates the existing structure. However, the present formula has evolved gradually over time and may not be the appropriate policy for the future. As long as a new formula must be constructed, the appropriateness of the tilt, or progressivity, in the formula should be given serious consideration.

Some advocates of a progressive benefit formula base their arguments on the fact that the existing overall income distribution is unsatisfactory and that social security expenditures should be used to achieve a more equitable result. Since benefit payments for OASDI currently account for almost 20 percent of the federal budget, they feel there is no reason to exempt such a large expenditure from the redistributive effort.

However, redistribution through the social security benefit structure is inefficient. Some retirees receive disproportionately high benefits regardless of whether their low average earnings are due to consistently low wage rates or simply to short periods in covered employment at higher wage levels. Thus, many of the progressive benefits simply go to the beneficiaries of other government pension programs who have spent a minimum period in OASDI-covered industry. In addition, social security imposes no means or assets tests, paying equal amounts to those with substantial savings and those with no other income. Redistribution could be accomplished efficiently by channeling funds to low-income families through an expanded means-tested supplemental security income (SSI) program and returning social security to a wage-related benefit system. With this approach, funds would be directed to those who are poor rather than to those who simply have low average earnings in covered employment but have other income.

Another argument favoring a progressive benefit formula can be couched in the context of the goals of the social security program itself, rather than in terms of the overall distribution of income. To prevent a serious decline in income upon retirement, retirees require about 70 percent of their gross preretirement earnings. (This low percentage reflects the decline in work-related expenses, the tax-free status of social security income, and the health insurance available to the elderly.) Guaranteeing all workers 70 percent of their previous earnings in retirement would be very expensive and would require almost double the present payroll taxes. The pragmatic compromise, therefore, is to provide higher replacement rates for low-income workers who cannot save on their own and lower replacement rates for high-income workers who can supplement their benefits with private pensions and saving.

However, there are two possible methods of achieving a system of progressive replacement rates. On the one hand, the present social security benefit structure could be retained with its minimum benefit and steeply progressive benefit formula. The alternative is to provide proportional benefits to all retirees through the social security program, combined with SSI for low-income workers. This approach would completely separate the goals of earnings replacement and income maintenance into two programs. The earnings replacement function would be performed by social security as a strictly wage-related system, with replacement rates equal across all earnings levels. The income support function would be transferred to SSI, which is financed by general revenues. There are four advantages to this approach.

First, shifting the welfare function to SSI would rationally redistribute, though not necessarily reduce, the total financial burden of income maintenance for the aged. A proportional social security program would establish a logical basis for separating the financing of earnings replacement and welfare. Social security benefits would be strictly related to past contributions and therefore appropriately financed by the payroll tax. All supplementary payments to low-income retirees under SSI would be financed by high-income taxpayers through the personal income tax. This transfer would be more effective than the present scheme, in which the progressive benefits provided for the elderly by social security are financed by low- and middle-income workers through the regressive payroll tax.

Second, a proportional social security benefit structure would ensure that all future workers received an equitable return on their contributions. In the past, the expansion of coverage and the growing labor force yielded adequate revenues to allow social security simultaneously to provide a positive return to all workers and to pursue the goal of social adequacy through a progressive benefit structure. These factors are reflected in the substantial real rates of return (shown in table 3-4) accruing to workers retiring at sixty-five in 1976. However, coverage is now virtually complete (with the exception of federal employees and some state and local workers) and population growth is expected to cease; therefore, the real rate of

Table 3-4. Real Rates of Return[a] to Workers Retiring at the Age of Sixty-five in 1976 and 2019

Worker and beneficiary	Percent of return		
	Low earnings	Median earnings	High earnings
Retirement in 1976			
Male			
Worker only	10.00	9.00	7.75
Worker, wife, survivor	12.00	11.00	9.50
Female			
Worker only	10.50	9.50	8.25
Worker, husband, survivor	12.50	11.50	10.00
Retiring in 2019			
Male			
Worker only	3.50	2.50	1.00
Worker, wife, survivor	5.25	4.50	3.00
Female			
Worker only	4.50	3.50	2.00
Worker, husband, survivor	6.25	5.50	4.00

Source: Social Security Administration, Office of the Actuary.
a. Assumes decoupled system with tax rate equal to costs. Difference between male and female workers caused by differing life expectancies.

return on social security contributions will be substantially lower for future retirees. By 2019, even with a decoupled system and before the peak of the demographic bulge, the real rate of return to a high-wage worker may be too low to justify participation in the program. In this setting, the goals of fair return and social adequacy come into direct conflict, since a steeply progressive benefit structure will probably yield minimal returns to workers with above-average earnings. Once this happens, support for the social security program might decline.

A third argument in favor of a more strictly wage-related social security program is based on workers' perception of their social security contributions. To the extent that workers perceive the social security levy as another tax that reduces take-home wages, the effect will be to discourage participation in the labor force, particularly of secondary workers. However, if the tax were clearly identified as saving, workers might perceive their contribution as part of their net wage, eliminating any distortions in work effort.

Finally, if benefits were strictly proportional to contributions, people could have the choice of opting out of the program (perhaps with some penalty), provided they accumulated funds for retirement elsewhere.[16] With the current progressive structure such an option is impossible, because those electing to opt out would probably be the high-contribution/ low-benefit workers, leaving inadequate funds to pay the disproportionately high benefits to low-income workers. Even with a proportional benefit structure, supplemental revenues would be required during a transition period to finance the accrued benefits to current retirees. Those who chose to save outside of the social security system would contribute to private capital formation, as will be discussed in chapter 6.

Table 3-5 presents a simple example of how a proportional benefit structure could be combined with an expanded SSI program to guarantee adequate protection to all retirees and supplemental benefits to low-income people.[17] In the example, social security benefits are set at 40 percent of preretirement earnings, approximately equivalent to the current replacement rate for workers with median earnings. The example is also based on an expanded supplemental security income program, where the SSI payment is reduced by only 50 cents for each dollar of unearned income, rather than the present dollar-for-dollar reduction. With this reduced rate, the $20 exception would be eliminated. Reducing the implicit tax would extend assistance to those who earn up to the median income level, thereby insulating affected low-wage earners from a decline in retirement income with the introduction of a proportional benefit formula. This reduction in the implicit tax on unearned income, specifically social security benefits, will naturally raise the cost of the SSI program, but a proportional social security system is not desirable unless low-income people can be adequately protected by this means-tested program. Furthermore, reducing

16. Some critics of the present social security system have suggested a scheme in which those who do not choose to participate in the program as it now stands have the option of purchasing special Treasury bonds on the open market. Thus there would still be forced saving but not necessarily within the social security program. Those who do participate in the Treasury bond program would purchase them through payroll deductions, a modified payroll tax system. Each worker would be guaranteed a positive return on bond purchases. For a fuller discussion, see James M. Buchanan, "Social Insurance in a Growing Economy: A Proposal for Radical Reform," *National Tax Journal*, vol. 21 (December 1968), pp. 386–95.

17. If social security benefits were based on wage-indexed earnings histories while SSI benefits continued to be indexed by prices, over time the percentage of workers qualifying for SSI would decline substantially because the real level of social security benefits would rise beyond the SSI eligibility standards. This phenomenon would result in proportional replacement rates for all income classes. If it is desirable to maintain a progressive combined social security–SSI benefit structure, both programs must use the same indexing variable.

Table 3-5. Comparison of Benefit Levels and Replacement Rates for Males Retiring at Sixty-five in January 1976 under Current and Proposed Systems

Earnings[a]	Monthly earnings,[b] 1975 (dollars)	Social security benefit (dollars)	Replacement rate	SSI benefit[c] (dollars)	Combined benefit (dollars)	Combined replacement rate
			Current system			
60 percent of minimum wage	218.40	165.50	0.758	12.20	177.70	0.814
Low[d]	286.58	178.50	0.623	0.00	178.50	0.623
Low middle[e]	487.25	238.20	0.489	0.00	238.20	0.489
Median	687.92	298.50	0.434	0.00	298.50	0.434
High middle[f]	931.46	329.30	0.353	0.00	329.30	0.353
High	1,175.00	364.00	0.310	0.00	364.00	0.310
			Proposed proportional benefit system			
60 percent of minimum wage	218.40	87.36	0.400	114.02	201.38	0.922
Low[d]	286.50	114.63	0.400	100.38	215.01	0.750
Low middle[e]	487.25	194.90	0.400	60.25	255.15	0.524
Median	687.92	275.17	0.400	20.11	295.28	0.429
High middle[f]	931.46	372.58	0.400	0.00	372.58	0.400
High	1,175.00	470.00	0.400	0.00	470.00	0.400

Sources: Table 3-2 and minimum wage and social security provisions effective in 1975.

a. A smooth yearly income growth is assumed.

b. Upon retirement at sixty-five in January 1976, average monthly earnings calculated by the Social Security Administration are $157, $184, $313, $442, $514, and $586, respectively.

c. Under proposed system there would be a 50 percent implicit tax and no $20 deductible as in the actual SSI law.

d. Represents a person who worked steadily at slightly below the minimum wage (typical of the earnings of the many workers covered by social security not affected by federal standards).

e. Income midway between low and median.

f. Income midway between median and high.

the SSI tax rate on social security benefits will ensure that workers receive some payoff for a lifetime of payroll taxes, and making the cut-off point for SSI less abrupt will eliminate some serious horizontal inequities between those who qualify for SSI and those who must rely on social security.[18]

18. While the benefits in the example are presented in terms of proportional replacement rates, benefits may be calculated on the basis of workers' contributions plus accumulated interest. Workers would receive the life annuity value of the present value of their lifetime tax payments. The appropriate interest rate for the value calculation should probably be the actual rate of growth of gross national product or some other index of aggregate activity. For discussions of this see Buchanan, "Social Insurance"; Paul A. Samuelson, "An Exact Consumption-Loan Model of Interest With or Without the Social Contrivance of Money," *Journal of Political Economy*, vol. 66 (December 1958), pp. 467–82; and Henry J. Aaron, "The Social Insurance Paradox," *Canadian Journal of Economics and Political Science*, vol. 32 (August 1966), pp. 371–74.

Two objections could be raised to expanding the SSI program, as suggested above. First, some might argue that subjecting an increasing proportion of the aged to the stigma of a means-tested program is undesirable. The Social Security Administration estimates that reducing the marginal tax on benefits from 100 percent to 50 percent would double the SSI rolls; reducing the eligible age for SSI to sixty-two would increase the rolls by somewhat less than 10 percent; and eliminating the minimum benefit and the spouse's benefit would increase the SSI rolls even more. With these changes, the number of people receiving SSI would more than double. It seems likely that a means-tested program that covered over half of the aged population would avoid much of the stigma of a program aimed specifically at the aged poor.

The second possible objection to an expanded SSI program is based on a political consideration. In contrast to OASDI, in which revenues are guaranteed by the earmarked payroll tax, SSI is financed by general revenue funds, subject to the vagaries of annual congressional appropriations. It may be unwise to transfer a large portion of income support for the aged from a program in which the funds are assured to one in which future appropriations are uncertain. If social security were changed to become strictly wage-related and the rolls of SSI were expanded, some procedures would have to be developed to ensure that general revenue funds would be available to meet the payments to SSI beneficiaries.

SPOUSE'S BENEFITS. The present structure of benefits for aged spouses has been subject to increasing criticism because (1) it is an inefficient way of funneling money to low-income people; (2) women's increased participation in the labor force means that most married women will be entitled to benefits on the basis of their own earnings records; and (3) awarding benefits on a family basis while taxing on an individual basis creates serious inequities.

If income redistribution is accepted as a goal of social security, a supplementary benefit for spouses is an extremely inefficient way to channel money to low-income families. As shown in figure 3-1, relatively few husband–wife families are poor. In fact, in 1974, 70 percent of these families had incomes in excess of $10,000 and only 9 percent had incomes of less than $5,000. Single people or one-parent families are generally much more in need and unable to provide for their own retirement.

Perhaps more important, it is no longer reasonable to design programs on the basis of the presumed dependency of a married woman on the male head of the household. There are several ways of looking at the change in

Figure 3-1. Income Distribution of Husband-Wife Families Compared to All Families and Individuals, 1974

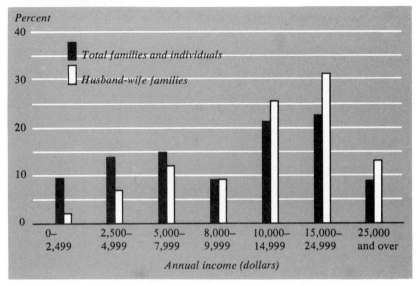

Source: Bureau of the Census, *Current Population Reports*, series P-60, no. 101, "Money Income in 1974 of Families and Persons in the United States" (GPO, 1976), pp. 18, 80.

the structure of the family that has taken place since the introduction of the social security program. Married couples in which both husband and wife work now make up the majority of families. In March 1975, there were 33.7 million husband-wife families in which the husband was between the ages of twenty-five and sixty-five. Of these families, 17.3 million, or 51 percent, were families in which both the husband and wife worked.[19]

Further evidence is provided by the labor force participation rate for married women, which nearly tripled between 1940 and 1970. As shown in table 3-6, the participation rate for married women increased from 14 percent in 1940 to 22 percent in 1950, 31 percent in 1960, and 40 percent in 1970.

The movement of married women into gainful employment has altered the economic relations within the typical household. Not only do many husband and wife families have two earners, but as a result of rising wages for women most families are now characterized by the mutual economic

19. Bureau of the Census, *Current Population Reports*, series P-60, no. 101, "Money Income in 1974 of Families and Persons in the United States" (GPO, 1976), tables 25, 37.

Table 3-6. Labor Force Participation Rates of Women Aged Fourteen and Over, by Age and Marital Status, Selected Years, 1940–70

Percent of population

Marital status and year	Total	Under 25	25–34	35–44	45–54	55–64	65 and over
Married, husband present							
1940	14	16	18	15	11	7	3
1950	22	25	22	27	23	13	5
1960	31	30	28	37	39	25	7
1970	40	45	38	46	48	35	8
Never married							
1940	46	36	79	73	64	47	17
1950	46	36	79	76	71	57	20
1960	43	33	79	78	76	65	23
1970	41	35	78	74	73	65	19
Other							
1940	34	52	65	62	47	27	6
1950	36	50	61	66	56	36	8
1960	39	48	60	68	67	48	11
1970	40	55	64	69	69	54	10

Source: Donald Cymrot and Lucy B. Mallan, "Wife's Earnings as a Source of Family Income," note 10 (Social Security Administration, Office of Research and Statistics, 1974), p. 14.

dependence of husband and wife. As table 3-7 shows, the majority of working wives provide between one-fourth and one-third of their families' total income. This represents a sizable earnings increase for dual earner families, who in 1974 had a median income 36 percent higher than that of families in which the wife was not employed.[20] Thus, many families rely on the incomes of both wife and husband for their living standards.

The implication of this evidence is that in the future a large majority of women will be covered under social security on the basis of their own earnings. By 1970, 68 percent of women forty-five to forty-nine years of age already had enough quarters of covered work to be insured for their own primary benefit.[21] Estimates for the year 2020 predict that about 70

20. Bureau of the Census, *Current Population Reports*, series P-60, no. 99, "Money Income and Poverty Status of Families and Persons in the United States, 1974" (GPO, 1975), p. 4, table 1.

21. Virginia Reno, "Women Newly Entitled to Retired-Worker Benefits: Survey of New Beneficiaries," *Social Security Bulletin*, vol. 36 (April 1973), pp. 4–5 (reprinted as *Preliminary Findings from the Survey of New Beneficiaries*, report 9, Social Security Administration, Office of Research and Statistics).

Table 3-7. Mean Family Income and Earnings of Wife in Husband-Wife Two-Earner Families, by Race of Husband and Weeks Worked by Wife in 1974

| | White | | | | Black | | | |
| | | | Wife's earnings | | | | Wife's earnings | |
Weeks worked by wife	Families[a] (percent)	Mean income (dollars)	Dollars	Percent of family income	Families[a] (percent)	Mean income (dollars)	Dollars	Percent of family income
50–52	53.4	20,170	6,313	31	57.0	16,352	6,147	38
27–49	21.6	16,566	3,662	22	21.9	13,527	3,835	28
1–26	25.0	14,533	1,284	9	21.1	9,647	1,434	15
All families	100.0	17,983	4,483	25	100.0	14,317	4,645	32

Source: Bureau of the Census, *Current Population Reports*, series P-60, no. 101, "Money Income in 1974 of Families and Persons in the United States" (GPO, 1976), tables 76, 77, 78.
a. There were 21.922 million husband-wife dual earner families in the United States in March 1975. Of these 20.101 million were white and 1.821 million were black.

percent of all aged wives of retired worker beneficiaries will be entitled to benefits on the basis of their own earnings records.[22]

A final criticism of the spouse's benefit is that many inequities of the social security program follow from the fact that the beneficiary unit and the taxpaying unit are not the same—the tax is levied on the individual, the benefit is awarded to the family. Compare two workers retiring at sixty-five with identical earnings histories, one single and one married with a nonworking spouse aged sixty-five. Both workers paid the same amount in taxes and receive equal primary benefits. However, the married worker receives an additional 50 percent of the primary benefit for support of his spouse, raising his wage replacement rate and giving him more benefits for his payroll tax dollar. For example, the replacement rate for a single worker with median earnings retiring at sixty-five in January 1976 was 43.4 percent, only two-thirds of the 65.1 percent replacement rate of a worker with a nonworking spouse.

The most serious inequity exists in the case of a two-earner family with a working wife who contributes to the social security system. At retirement she receives either the benefit based on her husband's earnings record or the benefit from her own earnings record. This family (call it family A) could contribute the same amount as a family with a nonworking wife (family B) but receive less in benefits. Assume that each spouse in family A earned 50 percent of the maximum taxable amount in effect in each year.

22. *Reports of the Quadrennial Advisory Council on Social Security*, p. 76.

If both had retired at sixty-five in January 1976, the husband's monthly benefit would be $229.20, the wife's $235.80, totaling $465.00. (The discrepancy in individual amounts is because of the shorter computation period for women, a discrepancy being corrected.) In family B, the husband earned the maximum taxable amount every year, the wife did not work. If he had retired at sixty-five in January 1976, family B would receive a benefit of $546.00 (150 percent of the husband's primary insurance amount). Thus, while both families contributed the same amount, the one-earner family would receive $972.00 more per year in benefits than the two-earner family.

One way to eliminate inequities between one- and two-earner couples is to use the family rather than the individual for both taxation and benefit calculation.[23] The primary insurance amount would be derived from the combined earnings of husband and wife up to the maximum taxable amount. Awarding 100 percent of this PIA plus the wife's regular benefit to all retired couples would equalize benefits among families with equal total earnings histories, regardless of the number of wage earners. Taxes, too, would be based on family income instead of individual income, equalizing the taxes of single earner families and dual earner families earning more than the maximum taxable amount. (This could be done by allowing multiple earner families to claim a refund on their income tax returns for social security taxes paid in excess of the earnings ceiling.)

Another possible way to accomplish equalization is to phase out benefits for aged spouses and convert to strictly wage-related benefits based on individual earnings records.[24] The proposal discussed by the 1975 Social Security Advisory Council called for gradually reducing the 50 percent supplementary benefit to 40 percent in six years, to 30 percent in the next six years, to 20 percent six years later, and so forth until the secondary retirement benefits are completely eliminated in the year 2006.[25] This ap-

23. Use of the family as the unit for benefit and tax calculation is discussed by Joseph A. Pechman, Henry J. Aaron, and Michael K. Taussig in *Social Security: Perspectives for Reform* (Brookings Institution, 1968), pp. 87–91, 222–26.

24. "This approach would eliminate most of the existing differences in treatment of singles and marrieds, for which this Subcommittee found no acceptable alternative, and would also eliminate the differences in treatment of the married woman who works and the married woman who does not work." *Reports of the Quadrennial Advisory Council on Social Security,* p. 146.

25. This pattern was suggested in the Report of the Subcommittee on the Treatment of Men and Women under Social Security of the 1975 Advisory Council, although the proposal of eliminating secondary benefits was not adopted by the entire committee. (See *Reports of the Quadrennial Advisory Council on Social Security,* p. 146.)

proach would also decrease the costs of the program. The exact amount of the cost reduction would depend on whether secondary survivors' benefits as well as retirement benefits were phased out. If only benefits for aged spouses were gradually abolished over the next thirty years as suggested above, the long-run saving to the system would be 0.52 percent of taxable payroll.[26] The largest saving would begin to be realized just after the turn of the century, when the actuarial deficit is projected to increase sharply in response to demographic shifts. (These changes in the age composition of the population and their implications for social security financing are treated in detail in chapter 5.)

While the elimination of benefits for aged spouses may be desirable to promote equity, such a move would produce considerable hardship for women who are primarily attached to the home. If it is decided that the wife's benefits should be eliminated, some provision must be made for the retirement income for nonworking wives.

One possible alternative within the system would be to allow women to receive benefits on the basis of imputed income for unpaid housework, either by earning credits or paying payroll taxes on the amount.[27] (The Social Security Administration has estimated the average 1972 value of a housewife's labor at $4,705 using a market cost approach, which applies wages for identical tasks performed in the marketplace to those same tasks performed by housewives.[28] Imputing wages to nonworking homemakers, however, is undesirable, because all workers—full-time, part-time, single, or married—also perform household chores. There is no logic to imputing a wage to the nonemployed homemaker without imputing at least some earnings to employed people who work around the house.

A solution preferable to imputing wages is a mandatory division of a married couple's contribution credits. Under this scheme, if the husband with a nonworking wife had earned the maximum in 1976 of $15,300, each would have been credited with $7,650. The same procedure would be used for the earnings of a husband and wife who are both employed— their earnings (up to the maximum) would be added together and divided by two, half credited to each account. Therefore, if the wife had earned the maximum of $15,300 in 1976 and the husband earned $6,700 each would

26. Social Security Administration, Office of the Actuary.

27. In 1972, Representative Bella Abzug introduced a bill to amend Title II of the Social Security Act, extending coverage to dependent homemakers for their work at household maintenance. They would receive benefits on the basis of imputed wage credits rather than on the basis of dependency status.

28. Wendyce H. Brody, "Economic Value of a Housewife," note 9 (Social Security Administration, Office of Research and Statistics, 1975), p. 5.

have been credited with $11,000 (($15,300 + $6,700)/2 = $11,000) of covered earnings. This approach seems equitable, since the decision on whether or not the wife works is probably made by the family. The non-working wife would have a permanent earnings base for future retirement benefits. Even if she should later become divorced she would retain the credits she earned during her marriage.

However, without some adjustment in benefit levels, eliminating the spouse's benefit and splitting earnings records would involve a drastic reduction in replacement rates for married couples with a nonworking spouse. A small portion of the loss of the spouse's benefit would be offset by the splitting of earnings, thereby concentrating a greater portion of the worker's AME in the high replacement rate brackets of the progressive benefit formula. Nevertheless, any sizable reduction in the couple's replacement rate for current workers is probably politically unacceptable.

Even if the overall replacement rate for couples could be maintained, the mandatory division of the couple's credits raises a serious problem if the working spouse is older than the nonworking spouse. Consider the case of a male worker aged sixty-five who wishes to retire but whose nonworking wife is too young to collect her benefits. With the mandatory division suggested above, the husband can collect only half the benefits the couple is entitled to and thus may not be able to afford retirement until the wife retires.

The Consultant Panel on Social Security proposed a scheme that maintains current replacement rates for couples and addresses the problem arising when there is a large age difference between husband and wife. This scheme would allow each spouse to build individual earnings records with additional individual contributions. A nonworking spouse would be assumed to earn 50 percent of the earnings of the working spouse; that 50 percent would be taxed as self-employed income. Eventually, an earnings history would be established for the nonworking spouse of every covered employee. The spouse who retired first would receive a benefit based on his own earnings record until the retirement of both, when the couple could choose between benefits based on individual earnings records or benefits based on the average of the couple's two AMEs.[29]

29. The family benefit would be divided between the spouses in proportion to the PIAs corresponding to their individual AMEs. Such division would be subject to a minimum of one-third and a maximum of two-thirds. If AMEs had been averaged before the death of a spouse, the surviving spouse would receive two-thirds of the total family benefit. If a spouse died before AMEs had been averaged, the surviving spouse could choose between a benefit based on his or her own AME or on the

Allowing couples to average their earnings records upon retirement provides a more generous benefit to couples than to single retirees as long as the benefit formula is progressive. Thus, while the nonworking wife would be provided for and one-earner and two-earner families treated fairly, the inequity between couples and single retirees with identical earnings records would remain. This imbalance is the inevitable result of averaging earnings records in a progressive benefit structure.

The panel proposal has many advantages, and with a slight modification might also improve the welfare of the nonworking spouse in case of divorce. If the earnings credits of the couple were averaged annually rather than at retirement, each spouse would have a permanent earnings history equal to at least 75 percent of the highest paid spouse's earnings. If the couple divorced, the wife would have an independent earnings history on the basis of which she would be entitled to retirement benefits. And in the event that one spouse wished to retire before the other, he would be entitled to at least 75 percent of the benefit he would receive under the current system. This modification could be viewed as a compromise solution for the problem of divorced couples and that of couples with significant age differences.

THE MINIMUM BENEFIT. A $10 minimum benefit was introduced in 1939 primarily for reasons of administrative efficiency. Over time, in response to criticism that the minimum benefit was inadequate to meet basic needs, it has been increased more than twice as fast as average benefits. Recently, however, the gradual elimination of the minimum benefit has been suggested by several groups, among them the 1975 Social Security Advisory Council. The supplemental security income program duplicates its social welfare objective.

Furthermore, there is evidence that a large portion of minimum benefits are paid to those who were not primarily dependent on earnings in covered employment during their working years and are not primarily dependent on social security benefits during their retirement years—in other words, the minimum benefit for them is consistent with neither a social adequacy objective nor an earnings replacement goal. Minimum benefits are payable on the basis of average monthly earnings under social security of $76 or less. Earnings at this level suggest very weak attachment to the labor force,

---

average of both AMEs. A couple who had averaged their AMEs before obtaining a divorce would continue to receive benefits based on this averaging if they had been married sufficiently long. Since AME averaging can be done only once, if either person remarried no change would be made.

since a man retiring at sixty-five in January 1976 who worked throughout
his life at the prevailing minimum wage would have average monthly earnings of $237.87. Under the present system, workers entitled to other major
pensions, such as federal civil service retirement benefits, can easily achieve
insured status under social security (one quarter for every year after 1950
or the age of twenty-one and before sixty-two) and receive the minimum
benefit in addition to their regular pensions. The extent to which dual benefits are received is considerable. It was estimated in 1968 that approximately 40 percent of those receiving civil service retirement benefits were
also receiving social security benefits.[30] In direct conflict with its stated welfare objective, the minimum benefit thus often serves to supplement the
income of those relatively affluent retirees who receive other pensions. The
minimum benefit should be phased out because it is not an efficient welfare
device, is not consistent with a wage-related benefit structure, and with the
advent of SSI, is no longer needed to achieve social adequacy.

Horizontal Equity: Treatment of Differing Wage Histories

The collapsing of an entire earnings history into a single number raises
two important questions. First, should earnings be indexed so that wages
in one year can be realistically compared with those in another? Second,
over how many years should earnings be averaged in the AME calculation?

INDEXING. Many proposals for revising the benefit computation procedure call for indexing the worker's earnings before calculating the average monthly earnings. The rationale for indexing earnings in a dynamic
economy is straightforward. Any benefit computation scheme uses a calculation of preretirement earnings as an average over a period of years,
and therefore some adjustment is required for a meaningful comparison
of dollars earned in one year with those earned in other years. The resulting indexed earnings provide an inflation-adjusted basis on which to calculate benefits.[31]

Two indexes have frequently been suggested—an index of consumer
prices and an index of wage levels in the economy as a whole. Price indexing translates earnings in previous years into the quantity of goods and

30. James R. Storey, "Public Income Transfer Programs: The Incidence of
Multiple Benefits and the Issues Raised by Their Receipt," in *Studies in Public
Welfare*, paper 1, prepared for the Subcommittee on Fiscal Policy of the Joint
Economic Committee, 92:2 (GPO, 1972), p. 31.

31. Discussion is based on the work of John Palmer, Jane Ross, Lawrence
Thompson, and Paul Van de Water.

services it could purchase today. For example, because consumer prices have doubled since 1956, a social security taxable wage of $4,000 earned in 1956 would buy $8,000 worth of goods and services in 1975, and price indexing would treat the 1956 wage of $4,000 as equivalent to $8,000 earned in 1975.

Wage indexing translates earnings in previous years into what the worker would earn in an equivalent job today.[32] For example, average wages increased 150 percent between 1956 and 1975, so that a job paying $4,000 in 1956 paid $10,000 in 1975. Wage indexing would thus treat the 1956 wage of $4,000 as equivalent to $10,000 earned in 1975.

Choosing between the two indexes involves both philosophical and distributional considerations. On the philosophical level, the choice of an index is related to how a standard of living should be measured. Are earnings to be measured in real terms (the command over goods and services) or are they to be measured in relative terms (the position of the worker relative to other earners)? Price indexing expresses each year's wage in terms of the goods and services it could now purchase and thereby measures a standard of living in real or absolute terms. Wage indexing expresses each year's wages in terms of the wage in a similar job today and therefore measures a standard of living in relative terms.

The choice between wage and price indexing will also have a significant effect on how a given level of benefits are distributed among workers with different wage histories. Table 3-8 shows the two series of suggested indexes for twenty-five years, beginning in 1951. Indexing earnings histories by either wages or prices shifts the distribution of benefits toward workers with high earnings early in life and slower wage growth thereafter. However, because wages rise more rapidly than prices, wage indexing gives greater weight to early years and thus favors these workers more than price indexing. For two people with the same average wages, the one with high earnings at the beginning but slow wage growth will do better if earnings are indexed by wages, while the one with rapid wage growth and high earnings later in life will do better if earnings are indexed by prices.

Workers who have their highest wages early in their earnings histories include blue-collar workers, whose earnings usually peak early, women who enter the labor force early and then leave, and workers who retire

---

32. Actually, average wages—and thus wage-indexed earnings—also reflect the changing composition of labor services and productivity increases, which not only affect only certain workers but affect them differently because of nonhomogeneity of labor services and markets.

Table 3-8. Data for Indexing Earnings Record for Worker Retiring in 1976

Year	Wage indexing		Price indexing	
	Earnings[a]	Factor[b]	CPI[c]	Factor[b]
1951	2,813	3.068	77.8	2.072
1952	2,970	2.906	79.5	2.028
1953	3,162	2.730	80.1	2.012
1954	3,204	2.694	80.5	2.002
1955	3,324	2.597	80.2	2.010
1956	3,514	2.456	81.4	1.980
1957	3,709	2.327	84.3	1.912
1958	3,830	2.254	86.6	1.861
1959	3,955	2.182	87.3	1.847
1960	4,126	2.092	88.7	1.817
1961	4,256	2.028	89.6	1.799
1962	4,437	1.945	90.6	1.779
1963	4,544	1.899	91.7	1.758
1964	4,683	1.843	92.9	1.735
1965	4,757	1.814	94.5	1.706
1966	4,966	1.738	97.2	1.658
1967	5,281	1.634	100.0	1.612
1968	5,652	1.527	104.2	1.547
1969	5,944	1.452	109.8	1.468
1970	6,250	1.381	116.3	1.386
1971	6,630	1.302	121.3	1.329
1972	7,210	1.197	125.3	1.287
1973	7,580	1.139	133.1	1.211
1974	8,031	1.075	147.7	1.091
1975	8,631	1.000	161.2	1.000

Sources: Robert J. Myers, "The Case for Indexing of Social Security Benefits for Changes in Wage Levels" (Temple University, June 1975; processed), p. 11a; *Economic Report of the President, January 1976*, p. 220; *1976 Annual Report of the Board of Trustees of the Federal OASI and DI Trust Funds*, p. 80.

a. Annualized average earnings in dollars for people with covered nonagricultural wages in first quarter of year.

b. Multiplied by yearly earnings yields indexed earnings for year.

c. Consumer price index figures on basis of 1967 = 100.

early. People whose highest earnings are likely to occur later in life include white-collar workers, people with long periods of training or education, and women who have children early and join the work force later. Wage indexing thus tends to favor the former group, whereas price indexing will help the latter.

While wage indexing may appear preferable on distributional grounds, it does introduce greater variability in year-to-year changes in real benefit awards. Indexing earnings by average wages ensures that benefits are a predictable fraction of real earnings in the year immediately preceding retirement, while price indexing guarantees that they are some predictable fraction of real earnings averaged over several years before retirement. The two schemes can yield significantly different results, since the real-wage growth of money wages varies considerably from year to year. On average, real earnings increase 2 percent a year; however, real earnings rose 3.1 percent in 1972 and 0.1 percent in 1973 but declined 2.5 percent in 1974 and another 0.3 percent in 1975.[33] Under wage indexing, real social security benefits would have varied from year to year in exactly the same pattern as yearly real wages, while under price indexing, benefits would have grown each year at roughly the trend rate of growth of real wages. This variability in the benefit awards penalizes and rewards particular workers depending upon the current vagaries of the economy.[34]

It must also be decided whether the same index used for earnings histories should be used to adjust benefits after retirement. Currently, benefits to retired workers are indexed by the CPI, thus maintaining the purchasing power of the initial benefit award. This approach is consistent with indexing earnings by their command over goods and services, or price indexing. Indexing benefits by wages would permit retirees not only to keep pace with inflation but also to share in the growth in the economy, thereby preventing a deterioration in their position relative to employed workers. This approach is consistent with indexing earnings histories by wages, where wages in the early years are adjusted to reflect increases in productivity as well as price level, thereby permitting workers to maintain their relative positions in the earnings scale. Whatever the choice, philosophically it would seem reasonable to use the same index for both earnings histories and benefits after retirement. However, long-run cost considerations may dictate choosing the alternative that costs the least, in which case benefits after retirement would continue to be indexed by prices regardless of the index applied to earnings histories.

THE AVERAGING PERIOD. The appropriate length of the averaging period depends partially on one's perception of the social security program.[35] If the system is viewed as an annual tax transfer program, there is

33. *Economic Report of the President, January 1976,* p. 204.

34. A wage indexing scheme that does not produce year-to-year variability in real benefits can be devised by using an average figure for the final-year index rather than wages for just that particular year.

35. This discussion assumes that the benefit structure is appropriately indexed for inflation. Otherwise, averaging over the last few years can be used as an inflation adjustment.

little rationale for requiring more than a minimal period for coverage and averaging. In this setting, where the goal is to channel money to relatively poor retired workers, eligibility criteria should be as lenient as possible.

At the other extreme, a completely wage-related annuity program would use lifetime contributions as the appropriate base on which to award benefits. Under the current law, the averaging period will increase gradually to an ultimate thirty-five years (after 1950 or the age of twenty-one and before sixty-two excluding five years of lowest earnings) for workers attaining the age of sixty-five in 1994 or after. This move toward lifetime averaging is consistent with a strictly wage-related system. Actually, it might be preferable to extend the period even further to include earnings after the age of eighteen rather than twenty-one. This lengthening of the averaging period to thirty-eight years would in general increase the figure for average wage used in the computation of benefits for those workers who work for a relatively long time. It would particularly help low-income workers who begin working at an early age and pay social security taxes on those early wages but receive no benefits from them. It would also aid workers who retire relatively later.

Averaging wages over an extended period provides a very imperfect adjustment for differing lengths of service in covered employment when benefits are based on a progressive formula. Consider two workers, A and B, with the same earning potential. If worker A works twice as many years as worker B, his lifetime wages will be twice as high. However, A's benefit will not be twice that of B's, since the progressivity of the benefit formula favors workers with low average earnings. This discrepancy arises because the progressive benefit structure cannot differentiate between workers with low wage rates and workers with limited years in covered employment.

Indexing earnings histories would improve the implicit length-of-service adjustment by giving earnings early in a worker's career as much weight as later earnings. For example, consider two workers retiring in 1976 who had earned median taxable earnings in all years. Assume, however, that worker A worked in covered employment all his life while worker B worked in covered employment only from 1966 to 1975, the minimum number of years necessary to receive retirement benefits. With earnings histories not indexed, worker A will receive a retirement benefit 33 percent greater than worker B's; while if earnings were indexed by wages, worker A would receive 53 percent more than worker B. The difference arises because earnings in early years are indexed upwards ($3,750 earned in 1960 is equivalent to $7,845 in the 1975 wage scale); however, years of zero earnings, when indexed, are still years of zero earnings. In this way, indexing increases the average monthly earnings of both workers, but it increases worker A's AME more than worker B's.

Even indexed earnings histories would not, however, differentiate between a worker with low average earnings resulting from many years in covered employment at low wages and a worker with the same average resulting from few years in covered employment at high wages—high-wage workers with short periods in covered employment would still profit unfairly from a benefit formula intended to aid low-wage workers.

In this setting, some explicit length-of-service adjustment might be preferable to an extended averaging period. One possibility is to use a variable averaging period, basing average monthly indexed earnings only on those years in which workers had covered earnings, up to a maximum of thirty-five years. The PIA would then be calculated from the AMIE and, finally, the PIA would be adjusted for length of service. Workers with minimum coverage (ten years) would receive 100 percent of their PIAs. For each year of coverage in excess of ten, benefits would increase 10 percent. Thus, if worker A has the same AMIE as worker B but twice as many years of coverage, A will get double the retirement benefit that B will. In this scheme, the length-of-service adjustment is totally explicit. The implicit adjustment is eliminated, since periods outside covered employment are not included in the averaging period.

Other length-of-service adjustment schemes have been suggested using a lifetime averaging period and basing the adjustment factor on the ratio of the worker's number of years in covered employment to the maximum number of years possible for that worker. Again, if worker A and worker B have the same AMIE, but A has twice the number of years in covered employment, A will receive twice the benefit that B will.

If social security were to move toward a strictly wage-related system with a proportional benefit formula, extended lifetime averaging of indexed earnings would provide a perfect length-of-service adjustment. However, under the progressive structure, explicit length-of-service adjustments should be seriously considered as a method of differentiating between low wages and limited service in covered employment.

Intertemporal Equity: Replacement Rates Now and in the Future

One of the foremost problems in designing a benefit structure is determining an appropriate level of replacement rates; that is, what percentage of preretirement earnings should be provided as benefits in retirement. Resolution of this issue requires balancing the financial needs of retired people with the increased tax burden on workers. Once replacement rates are established, the more difficult issue of how they should vary over time must be addressed. The future path of replacement rates is the key issue in the decoupling controversy over whether the break points in the benefit formula should be indexed by wages or by prices.

The selection of the level of replacement rates is necessarily a value judgment, but the decision is also conditional upon the role of social security. If social security benefits are to be the sole source of support in retirement, replacement rates must be considerably higher than if social security is to provide only a base, supplemented by other sources. The decision about replacement rates, therefore, comes back to two questions: (1) can personal saving, private pension plans, and individual retirement accounts (IRAs) adequately supplement social security benefits for workers above the median, and (2) can SSI provide the needed support for low-wage workers?

Table 3-9 presents, for married couples in various income classes, estimates of the percentage of preretirement income required in retirement to maintain the same standard of living. Because of reduced expenses and lower taxes, retirees require only 65–80 percent of preretirement earnings. A man with a history of median earnings who retired at sixty-five in January 1976 has about 43 percent of his earnings replaced by social security. The comparable ratio for a low-wage worker is 62 percent, and for a worker with maximum taxable earnings it is 31 percent. Workers with private pensions as well as social security receive an additional 30–40 percent of preretirement earnings.

In dollar terms, a worker with a median-wage earnings history received a monthly social security benefit of $318, or $3,816 per year, in 1976— enough to meet the minimum retirement needs of a worker with median earnings. Additional income from private pensions, saving, or the new IRAs may have improved the retiree's standard of living.

Once the level of replacement is determined, the problem remains of deciding how replacement rates should vary over time. The higher the replacement rate, the higher the tax rates required to finance the benefits. Social security taxes must be increased by about 10 percent in the next few years simply to finance the current level of replacement rates. Furthermore, current projections indicate that, because of demographic shifts, social security tax rates will increase 70 percent by the middle of the next

**Table 3-9. Retirement Income Equivalent to Preretirement Income for
Married Couples Retiring January 1976, Selected Income Levels**

Pre-retirement income (dollars)	Preretirement tax payment (dollars)			Reduction in expenses at re-tirement[b] (dollars)	Equivalent retirement income[c]	
	Federal income	OASDHI	State and local income[a]		Dollars	Percent of pre-retirement income
4,000	28	234	4	544	3,190	80
6,000	330	351	43	816	4,460	74
8,000	679	468	89	1,088	5,676	71
10,000	1,059	585	139	1,360	6,857	69
15,000	2,002	824	262	2,040	9,872	66

Sources: Commerce Clearing House, *1976 U.S. Master Tax Guide* (CCH, 1975); Bureau of Labor Statistics, *Revised Equivalence Scale for Estimating Equivalent Incomes or Budget Costs by Family Type*, Bulletin 1570-2 (GPO, 1968), p. 4; estimates of state and local income tax receipts as a percentage of federal income tax from Bureau of Economic Analysis.

a. In 1974 state and local income tax receipts were 13.1 percent of federal income tax receipts. This percentage probably rose in 1975 because federal taxes were decreased while state taxes increased. Therefore the percentage of preretirement income needed to maintain living standards is probably slightly overstated.

b. Consumption requirements for a two-person husband-wife family after retirement are 86.4 percent of those for a like family before retirement (aged 55 to 64). Savings are therefore estimated at 13.6 percent of preretirement income.

c. Assumes that retirement income is not subject to tax. If retirement income is subject to taxation, a larger preretirement disposable income would be needed to yield the equivalent retirement income.

century—this assumes the system is decoupled and the break points are indexed by wages, thus stabilizing replacement rates at their present levels. Most of this projected tax increase could be eliminated if the break points in the benefit formula were indexed by prices, permitting replacement rates to decline gradually over time.

The debate over wage versus price indexing is, in fact, a debate over the intertemporal behavior of replacement rates. The implicit assumption in most analyses is that the replacement rate should remain constant over time. Many feel that it would represent a tremendous deliberalization of the system to lower the levels of replacement. On the other hand, an argument can be made for simply maintaining the real purchasing power of today's benefits which, combined with rising real wages, would result in declining replacement rates. Assuming current benefit levels allow retired workers to meet their minimum needs, it could be argued that the goal of social security should be merely to continue to provide a level of benefits that satisfies these same needs by adjusting benefit levels over time for changes in prices. Future retirees could supplement retirement incomes with private saving out of their higher real wages. Furthermore, declining replacement rates would leave Congress some leeway for legislative adjustment of benefits.

The behavior of replacement rates over time is dependent on the design of the benefit formula. As noted in the discussion of overindexing, without constant widening of the formula brackets a progressive benefit formula in a period of rising wages leads to declining replacement rates. The same effect is produced in a progressive structure if the break points are indexed by prices. On the other hand, indexing the break points by wages or introducing a proportional benefit structure would result in constant replacement rates. In short, there are important intertemporal implications in the selection of a particular benefit structure. Therefore, the path of replacement rates over time is also an important issue, which should be opened for debate.

Summary

The overindexing of the benefit structure is an error that must be corrected as soon as possible. In the course of reaching the optimal decoupling scheme the opportunity to redesign the benefit structure will arise. Designing a decoupled system is quite simple in a technical sense but requires resolution of a number of fundamental issues about the nature of the social security program. Each issue should be addressed directly and resolved explicitly.

In a strictly wage-related benefit program, the minimum benefit and dependents' benefits could be eliminated and the benefit formula made less progressive. However, such a system would require a liberalized SSI program to supplement the income of low-wage workers. The SSI could be most easily expanded by reducing the implicit tax on unearned income from 100 percent to 50 percent. In the absence of an expansion of SSI, there would be compelling reasons to maintain progressivity in the social security benefit structure, since low-income people require very high replacement rates simply to meet their basic needs. If progressive benefits are retained it will be desirable to revise the method of treating married couples so that the benefits of working spouses are better related to their earnings.

Changing the formula for calculating average monthly earnings would also affect the level and distribution of benefits. Either method of indexing earnings histories would permit a comparison of wages earned in different years and provide an inflation-adjusted basis on which to calculate benefits. The appropriate length of the averaging period depends on the nature of the social security program. Use of an averaging period that includes all years in covered employment is consistent with a strictly wage-related system and proportional benefit formula and permits distinction between low-wage and short-term workers. In a system committed to social adequacy, however, the averaging period may be shorter, with some length-of-service adjustment to distinguish workers with low wages from those with only a few years in covered employment.

The method of decoupling, whether by wages or prices, has important implications for the intertemporal behavior of replacement rates. Wage indexing will produce replacement rates that are constant over time, while price indexing will result in gradually declining replacement rates. How replacement rates should behave over time is an unresolved issue, but one that is at the heart of the decoupling controversy.

chapter four Social Security and Retirement Patterns

Participation in the labor force of men sixty-five years of age and over declined from 45.8 percent to 21.7 percent during the twenty-five years from 1950 to 1975. During this same period, the percentage of insured men sixty-five and over receiving social security benefits rose from 59 percent to 94 percent.[1] Has the dramatic reduction in work effort of the aged resulted from increasing eligibility for retirement benefits and other provisions of the social security program? Or have other factors figured in the decline?

Studies by the Social Security Administration generally conclude that early retirement is the result primarily of poor health and difficulties in finding and keeping jobs, with the availability of social security benefits playing only a secondary role. Other studies, however, find that social security has a much greater effect than poor health on the labor force activity of the aged. Recent research confirms the importance of both health and social security in the retirement decision. The evidence indicates that health and financial considerations are highly interactive. That is, many people of retirement age do have health problems, which, while they do not preclude work, make it less desirable. For this group, who are predisposed to retire, social security eligibility is a very important factor.

The trend toward early retirement has high social and financial costs, not only to the elderly but to society as a whole. If the trend is to be reversed, the causes must be understood. This chapter evaluates social security's role in the retirement decision and in the trend to early retirement and proposes changes in social security—such as modification of the earnings test or expansion of the delayed retirement credit—that may be required to encourage the elderly to remain in the work force.

1. The statistics are from Bureau of Labor Statistics and the Social Security Administration.

The Effect on Labor Force Participation

Social security affects retirement in three ways. First, retirement benefits moderate the reduction in income that workers must face when they
retire. Consequently, there is a pure income effect that encourages older
workers to choose leisure instead of work. Second, the earnings test makes
it impossible for most workers to receive benefits without cutting back on
work effort. Finally, social security may condition both employers and
employees to the idea that sixty-five is the "normal" retirement age. The
adoption of compulsory retirement rules by private industry may therefore
be an indirect result of the expansion of the social security program.

The Benefit Effect

Social security benefits lessen the reduction in income that workers
must face upon retirement. If benefits completely replace preretirement
earnings, there is little incentive to remain in the labor force; as this
replacement rate declines and benefits replace a smaller proportion of
earnings, the desire to work in order to augment income increases.

Replacement rates from 1952 to 1976 for five hypothetical workers are
shown in table 4-1. The worker under minimum wage represents workers steadily employed at low wages, while the worker in the construction
industry represents high-earnings, maximum-benefit workers. The figures
are based on full benefits awarded to a male worker at the age of sixty-five
(the rates would be lower if the worker elected early retirement with
actuarially reduced benefits). The table shows that, while replacement
rates were relatively constant from 1952 to 1969, there has been a strong
upward trend in the ratio of benefits to preretirement earnings in all five
wage categories during the last eight years. This trend is largely the result
of seven benefit increases, averaging 12 percent, over the last eight years.

The replacement rates in table 4-1 probably understate the actual replacement of earnings in retirement. Social security benefits are not taxed,
while preretirement earnings are subject to the federal income tax, the
social security payroll tax, and state or municipal income taxes. Thus,
using after-tax income net of expenses as the denominator would result in
even higher replacement rates. Furthermore, expenses for transportation,
clothing, and food away from home are incurred in maintaining a job. The
Bureau of Labor Statistics estimates that retirement lowers expenses by

Table 4-1. Social Security Benefits[a] as a Percentage of Earnings in Year before Retirement, Five Single Male Workers at Differing Wage Levels Retiring at the Age of Sixty-five, 1952–76

Retirement date[b]	Minimum wage[c]	Retail trade	Service industry	Manu-facturing	Construction industry
1952	38	30	29	22	19
1953	42	36	34	28	24
1954	41	35	33	28	23
1955	44	39	36	32	26
1956	43	38	36	31	26
1957	42	37	35	31	26
1958	41	37	34	30	25
1959	43	38	36	32	26
1960	41	37	35	31	25
1961	40	36	34	31	24
1962	39	36	33	30	24
1963	38	35	32	29	23
1964	37	35	31	28	22
1965	38	36	32	29	23
1966	37	35	31	28	22
1967	36	35	30	27	21
1968	35	34	29	27	21
1969	38	37	31	29	22
1970	43	40	34	32	24
1971	46	43	36	35	25
1972	45	42	34	34	23
1973	53	48	39	38	27
1974	51	47	38	37	26
1975	55	49	40	39	29
1976	58	51	41	40	31

Sources: 1952–72 from Peter Henle, "Recent Trends in Retirement Benefits Related to Earnings," *Monthly Labor Review*, vol. 95 (June 1972), pp. 12–20; 1973–76, author's estimates.
a. Primary insurance amounts.
b. As of January 1.
c. Uses 4 percent annual increase to avoid erratic changes resulting from following statutory increases in the federal minimum wage.

about 13.6 percent of take-home pay.[2] If the retiree moves to a warmer climate, living expenses may decline even further. Medicare benefits, available at the age of sixty-five regardless of employment status, also tend to reduce income requirements.

Furthermore, the replacement ratios in table 4-1 are for a single worker. If a retired male worker is married, he would receive an additional

2. Bureau of Labor Statistics, *Revised Equivalence Scale for Estimating Equivalent Incomes or Budget Costs by Family Type*, bulletin 1570-2 (GPO, 1968), p. 4.

37.5–50 percent of the basic benefit (depending upon the age at which his wife retired). About 40 percent of men who retired in 1975 were married, and the couple received the supplementary benefit.[3] For this group of beneficiaries, replacement rates would be 37.5–50 percent higher than those shown in table 4-1.

With these qualifications, replacement rates are a good measure of expected income in retirement. The effect is such that the larger the replacement rate, the higher the retirement benefits, and the stronger the desire to reduce work effort and opt for leisure. This is the pure income effect of social security benefits.

The Earnings Test

The earnings test affects the retirement decision by placing a high marginal tax rate on earned income. In 1976, a person's social security benefit was reduced a dollar for every $2 earned in excess of $2,760 a year ($230 a month) until the benefit was completely exhausted. The earnings limit is scheduled to increase automatically in line with the growth in average wages. The limit is predicted to grow to $3,000 in 1977, $3,480 in 1979, and $4,200 in 1981.[4]

The earnings test reflects the basic philosophy that the social security system was designed to provide income support to people who have retired rather than an annuity to everyone who reaches the age of sixty-five. In 1939, this provision was also seen as a method of reducing unemployment by releasing jobs for unemployed younger workers.

Congress has never been persuaded of the desirability of a strict earnings test, and the constant controversy has led to its gradual liberalization over the years. Even before the first benefits were paid in 1940, the original act was amended to permit monthly earnings up to $15 without loss of benefit. This limit was subsequently raised several times and in 1960 the penalty was relaxed, so that only a dollar of benefits was forfeited for each $2 of earnings between specified amounts, and dollar for dollar thereafter. In 1972, the test was further liberalized and simplified to its present form, in which benefits are reduced by a dollar for every $2 of all earnings over a specified amount.

3. *Social Security Bulletin*, vol. 39 (June 1976), pp. 47, 71.
4. *1976 Annual Report of the Board of Trustees of the Federal Old Age and Survivors Insurance and Disability Insurance Trust Fund*, H. Doc. 94-505, 94:2 (GPO, 1976), p. 22.

The earnings test has been liberalized not only by raising the limit on exempt earnings and reducing the per-dollar loss of benefits, but also by exempting an increasing portion of the aged population. Beginning in September 1950, all beneficiaries aged seventy-five and over were no longer subject to the earnings test. After December 1954 this age exemption was extended to beneficiaries seventy-two and over. At the end of 1975, of the total 16.6 million retired beneficiaries, about 50 percent were seventy-two or older and therefore not subject to any earnings test.[5]

For many aged workers, the earnings test is equivalent to a marginal tax rate of 50 percent on earnings in excess of $230 in any given month; and this high tax rate may have a significant effect on work effort.[6] The test affects only those who, in its absence, would continue to work and would earn more than $230 a month. People with substantial flexibility in working hours might choose to continue to earn up to the allowable limit and then withdraw from employment rather than face the 50 percent tax on monthly earnings over $230. Most people, however, cannot work part time or a few months a year at their regular jobs, and for them retirement is total and abrupt. It is not surprising that the self-employed and professional workers, who control their own employment and have greater flexibility in adjusting their hours, are less likely to retire than other workers. Nor is it surprising that many retirees find supplementary jobs with flexible hours that permit them to earn just $230 per month or to concentrate work in a few months of the year.

A study by the Social Security Administration in 1973 revealed that nearly 16 percent of retired worker beneficiaries incurred reduced benefits as a result of the earnings test (see table 4-2). Men were most affected by the test, since relatively fewer women worked and those who did had lower earnings. Data from a similar study in 1971 indicate that the 1.5

5. Though 50 percent of retired beneficiaries are not subject to the earnings test because they are seventy-two or over, few persons in this age bracket are actually gainfully employed. A 1971 survey revealed that of nonmarried individuals seventy-two and older only 10 percent had earnings. Though for married couples the figure is considerably higher (30 percent), this probably reflects some earnings of spouses under seventy-two, who are more likely to be employed. Gayle B. Thompson, "Work Experience and Income of the Population Aged 60 and Older, 1971," *Social Security Bulletin*, vol. 37 (November 1974), p. 6.

6. For aged workers who earn more than $230 per month and whose earnings are subject to the personal income tax, the payroll tax, state tax, and local tax, the marginal tax rate can be considerably higher.

Table 4-2. Beneficiaries Affected by the OASDI Earnings Test, 1973[a]

Sex and age	Beneficiaries (thousands)		Percent on rolls affected by earnings test[b]
	On rolls at end of year	Affected by earnings test	
Men			
62–71	4,992	976	19.6
62–64	773	131	16.9
65–71	4,220	845	20.0
Women			
62–71	3,767	410	10.9
62–64	816	83	10.2
65–71	2,950	327	11.1
All beneficiaries	8,759	1,386	15.8

Source: Social Security Administration, Office of Research and Statistics.
a. In 1973, beneficiaries could earn up to $2,100 with no reduction in benefits. Benefits were reduced $1 for each $2 of earnings in excess of $2,100.
b. There are some retired workers who may not file because high earnings will defer benefits completely. However, most people sixty-five or older file to become eligible for Medicare even though their retirement benefits are deferred.

million workers affected by the test lost roughly 70 percent of the benefits to which they were entitled, or a total of $2.2 billion.[7]

Compulsory Retirement Rules

Since the end of World War II there has been a large increase in compulsory retirement provisions in union contracts and company personnel practices. The spread of compulsory retirement is due, in large part, to the growth of private pension plans, but the existence of social security retirement benefits must also have influenced employers' attitudes toward their older workers. It is much more conscionable to dismiss workers who are assured retirement benefits than workers who face destitution. Indeed, in the 1930s, part of labor's enthusiasm for the social security program was the hope that it would move older workers out of the labor force to make room for younger workers.

It seems extremely likely that the social security program influences the work effort of the elderly through the three mechanisms described above—the benefit effect, the earnings test, and compulsory retirement rules. Because the aged are becoming an increasing proportion of the popula-

7. Barbara A. Lingg, "Retired-Worker Beneficiaries Affected by the Annual Earnings Test in 1971," *Social Security Bulletin,* vol. 38 (August 1975), p. 25.

tion, their labor force participation affects the costs of the social security program dramatically.

Empirical Evidence

Past evidence of the impact of social security on retirement has been ambiguous. The Social Security Administration, which periodically asks people why they retire, has usually found health cited as the primary reason, though outside studies usually attributed a major role to the social security program. Recent findings, however, indicate that both health and social security are important in the retirement decision.

Studies by the Social Security Administration

The earliest study undertaken by the Social Security Administration was a 1941–42 survey of retirees. Only 5 percent of the sample indicated that they had retired voluntarily and were in good health when they retired. The report concludes, "The fact that only 3–6 percent of the beneficiaries retired voluntarily in order to enjoy leisure is significant in evaluating the part old-age insurance benefits have played in influencing aged workers to leave the labor market."[8]

A report on surveys conducted during the 1940–47 period also revealed that only about 5 percent of the respondents said that they had quit their jobs simply because they wished to retire. This report concludes that "most old people work as long as they can and retire only because they are forced to do so."[9] A 1951 survey confirmed these earlier findings —only 3.8 percent of the 1951 respondents had retired voluntarily and in good health. The later survey reaffirms the earlier finding that "most retired workers who are beneficiaries under the old-age and survivors insurance program do not leave their jobs because they want to; if their health permits and there is a market for their services, they would rather continue in gainful employment."[10]

The 1960 surveys revealed a dramatic increase in voluntary retire-

8. Edna C. Wentworth, "Why Beneficiaries Retire," *Social Security Bulletin,* vol. 8 (January 1945), pp. 16–20 (p. 18 for quotation).

9. Margaret L. Stecker, "Beneficiaries Prefer to Work," *Social Security Bulletin,* vol. 14 (January 1951), p. 15.

10. Margaret L. Stecker, "Why Do Beneficiaries Retire? Who Among Them Return to Work?" *Social Security Bulletin,* vol. 18 (May 1955), p. 3.

ments. In the 1963 Survey of the Aged, 19 percent of men who retired at the age of sixty-five and 11 percent of early retirees cited a preference for leisure as their reason for retirement.[11] The trend toward voluntary retirement was confirmed by the 1968 Survey of Newly Entitled Beneficiaries. Although health was still given most frequently as the primary reason for withdrawing from the labor force, in a separate question, 46 percent of the respondents indicated that they wanted to retire. In addition, two-thirds of those who wanted to retire indicated that eligibility for retirement benefits was influential in their decision to retire.[12] The Social Security Administration's Retirement History Study, a longitudinal study of a cohort of workers reaching retirement age in the early 1970s, will show whether the trend toward voluntary retirement is continuing. Preliminary findings from this study indicate that 42 percent of male retirees aged sixty-two to sixty-three in 1973 who had been employed in 1969 had left their jobs voluntarily and for nonhealth reasons. Half of these men cited pension eligibility as their primary motivation. In addition, 52 percent of men aged sixty-four to sixty-five and 54 percent of men aged sixty-six to sixty-seven who left the labor force between 1969 and 1973 cited reasons other than health or job displacement as their main reason for retiring.[13]

It is important to keep in mind that the use of the interview technique may yield unreliable results, since in interviews people tend to give socially acceptable reasons for not working. Poor health is a very legitimate reason for withdrawing from the labor force, while a desire for leisure might be considered reprehensible laziness. Even though the interview technique thus tends to understate the extent of voluntary, nonhealth-related retirement, the evidence still points to a definite trend toward voluntary retirement, which coincides with the expansion of social security.

Independent Studies

The Census Bureau data on labor force participation presented in table 4-3 reveal a sharp decline in activity at the age of sixty-five, the year when workers become eligible for full retirement benefits. The decline at sixty-

11. Erdman Palmore, "Retirement Patterns Among Aged Men: Findings of the 1963 Survey of the Aged," *Social Security Bulletin,* vol. 27 (August 1964), p. 9.

12. Virginia Reno, "Why Men Stop Working at or Before Age 65: Findings from the Survey of New Beneficiaries," *Social Security Bulletin,* vol. 34 (June 1971), pp. 3–17.

13. Lenore E. Bixby, "Retirement Patterns in the United States: Research and Policy Interaction," *Social Security Bulletin,* vol. 39 (August 1976), pp. 3–19.

Table 4-3. Labor Force Participation Rates for Males and Females Fifty-five and Older, Selected Years, 1940–70

Percent

	Male				Female			
Age	1940	1950	1960	1970	1940	1950	1960	1970
55	89.5	87.8	89.9	88.9	19.9	27.9	42.5	49.6
56	89.1	87.8	89.0	88.3	19.2	26.7	40.7	48.7
57	87.8	86.7	87.8	86.7	18.0	25.4	39.7	48.0
58	86.9	86.1	86.7	85.8	17.7	24.8	38.6	46.5
59	85.6	85.1	85.1	83.7	17.4	24.1	37.0	45.1
60	81.9	82.1	83.2	81.3	16.8	23.1	34.7	42.9
61	81.4	81.4	80.7	79.2	15.3	21.0	32.1	40.2
62	79.7	80.0	78.6	72.7	14.9	20.9	29.3	35.9
63	76.9	77.6	75.7	67.5	13.8	19.1	26.1	32.6
64	74.4	75.2	70.0	63.1	12.4	18.0	24.3	29.3
65	66.9	67.7	53.6	47.1	12.0	16.3	20.3	22.0
66	62.0	62.9	45.9	41.9	9.6	13.4	17.6	18.8
67	57.8	58.2	41.9	38.6	8.9	12.2	16.2	17.0
68	54.9	54.2	39.5	35.4	8.2	11.4	14.6	14.7
69	51.4	51.2	36.6	31.5	7.5	10.1	13.2	12.9
70	44.0	44.5	33.2	26.9	6.3	8.1	11.7	11.1
71	40.8	42.0	29.0	24.6	5.4	6.7	10.2	9.8
72	37.4	39.0	27.8	22.1	5.2	6.0	9.0	9.1
73	34.5	34.0	26.9	19.8	4.0	5.4	8.8	7.8
74	31.4	30.8	25.1	17.4	3.9	5.0	7.6	7.1
75 and over	18.2	18.7	15.6	12.1	2.3	2.6	4.3	4.7

Source: Bureau of the Census, *Census of Population, 1970*, Final Report PC(2)-6A, *Employment Status and Work Experience* (GPO, 1973), pp. 31–32.

five was significantly larger in the 1960 and 1970 censuses than in 1940 and 1950, probably reflecting the rapid expansion of social security coverage and benefits during the 1950s.[14] In 1940, 1950, and 1960 work force participation declined gradually by about 2 percent each year between the ages of fifty-five and sixty-five, at which point activity dropped off sharply. For males, this sudden drop amounted to 7 percentage points in 1940 and increased to 16 percentage points in 1960, after expansion of the social security program. The data for 1970 show a slightly different pattern, since beginning in 1962 men became eligible for reduced benefits

14. Farm and domestic workers were brought into the system in 1950 and most professionals and members of the armed forces were covered by 1956. In addition, between 1950 and 1960 the average monthly benefit awarded to a retired worker increased from $29.03 to $81.73. *Social Security Bulletin, Annual Statistical Supplement, 1974* (GPO, n.d.), p. 89.

at the age of sixty-two. Therefore, in 1970 there are two sharp drops in labor force participation, one at sixty-two and the other at sixty-five. This information alone, however, does not separate the impact on retirement of social security from that of factors such as health and occupation.

Several economists have analyzed the statistical data on labor force participation to determine the relative importance of various factors affecting retirement behavior. One study, by Bowen and Finegan, concludes that social security plays a major role in the declining labor force participation of the aged.[15] They performed two separate analyses. Both analyses pointed to the role that social security plays through its income effect, its earnings test, and its less easily quantifiable effect on attitudes toward retirement.

Bowen and Finegan first focused on the difference in labor force participation of men between the ages of sixty-four and sixty-seven. The factors in the total decline of 32.9 percent were:

	Percent
Earnings test, compulsory retirement, and attitudes toward 65 as the appropriate retirement age	17.0
Other income (primarily social security)	11.6
Three years of aging	4.0
Schooling, marital status, color	0.3

Their second study was the 1948–65 decline in employment of 18.9 percent for males aged sixty-five and over, plus 6.3 percent to allow for the *encouraging* influence of the reduced workweek.[16] The factors making up the total hypothetical decline were:

	Percent
Other income	9.8
Compulsory retirement	5.0
Demographics	2.9
Unemployment in 1950s	2.7
Other[17]	3.4
Residual	1.4
Total	25.2

15. William G. Bowen and T. Aldrich Finegan, *The Economics of Labor Force Participation* (Princeton University Press, 1969).

16. The most important factor, accounting for over half of the predicted increase in labor force participation by the elderly, is the reduced workweek.

17. These factors include a decline in health of older males, a reduction in the self-employment mix, and a general rise in the percentage of all males aged fourteen and over in the labor force, which increased the competition for jobs.

In another study, Michael Boskin examined the retirement decisions of 131 white married males, aged sixty-one to sixty-five in 1968, who were interviewed annually during the period 1968–72.[18] In constructing a model of their retirement behavior, variables representing the social security system—benefits and net earnings (a proxy for the earnings test)—were found to have a large effect on the probability of retirement, whereas other variables—income from assets, spouse's earnings, hours ill, and age —had a relatively small impact. Boskin's results suggest that a decrease in the implicit tax on earnings from one-half to one-third would reduce the annual probability of retirement by almost 60 percent. Boskin used his cross-sectional results to explain the long-term decline in the labor force participation rate of elderly males. He concludes that social security has been the major force behind the trend toward early retirement. His results must be interpreted with care, however, since he does not include a variable for private pension benefits. Thus, his estimates may overstate the effect of social security, since some of the impact of the social security variables may actually represent the influence of the private pension annuities.

Noticeably absent from both the Boskin and the Bowen and Finegan results is deteriorating health as an important reason for declining labor force activity. In fact, Bowen and Finegan found that only a small portion of the decline in labor force participation from sixty-four to sixty-seven was the result of three years of age or worsening health. For the long-run decline in participation, Bowen and Finegan found little support for the argument that health is a major factor.

Some recent work on retirement patterns of men in their early sixties provides evidence that recognizes both poor health and retirement benefits as primary incentives to retire. A cross-sectional analysis of a 1966–67 sample of retirees by Barfield and Morgan indicate that health was important but that health and financial factors are interdependent. The conclusion reached was:

Economic factors provide the basic enabling framework for the retirement decision. If one can afford to retire, then his decision will be affected by his health and by his attitudes toward work and retirement. But if one feels economically unable to retire, only rather severe problems with (say) health or work may induce retirement.[19]

18. Michael J. Boskin, "Social Security and Retirement Decisions" (National Bureau of Economic Research, 1975; processed).

19. Richard E. Barfield and James N. Morgan, *Early Retirement: The Decision and the Experience and a Second Look,* University of Michigan (Survey Research Center, reprinted 1974), p. 70.

This kind of interaction between health and financial variables was confirmed in a 1975 study by Joseph Quinn based on the 11,000 respondents aged fifty-eight to sixty-three in the Social Security Retirement History Survey.[20] In the aggregate regressions, the strongest reasons for retirement status turn out to be health, eligibility for social security, and eligibility for other retirement benefits. The interaction between health and financial security was then clarified by disaggregating the group of white married males according to health status. The results show that the aggregate social security effect was the average of two quite different components—a very large impact on those with some health limitation and a very small effect on those without. This study concludes that

Health and financial considerations are highly interactive. Many people of early retirement age have health problems which are not serious enough to preclude work, but which are serious enough to make continued labor force participation less desirable. For these people, who are *predisposed* to retire, Social Security eligibility is a very important factor.[21]

Retirement Age

The evidence developed in the previous section indicates that social security benefits and the earnings test encourage workers to withdraw from the labor force. Retirement is also facilitated by the availability of actuarially reduced benefits before the age of sixty-five. The trend toward early retirement has far-reaching consequences both for the welfare of the aged and for the costs of the social security system. In view of the increasing physical capacity of the aged to continue working, the growing proportion of elderly in the population, and the forecast rise in social security costs, an attractive option is to encourage later retirement by moving the normal retirement age forward, perhaps to sixty-eight.

Reduced Benefits for Early Retirees

Until 1956, retirement benefits were not paid until a worker reached sixty-five. However, beginning in November 1956 for women and August 1961 for men, permanently reduced benefits were made available at sixty-two. The reduction in benefits is calculated so that there is no additional cost to the system (benefits are reduced 5/9 of 1 percent for each month

20. Joseph F. Quinn, "The Microeconomics of Early Retirement: A Cross-sectional View," (Ph.D. dissertation, Massachusetts Institute of Technology, 1975).

21. Ibid., p. 213.

Table 4-4. **Growth in Early Retirement of Eligible Men and Women, Selected Years, 1956–75**

Year[a]	Men	Women	Both sexes
	Percent of eligible insured aged 62–64 receiving OASI benefits		
1957	. . .	16	16
1960	. . .	44	44
1965	32	47	38
1970	34	46	39
1973	41	52	46
1974	44	54	48
1975	46	55	50
	Percent of total OASI benefits received by early retirees		
1956	. . .	31	12
1960	. . .	59	21
1965	43	59	49
1970	49	66	56
1973	56	70	61
1974	58	73	64
1975	59	72	65

Source: Social Security Administration.
a. As of January 1.

of retirement before sixty-five, which amounts to a 20 percent reduction for retirement at sixty-two).

The tremendous popularity of the early retirement option is demonstrated in table 4-4 and in statistics on labor force participation. After the introduction of the early retirement option, the drop in labor force participation for women between sixty-one and sixty-two was 2.8 percentage points in 1960 and 4.3 percentage points in 1970 compared to less than 0.5 points in 1940 and 1950. After the option was extended to men in 1961, the drop in their participation rates between the ages of sixty-one and sixty-two was 6.5 points in 1970 compared to 1.4–2.1 points in earlier years.

More women than men elect the early retirement option because more women work part-time and can adjust their earnings to qualify for benefits under the provisions of the earnings test. Furthermore, a married female worker can receive her benefit at sixty-two and, when her spouse retires, qualify for the dependent spouse's benefit (adjusted for early retirement) if it is larger. (An aged woman who has not worked is not entitled to benefits until her spouse retires.)

The actuarial reduction of early retirement benefits has not had the expected inhibiting effect on the retirement decision of potential bene-

Table 4-5. Number of Newly Entitled Beneficiaries and Average Amount of Benefit, by Type of Award and Sex of Retired Worker, 1974

Type of award	Male Benefi-ciaries (thou-sands)	Male Percent of all awards	Male Average benefit (dollars)	Female Benefi-ciaries (thou-sands)	Female Percent of all awards	Female Average benefit (dollars)
Currently payable	**641**	**76.7**	**201.48**	**512**	**88.7**	**149.08**
Without reduction	58	6.9	212.90[a]	50	8.7	170.90[a]
With reduction	484[b]	58.0	191.40	420	72.7	139.60
Aged 62	184[b]	22.0	181.03	226[b]	39.1	128.21
Aged 63	96[b]	11.5	194.91	68[b]	11.8	145.67
Aged 64	63[b]	7.5	214.96	37[b]	6.4	168.30
Aged 65 and over[c]	141[b]	16.9	227.30	89[b]	15.4	188.54
Disability conversions and transitionally insured	99	11.9	221.65	42	7.3	172.40
Not currently payable[d]	**194**	**23.2**	**258.30[a]**	**66**	**11.4**	**225.40[a]**
Conversions of previously deferred awards	**224**	...	...	**135**	...	...

Source: Social Security Administration, *Social Security Bulletin, Annual Statistical Supplement, 1974* (GPO, n.d.), pp. 86, 87, 94, 95, 105.
a. Average for all awards; includes benefits to retirees who received first awards in previous years.
b. Estimate.
c. Filing retroactively.
d. Conditional and deferred awards suspended immediately, mainly because of earnings. Since September 1965 most of these awards have been made primarily for the purpose of assuring eligibility for hospital insurance benefits.

ficiaries. A worker's immediate economic needs seem to be the determining factor of whether or not he or she elects early benefits. In fact, in the 1968 Survey of Newly Entitled Beneficiaries, 20 percent of the men who received reduced benefits were either sixty-five or within three months of that age.[22] These men could easily have avoided any reduction in their benefits but elected deliberately to be entitled retroactively and incur the benefit reduction.

Table 4-5 presents a breakdown by type of benefit of awards for 1974, when well over half the men and two-thirds of the women received reduced benefits. The average reduced benefit for men was $191, 10 percent below the average $213 benefit awarded to sixty-five-year-old men that year. The lowest average award of $181 (to men aged sixty-two) reflected about a 15 percent actuarial reduction. Those workers who re-

22. Patience Lauriat and William Rabin, "Men Who Claim Benefits before Age 65: Findings from the Survey of New Beneficiaries, 1968," *Social Security Bulletin,* vol. 33 (November 1970), p. 22.

ceived reduced awards at sixty-five or older retired before reaching that age and later claimed benefits retroactively.

Although male early retirees received benefits averaging 10 percent less than men retiring at sixty-five, women retiring early received benefits averaging over 18 percent below those awarded women at sixty-five. For women retiring at sixty-two, the average reduction in benefits was 25 percent. This discrepancy is explained by the fact that women workers who retire early are twice as likely to be a secondary earner as women claiming benefits at sixty-five.

The popularity of reduced benefits is quite understandable. Anyone doubtful about how long he or she will live finds it attractive to begin receiving benefits three years earlier. Furthermore, there is the possibility of supplementing social security pensions with part-time earnings and private pensions. The 1968 Survey of Newly Entitled Beneficiaries revealed that approximately two-thirds of the men choosing benefits at sixty-two had either earnings or a second pension, or both.

Retirement Age and Cost

The actuarial reduction in benefits awarded before sixty-five ensures that there is no increased benefit cost to the system, although there is a loss in revenues, since the worker stops contributing to the system at sixty-two instead of sixty-five. The result of the actuarial reduction, however, is that many of the least fortunate workers receive permanently lower benefits throughout their retirement. The popularity of early retirement has, therefore, led to pressure for further liberalization by lowering the age requirement and eliminating the actuarial reduction. These two changes would greatly increase the cost of the system.

The argument for lowering the minimum retirement age gains strength from the lack of employment for workers just below sixty-five. Early retirement, however, is not always the appropriate solution to the problem of unemployment among the aged. The solution must be related to the cause. If, as some suggest, older workers are unemployed because they have been displaced by automation, early retirement may be the logical course, since retraining the aged may be impractical.[23] However, if it is physical disability that prevents the aged from working, the appropriate way to provide for them is an extended disability program and not a retirement program that pays benefits to everyone.

23. See Robert J. Myers, *Social Security* (Irwin for McCahan Foundation, 1975), p. 187.

Table 4-6. Tax on Workers Required to Finance Benefits at Various Hypothetical Retirement Ages, 1975

Retirement age	Population (thousands)[a]		Tax in cents per worker for $1 of benefits per retiree
	Retired	Working[b]	
55	42,099	105,077	40
60	31,568	115,608	27
62	27,733	119,443	23
65	22,330	124,846	18
68	17,184	129,992	13

Sources: Bureau of the Census, *Current Population Reports*, Series P-25, no. 541, "Projections of the Population of the United States, by Age and Sex, 1975 to 2000, with Extensions of Total Population to 2025 (Advance Report)" (GPO, 1975), table 2, p. 8; for retirement at sixty-eight, Bureau of the Census.

a. Population figures equal sum of resident population and armed forces stationed outside the United States.

b. All people between eighteen and retirement age.

If the elderly disabled are to be removed from the retirement program, some mechanism that takes into account the degree of disability should be established. A Brookings study suggests that an appropriate procedure might be one analogous to that used to determine eligibility for veterans' disability pensions.[24] Under this procedure, permanent and total disability is required for receipt of pensions before the age of fifty-five, 60 or 70 percent disability is sufficient between the ages of fifty-five and fifty-nine, and only 50 percent disability is required between sixty and sixty-four.

Although transferring elderly workers with health problems from the retirement to the disability program would involve increased costs for the disability insurance program, such a move would reduce the pressure for full benefits before people reach sixty-five, and avoid the even greater costs associated with a reduction in the normal retirement age.[25] The system's costs are extremely sensitive to retirement age. As table 4-6 indicates, the tax required to finance a dollar of benefits would increase almost 30 percent if the normal retirement age were lowered from sixty-five to sixty-two.

24. Joseph A. Pechman, Henry J. Aaron, and Michael K. Taussig, *Social Security: Perspectives for Reform* (Brookings Institution, 1968), p. 141.

25. Data from the 1972 Survey of the Disabled indicate that about 30 percent of the civilian noninstitutionalized population aged fifty-five to sixty-four were disabled to some degree in 1972. This represents about 5.6 million people, all of whom could be eligible for partial disability benefits and only 1 million of whom reported receiving disability insurance benefits.

Table 4-7. Life Expectancy at the Age of Sixty-five, by Sex, Selected Periods, 1929–71

	Average remaining years to live		
Period	Male	Female	Both sexes
1929–31	11.7	12.8	12.2
1939–41	12.1	13.6	12.8
1949–51	12.7	15.0	13.8
1959–61	13.0	15.8	14.4
1969–71	13.0	16.8	15.0

Sources: Public Health Service, *United States Life Tables: 1969–71* (GPO, 1975), tables 1, 2, 3; and Department of Health, Education, and Welfare, *Health, Education, and Welfare Trends, 1966–67* (GPO, 1968), pp. S-16, S-29.

Postponing Retirement

Considering the improved health and life expectancy of today's elderly (see tables 4-7 and 4-8), it is more logical to prolong their working life than shorten it, and to encourage them to active and productive employment beyond the customary retirement age of sixty-five. Increased labor force participation by the elderly who are physically able and who want to continue working would be beneficial to them, to the social security system, and to society as a whole. Many of the problems afflicting the elderly are directly related to the economic hardship caused by retirement, and naturally these would be relieved by earnings from continued employment. Working might also alleviate their isolation in a society that seems to have no place for them, and restore their dignity and self-reliance.

The 1975 Social Security Advisory Council's report recommends that "serious consideration be given to gradually extending the retirement age."[26] It suggests that one way to accomplish this is to increase the retirement age by one month every six months beginning in 2005 and ending in 2023. By 2023, the retirement age would have increased to sixty-eight and the early retirement age to sixty-five. If adopted, this proposal would reduce the tax rate by 1.5 percentage points in the period 2025–50.

If the trend toward early retirement is ever to be reversed, measures that discourage the elderly from remaining in the work force should be eliminated and the social security program should be modified so that people have a greater choice about when they wish to retire.

INCREASE DELAYED RETIREMENT CREDIT. A straightforward way

26. *Reports of the Quadrennial Advisory Council on Social Security*, H. Doc. 94-75, 94:1 (GPO, 1975), p. 117.

Table 4-8. Average Days Sick for Those Aged Sixty-five, by Sex, 1958–74

Year	Average restricted activity days[a]		
	Male	Female	Both sexes
1958	45.2	49.1	47.3
1959	35.9	39.7	38.0
1960	36.8	38.6	37.8
1961	38.7	41.2	40.1
1962	33.3	38.9	36.4
1963	35.3	38.6	37.1
1964	34.7	41.1	38.2
1965	35.6	40.8	38.5
1966	32.7	34.8	33.9
1967	33.0	38.0	35.8
1968[b]	31.2	30.3	30.7
1969	30.9	35.5	33.5
1970	27.9	32.7	30.7
1971	30.9	36.2	34.0
1972	33.2	38.8	36.5
1973	29.9	36.0	33.5
1974	36.8	38.8	38.0

Sources: U.S. Public Health Service, National Center for Health Statistics, *Current Estimates from the Health Interview Survey, United States—1974*, Vital and Health Statistics, series 10, no. 100 (GPO, 1975), and preceding issues in the series, table 16 in each.
a. A day on which a person reduces usual activities because of illness or injury.
b. For those sixty-five to seventy-four.

to encourage late retirement is to expand the delayed retirement credit, which permanently increases benefits for late retirees. The present credit, introduced in 1972, raises benefits by only 1 percent for each year that a worker receives no benefits between the ages of sixty-five and seventy-two. In order to keep the actuarial value of a worker's benefit unaffected by his age of retirement, the benefit would have to be increased by about 10 percent for each year of employment beyond sixty-five. This adjustment would cost exactly the same as eliminating the earnings test—$2 billion to $3 billion—as is discussed in the next section. The advantage of actuarially increasing benefits, compared to eliminating the retirement test, is that it is completely consistent with the current goals of the system. Social security benefits are designed to replace wage income upon retirement, and under this scheme increased benefits would be withheld until the worker leaves his job.

EXEMPT EARNINGS FROM PAYROLL TAX. A considerably less expensive way to encourage later retirement is to exempt workers aged sixty-five and over (but not their employers) from the OASDI payroll tax. This would probably cost about $1 billion in 1977, although the costs might increase over time as the structure of the population changed. Exemption from the tax could be combined with either a delayed retirement credit or the elimination of the earnings test. The popular rationale for exempting earnings is to avoid penalizing workers over sixty-five twice, first by withholding benefits and second by taxing earnings. On the other hand, it could be argued that there are several reasons that their earnings should be taxed. First, some workers may use earnings after sixty-five to establish credentials for social security benefits. Second, workers may substitute earnings after sixty-five for years of lower earnings to derive higher average monthly earnings and eventually higher benefits.[27] Third, insured workers receive a 1 percent increase in benefits for each year after sixty-five that retirement is delayed. If the program became an annuity system, however, and benefits were awarded at an agreed upon age there would be no logical reason to require employed workers to pay taxes after they qualified for that annuity. It is not certain, of course, that this tax exemption would encourage the elderly to work.

LIBERALIZE EARNINGS TEST. Another possible spur to employment is liberalization of the earnings test either by raising the annual exempt amount or by reducing the amount of benefits withheld for each dollar of earnings in excess of the exempt amount. This test has been the most controversial provision of the social security program and is widely regarded as being inequitable. However, the test has frequently been reviewed by public committees, most recently the 1975 Advisory Council on Social Security. Each committee has decided in favor of retaining it.

The primary argument for a retirement, or earnings, test is that it is consistent with social security's stated objective of replacing wage income when a worker retires; eliminating the test would change the nature of the system. A change may be appropriate at this time, but it must be recognized that awarding benefits without regard to labor force activity would represent a dramatic departure from the underlying principle of wage replacement.

Cost is also an important argument for retention of the test, especially with a program already calling for higher tax rates in the future. Robert M. Ball, Commissioner of Social Security from 1962 to 1973, argued for

---

27. If the present system were revised so that benefits were based on indexed earnings histories, the advantage of this substitution would be reduced, especially if earnings histories were indexed by wages.

continuing the retirement test "because the system can be more effective by restricting payment to those who have suffered a loss of income and using the money thus saved to pay a higher level of benefits."[28] The Office of the Actuary estimates that eliminating the earnings test would add $2 billion to $3 billion in benefits in the first year and a long-run cost of 0.33 percent of taxable payrolls. In 1975, the $2 billion to $3 billion extra would have caused an additional combined employer-employee contribution of $20 to $30 for each of the 101 million taxpaying workers.

The cost argument leads into the distributional implications of a change in the test. Under the present system, these additional revenues would be raised by a regressive payroll tax and the proceeds distributed as benefits to the elderly, who may be earning wages and as a result be relatively well off. As long as social security is structured as a system with both welfare and insurance attributes, it is difficult to justify the use of limited social security revenues to pay benefits to a relatively affluent minority of the aged. On the other hand, if social security were more analogous to private insurance—more strictly wage-related—then it would be more appropriate to award benefits at a given age regardless of other earnings.

However, there has been widespread criticism of the test as being unfair to those who contribute during their entire working career and are denied benefits simply because they choose to continue working. As noted earlier, it would be inconsistent with the present goals of the system to award benefits to workers who continued full time at their present jobs.

The earnings test has also been criticized because it does not take into consideration unearned income such as dividends, interest, rents, or other pension payments. A person with, for example, $25,000 a year in interest and dividends would qualify for the full benefit, while someone who continued to work full time, earning about $10,000, would have his benefit withheld. If the test took into account income other than earnings, it would no longer be an earnings test but an income test. The wage-replacement principle would be lost, and social security would become more of a means-tested welfare system than a social insurance program where individuals are eligible for benefits as a matter of right.

The wage-replacement principle of the current social security program requires at least partial retirement as a prerequisite for receiving benefits. However, given the improved health and life expectancy of the elderly and the costs of a large retired population, it may be more important to encourage the elderly to continue to work. Therefore it may be desirable

28. Robert M. Ball, letter to the editor, *New York Times*, May 6, 1974.

to modify the goals of the current program and award benefits as annuities at sixty-five.

Liberalization of the earnings test would not only promote labor force participation by the elderly but would muster public support for any reform package it was a part of. The 1975 Social Security Advisory Council recommended a schedule of withholdings for 1976 similar to the following. As under the existing law, no benefits would be withheld for earnings of $2,760 or less, and for all earnings in excess of $5,520, a dollar of benefits would be withheld for every $2 of earnings. However, for earnings between $2,760 and $5,520, benefits would be reduced $1 for each $3 earned, instead of the present $1 for every $2. This liberalization would cost about $700 million at 1976 levels. The new test would mean that a couple who received the maximum benefit in June 1976 of $581 a month would have continued to receive at least partial payments until their 1976 earnings exceeded $17,624.

In sum, there is good reason to be concerned about the provision of the social security law that discourages labor force participation of people over sixty-two who prefer to continue working. By limiting available income sources, such a deterrent reduces the welfare of the elderly. The burden falls particularly heavily on low-income people, who seldom have other sources of retirement income such as private insurance, pension benefits, or savings. In addition, any provision that encourages a smaller labor force in future years will force a significantly higher tax rate in the long run.

Summary

The social security system has contributed to the decline in the labor force participation of the elderly through the income effect of benefits, the tax on wages from the earnings test, and indirectly through the impact of social security on private pension plan provisions. The income effect of social security is inevitable and desirable. In fact, it was the intention of the program to provide benefits to replace earnings so that workers could retire. Few would argue for reducing benefit levels or replacement rates in order to stimulate work effort among the elderly. Furthermore, altering the retirement practices of private industry also would fail as a tool to encourage labor force participation of the elderly, since the influence of social security is only indirect.

The remaining and logical policy instrument is to revise the earnings test by either raising the exempt amount or reducing the tax rates on excess earnings or equivalently to increase the delayed retirement credit. Unfortunately, there are no empirical studies that could be used to predict how the aged would respond to changes in these parameters. Clearly, more analysis is required before any reform is enacted, since liberalizing or eliminating the earnings test might cost as much as $3 billion annually. However, if workers should be willing to pay an additional $30 a year in combined employee and employer taxes to finance them, these reforms should receive serious study.

chapter five **Financing Now and in the Future**

The problem of social security financing is two-dimensional, involving questions of form and adequacy. The issue of form centers on the appropriateness of relying on the payroll tax as the primary source of revenue. The arguments for and against payroll tax financing depend primarily on whether the social security system is viewed as a unified program of taxes and benefits or as two separate programs in which benefits are simply one component of a larger transfer of funds and payroll taxes are one component of federal revenues. While the appropriateness of the payroll tax is an old and much-debated problem, the adequacy of the existing financing, in the face of the increasing ratio of aged to working population and an overindexed benefit structure which produces rapidly rising benefits in inflationary periods, is a new and vitally important issue.

The Payroll Tax

The payroll tax is now the second largest source of federal revenue, and the fastest growing. As its importance has grown, so has the debate over exclusive reliance on this source of revenue to finance the social security program. When the tax was introduced in 1935,[1] the levy was considered a contribution for insurance, and its fairness was judged in the context of the entire social security tax and benefit system.

Individual benefits roughly proportional to individual contributions would mean a neutral net distributional impact. However, even in the beginning, a quid pro quo benefit structure did not exist, and since then such redistributional elements as the minimum benefit, dependents' bene-

1. Although the payroll tax was instituted in 1935 through the Social Security Act, payment of the tax did not begin until 1937.

84

fits, and a progressive benefit formula have increased in importance, lead-ing critics of the payroll tax to argue that social security benefits should be viewed not in insurance terms but as an expenditure program in an overall income maintenance system.[2] Within this framework, the payroll tax should be evaluated in relation to other taxes, not to benefits. However, even critics agree that it is best to retain the concept of contributory finance for social security, as it allows workers to receive benefits as an earned right rather than as a dole. Furthermore, earmarking revenue protects the system from the uncertainties of annual appropriations.

The Nature of the Tax

The initial payroll tax rate was 1 percent, payable by employees and employers on the first $3,000 of wage income. By 1977, the rate for retire-ment, survivors, and disability benefits was 4.95 percent, each, for em-ployers and employees on the first $16,500 of wage income, with the ceiling scheduled to rise automatically with the wage level.[3] Health insur-ance contributions raised the overall payroll tax rate to 5.85 percent. (Table 5-1 summarizes changes in tax base and rates since the beginning of the program.)

Total old age, survivors, disability, and health insurance receipts in 1975 amounted to over $75 billion, more than a sixfold increase since 1960 (table 5-2). Growth in dollars is paralleled by growth in the relative importance of the tax as a revenue source. In 1950, social security ac-counted for only 5 percent of all federal receipts, but its share has doubled every ten years since then. In 1975 the OASDHI taxes accounted for more than 25 percent of federal revenues, second in importance only to the personal income tax.

The Incidence of the Tax

The legislative intent of levying half the tax on the employer and half on the employee was to divide the burden between the two parties. It is

2. Joseph A. Pechman, Henry J. Aaron, and Michael K. Taussig, *Social Security: Perspectives for Reform* (Brookings Institution, 1968), pp. 74–76.

3. After 1974, the earnings base was adjusted for each year in which the benefit table increased. The adjustment factor is based on the ratio of first-quarter average wages in covered employment in the year of determination to either (a) first quarter of 1973, or (b) the first calendar quarter of the year in which the last automatic base increase became effective. The adjusted base is then rounded to the nearest multiple of $300.

Table 5-1. **Maximum Taxable Earnings, Tax Rates, and Maximum Tax, 1937-2011**

Years	Maximum taxable earnings (dollars)	Tax rate[a]				Maximum tax[a] (dollars)
		OASDHI	OASI	DI	HI	
		Actual experience				
1937–49	3,000	1.0	1.0	...	...	30.00
1950	3,000	1.5	1.5	...	...	45.00
1951–53	3,600	1.5	1.5	...	...	54.00
1954	3,600	2.0	2.0	...	...	72.00
1955–56	4,200	2.0	2.0	...	...	84.00
1957–58	4,200	2.25	2.0	0.25	...	94.50
1959	4,800	2.5	2.25	0.25	...	120.00
1960–61	4,800	3.0	2.75	0.25	...	144.00
1962	4,800	3.125	2.875	0.25	...	150.00
1963–65	4,800	3.625	3.375	0.25	...	174.00
1966	6,600	4.2	3.5	0.35	0.35	277.20
1967	6,600	4.4	3.55	0.35	0.5	290.40
1968	7,800	4.4	3.325	0.475	0.6	343.20
1969	7,800	4.8	3.725	0.475	0.6	374.40
1970	7,800	4.8	3.65	0.55	0.6	374.40
1971	7,800	5.2	4.05	0.55	0.6	405.60
1972	9,000	5.2	4.05	0.55	0.6	468.00
1973	10,800	5.85	4.3	0.55	1.0	631.80
1974	13,200	5.85	4.375	0.575	0.9	772.20
1975	14,100	5.85	4.375	0.575	0.9	824.85
1976	15,300	5.85	4.375	0.575	0.9	895.05
1977	16,500	5.85	4.375	0.575	0.9	965.25
		Projections according to current law				
1978	17,700[b]	6.05	4.35	0.6	1.1	1,070.85[c]
1979	19,200[b]	6.05	4.35	0.6	1.1	1,161.60[c]
1980	21,000[b]	6.05	4.35	0.6	1.1	1,270.50[c]
1981	22,800[b]	6.30	4.3	0.65	1.35	1,436.40[c]
1982–85	...	6.30	4.3	0.65	1.35	...
1986–2010	...	6.45	4.25	0.70	1.5	...
2011 and later	...	7.45	5.1	0.85	1.5	...

Source: Social Security Administration.
a. Employee and employer, each.
b. Estimate. Subject to automatic revisions.
c. Dependent on maximum taxable earnings (see note b).

unclear whether the employers' half was meant to fall on profits or consumers, but the intention was definitely to charge employees with only half of the contribution.

Most economists now think that, in spite of the intent of the law, the

Table 5-2. Federal Receipts, Selected Years
Billions of dollars

Source	Calendar year					
	1935	*1940*	*1950*	*1960*	*1970*	*1975*
Personal taxes and nontaxes	0.8	1.4	18.1	43.6	92.2	125.6
Payroll tax	0.1	2.0	5.9	17.6	49.7	94.3
OASDHI	...	0.6	2.7	11.9	39.7	75.6
OASI	...	0.6	2.7	10.9	30.3	56.8
DI	...	...	...	1.0	4.5	7.4
HI	...	...	...	...	4.9	11.5
Other[a]	0.1	1.4	3.3	5.7	10.0	18.5
Corporation income tax	0.8	2.6	17.2	21.4	30.8	42.6
Indirect business taxes and nontaxes	2.2	2.6	8.9	13.4	19.3	23.9
Total	4.0	8.6	50.0	96.1	192.1	286.5

Sources: Bureau of Economic Analysis and Social Security Administration. Figures are rounded.
a. Unemployment insurance, railroad retirement, federal civil service retirement, veterans' life insurance, and miscellaneous similar sources.

entire tax is borne by the employee.[4] They generally base their analysis on a model of the cost-minimizing behavior of firms: firms hire factors of production until the ratio of marginal-value-product to marginal-factor-cost is equal for all factors—that is, until the value of what is produced by an additional unit of a factor is just offset by the cost of hiring that unit. In figure 5-1 curve *D* represents the firm's demand price, or the wage the employer is willing to pay for a certain amount of labor. Since the imposition of the payroll tax has no effect on the productivity of labor, employers would continue to pay the same total cost for that unit of labor, reducing wages by the amount necessary to pay the employers' half of the tax. For example, if the employer were willing to pay a worker $9,000 before the tax, he would be willing to pay only $9,000 after the tax. With a 5 percent tax levied on the employer the $9,000 would consist of a wage of $8,550 and a payment to the government of $450. A worker cannot easily avoid the tax, since it is applicable to wages in practically all industries. (Though the only available recourse is to work less, the evidence suggests that labor supply is not responsive to the payroll tax.[5])

4. Richard A. Musgrave and Peggy B. Musgrave, *Public Finance in Theory and Practice* (McGraw-Hill, 1973), pp. 390–95.
5. Even if labor responded to the payroll tax by working fewer hours or withdrawing from the labor force, labor would not necessarily be able to shift the tax. Although wage rates might increase in these circumstances, employment would probably be reduced, and under plausible assumptions concerning the elasticity of demand

Figure 5-1. Incidence of the Payroll Tax under Perfect Competition

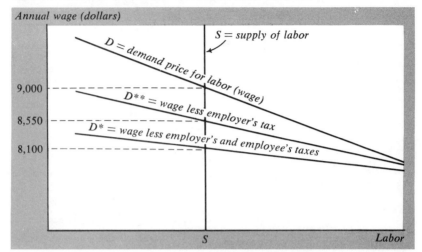

Unions and large corporations may complicate the picture, the unions resisting long-term reductions in wages and corporations resisting reduction in profits and, instead, raising the prices that they charge their customers. Under these circumstances the employer's share may be shifted forward in the form of higher prices to consumers.[6]

Ultimately, the question who pays the tax must be settled by empirical analysis. One of the few studies on the effect of payroll taxes, a cross-sectional analysis by John A. Brittain, concludes that, for any given level of productivity, industries in countries with relatively high employer payroll taxes pay a basic wage that is relatively lower by the amount of the tax. This evidence suggests that the full burden of payroll taxes—whether levied on employers or employees or both—rests on the workers.[7]

Figure 5-2 shows the 1966 distribution of the payroll tax burden in this country by income class under two different assumptions for the final bearer of the employer's tax: (1) the worker, who receives lower wages, or (2) the consumer, who pays higher prices. There is really little differ-

for labor, the aggregate wage bill would probably be reduced by at least as much as the proceeds of the tax. See John A. Brittain, *The Payroll Tax for Social Security* (Brookings Institution, 1972), pp. 39–44, 55–57.

6. For a discussion of this effect, see Musgrave and Musgrave, *Public Finance in Theory and Practice*, pp. 353–55.

7. Brittain, *The Payroll Tax for Social Security*, pp. 60–81. For a criticism of this approach, see Martin S. Feldstein, "The Incidence of the Social Security Payroll Tax: Comment," *American Economic Review*, vol. 62 (September 1972), pp. 735–38 and Brittain, "Reply," in the same issue, pp. 739–42.

Figure 5-2. Effective Rates of a 5 Percent Payroll Tax on Employers and Employees, by Income Level, 1966

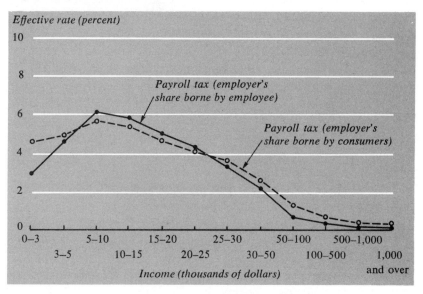

ence in impact between these two assumptions, since the distribution of consumption by income class is similar to the distribution of wages by income class. Under either assumption, the 1966 payroll tax proved very regressive, with the tax burden as a percentage of income declining as income rose. However, with the recent increases in the wage base the payroll tax is regressive at a significantly higher income level.

The Regressivity of the Tax

There are two causes for the regressivity of the OASDI payroll tax. First, it is levied only on wage income, thus excluding all income from capital, a source whose importance increases as income increases. Second, all wages above the maximum taxable limit are excluded.

For low-income families with children, the payroll tax is now partially offset by the earned income credit, a feature introduced into the personal income tax by the Tax Reduction Act of 1975. The credit was intended to ease the payroll tax burden on poor families and is financed through general revenue. Without the credit, the OASDI tax burden, measured as a percentage of wage income, would be proportional to earnings up to the ceiling and then would decline sharply. The earned income credit (available only to low-income workers who have dependent children and maintain a household) is 10 percent of the first $4,000 of earned income, after which it is reduced by 10 percent of adjusted gross income in excess of $4,000. The OASDI tax (9.9 percent of taxable pay) is zero for eligible families with incomes below $4,000, a progressive percentage of wages between $4,000 and $8,000, proportional between $8,000 and the ceiling ($16,500 in 1977), and regressive thereafter.[8]

The impact of the unearned income exclusion, the ceiling on taxable earnings, and the earned income credit are demonstrated in table 5-3, which presents the OASDI taxes for five hypothetical income recipients. If the tax burden is measured as a percentage of total income—both earned and unearned—excluding capital income from the tax base makes the tax regressive at a lower level and the burden decline faster. This pattern is important to note, because it underlines the fact that, even if the limit on taxable earnings were eliminated, at some point on the income scale payroll taxes as a percentage of total income declines as income rises, since the wage share declines as income rises.

Overall Evaluation of the Tax

Any evaluation of the payroll tax as the means for financing social security must take into account the issue of the intended effect of the program on the distribution of income. This distributional question can be viewed from either an annual or a lifetime perspective. Some argue that social security is best construed as an annual tax transfer program, which redistributes income from the relatively affluent wage earners to the relatively poor retired.[9] The more common perspective is the view of social security in a lifetime framework, where payroll taxes are considered compulsory saving for retirement.

The annual view—that social security is part of the federal government's tax and transfer schemes—leads to an evaluation of the tax inde-

8. The OASDI tax, 9.9 percent of taxable income, is thus completely remitted by the earned income credit for eligible families. The families still pay an additional 1.8 percent tax for health insurance, as well as state taxes for unemployment insurance under the assumption that labor bears the full burden of a payroll tax.

9. Pechman and others, *Social Security: Perspectives for Reform*, pp. 74–76.

Table 5-3. Distribution of Old Age, Survivors, and Disability Insurance Payroll Tax Burden at Selected Income Levels, 1976[a]

	Annual wage and salary income plus other income				
Item	5,250 (5,000[b] +250[c])	11,000 (10,000[b] +1,000[c])	18,000 (15,000[b] +3,000[c])	65,000 (50,000[b] +15,000[c])	130,000 (100,000[b] +30,000[c])
	Average amount (dollars)				
OASDI tax base	5,000	10,000	15,000	15,300	15,300
OASDI tax	495	990	1,485	1,515	1,515
Earned income credit[d]	275	...	...	...	...
Net OASDI tax	220	990	1,485	1,515	1,515
	Percent				
OASDI tax on wage income	4.4	9.9	9.9	3.0	1.5
OASDI tax on total income	4.2	9.0	8.2	2.3	1.2

Source: Calculated from legislative provisions as of 1976: payroll tax of 9.9 percent on maximum taxable earnings of $15,300 and earned-income credit for certain low-income workers.

a. The regressivity of the payroll tax is somewhat overstated here, because many families who earn more than the maximum taxable amount have two earners and therefore pay more than $1,515 in OASDI tax. Data for March 1975 show that dual earner families as a percent of the nonaged families rise in each successively higher income bracket, peaking at the $15,000–$24,999 level (53 percent). Thereafter, the portion of each bracket represented by two-earner families begins to decline. See Bureau of the Census, Current Population Reports, series P-60, no. 101, "Money Income in 1974 of Families and Persons in the United States" (GPO, 1976), tables 25, 37.

b. Wages and salary income.

c. Hypothetical nonwage income figures are based on Richard A. Musgrave and Peggy B. Musgrave, Public Finance in Theory and Practice (McGraw-Hill, 1973), p. 349.

d. Ten percent of first $4,000, reduced by 10 percent of income over $4,000. The credit applies only to poor families with dependent children, who account for 55 percent of the OASDI tax-paying units that are poverty-stricken. Bureau of the Census, Current Population Reports, series P-60, no. 99, "Money Income and Poverty Status of Families and Persons in the United States, 1974" (GPO, 1975), tables 17, 23.

pendent of the benefits, the inevitable conclusion being that the payroll tax clearly violates the ability-to-pay criterion for equitable taxation. The tax is levied without provision for number of dependents, affects only wages, and exempts wages over the maximum. Such regressivity in relation to the progressivity of the personal income tax is shown in the 1970 tax receipts: 67.6 percent of payroll tax receipts came from families with incomes of less than $15,000, while only 48.8 percent of personal income tax receipts came from this group.[10]

The earned income credit introduced in 1975 goes part way toward eliminating the burden of the payroll tax on the working poor. However,

10. Internal Revenue Service, Statistics of Income—1970, Individual Income Tax Returns (GPO, 1972), p. 7; Social Security Administration, Office of Research and Statistics, Reducing Social Security Contributions for Low-Income Workers: Issues and Analysis (GPO, 1974), p. 17.

this credit is limited to taxpayers with children and provides no relief for low-income childless couples or single people. Families with dependent children account for only 50 percent of nonaged low-income units.[11] Furthermore, limiting the maximum credit to earned income of $4,000 means that a family with two children still would pay a payroll tax on earnings not taxed under the personal income tax (which exempts the first $5,700).[12]

Advocates of the annual tax transfer perspective favor a more progressive source of revenue, either general revenue or a modification of the payroll tax. An expanded earned income credit, to include all low-income families, would probably provide sufficient relief at the low end of the income scale. At the high end, elimination of the limit on taxable earnings would reduce the regressivity of the tax.[13] However, on distributional grounds, the preferable alternative is to move to general revenue financing, since the income tax includes unearned as well as earned income in the tax base and is therefore more progressive than even a modified payroll tax.

An annual perspective, however, seems at variance with the existing structure of the social security program. The social security system is inappropriate as an annual redistributive scheme, since it transfers funds to all covered retirees irrespective of need. If the system were simply part of society's overall redistributive program, then it should be structured in line with an expanded supplemental security income program financed by general revenues.

In fact, the present system can best be understood when considered in a lifetime compulsory saving framework. Social security is a device to force people to save during their working years to ensure adequate income in retirement. Within the lifetime framework, the social security system

11. Percent calculated from Bureau of the Census, *Current Population Reports,* series P-60, no. 102, "Characteristics of the Population Below the Poverty Level, 1974" (GPO, 1976), pp. 36, 90.

12. In 1976 a family of four filing a joint return with $5,700 in income could claim $3,000 in personal exemptions (four exemptions at $750 each) plus a $1,900 low-income allowance (in lieu of the standard deduction). The tax on the resulting $800 of taxable income would be $112. The tax credit of $30 per personal exemption provided for in the Tax Reduction Act of 1975 would bring the family's tax obligation to zero.

13. However, without some modification in the current method of calculating benefits, this will necessarily lead to higher benefits for high-wage workers. For purely redistributive purposes, perhaps the limit could be removed for tax purposes but retained for benefits. However, this might be difficult to explain to taxpayers who link benefits to taxes paid.

can be either distributionally neutral or redistributive. The current social security system is a progressive redistributional scheme, since low-income workers are granted a much higher return on their tax contributions than high-income workers. In contrast, if benefits were strictly proportional to contributions over the worker's lifetime, this system would have a neutral distributional impact for most people. However, even in the proposed system, low-wage workers require special treatment.

In the lifetime perspective, where taxes and benefits are considered jointly, the payroll tax with an earned income credit is an appropriate method of financing a compulsory saving program. This would be especially true if the program functioned on the basis of an individual equity criterion and phased out the minimum benefit, dependents' benefits, and the steeply progressive benefit formula. The earned income credit, however, is essential to the acceptability of the payroll tax, since compulsory saving schemes simply do not make sense for low-income families. It is unreasonable to impose payroll taxes on incomes considered too meager to support personal income taxes and then justify those taxes on the ground of retirement benefits payable two or three decades hence. These families cannot afford to save. Forcing them to contribute to a social security program will merely compel them to borrow money at extremely high interest rates; accumulating social security contributions at a real rate of interest of 2 or 3 percent while borrowing at rates in excess of 10 percent cannot be viewed as distributionally neutral.

Fortunately, the earned income credit, once it is expanded to include all low-income families, provides a nice solution to the burden of the payroll tax on low-wage workers. In addition, the fact that tax relief occurs outside the social security program permits the program to function as a strictly wage-related system.

The Adequacy of Financing

There has been widespread concern in the past few years about the financial solvency of the social security system. Newspapers and magazines have been filled with headlines such as "social security system is on way to going broke" and "social security promising too much to too many?"[14] Projections of large long-term deficits have been accompanied

14. See, for example, the *Wall Street Journal,* February 27, 1975, and *U.S. News and World Report,* July 15, 1974.

by warnings of the more immediate danger that the trust funds will be
exhausted by 1981 or soon thereafter unless additional financing is
obtained.[15]

In fact, the social security system does have serious long-term financial
problems. If nothing is done to change the current social security law,
payroll taxes will have to rise very steeply in the future to finance scheduled benefits. However, a large portion of the long-term deficit is due to
overindexing, an irrational and correctable feature of the benefit formula
that tends to overcompensate workers for inflation. With this error recti-
fied, the projected deficit shrinks to a more manageable magnitude.

The short-run problem of declining trust fund balances arises primarily
from the current economic situation, which combines a high level of
unemployment and a downward shift in the trend growth of real wages.
In this situation, the trust funds are essentially fulfilling their role of
providing a buffer for temporary shortfalls in revenues.[16] Nevertheless, to
place both long-run and short-run difficulties in perspective, it is important
to clarify the nature of social security financing.

Social security functions on a pay-as-you-go basis: the government
collects payroll taxes and uses this money to finance current benefits for
retired workers, dependents, survivors, and the disabled, as well as medicare benefits for the aged. Pay-as-you-go financing runs counter to the
original intention that social security build up a large reserve fund, an intention abandoned in 1939, when it was decided to have the current labor
force contribute taxes to pay benefits for the current aged and to maintain
the trust fund as simply a contingency reserve. Thus, the system serves
primarily as a massive intergenerational transfer.

At the end of 1975, the combined OASDI trust funds held $44.3
billion, less than one year's benefits.[17] However, the fact that social
security does not have a large trust fund should not be a source of concern
in a social insurance program. A private pension program must have
sufficient assets to meet all prior and current commitments, because it
cannot be certain of receiving future premiums. In contrast, the social
security program, which relies on the government's taxing powers to meet

15. *1976 Annual Report of the Board of Trustees of the Federal Old Age and
Survivors Insurance and Disability Insurance Trust Funds,* H. Doc. 94-505, 94:2
(GPO, 1976), pp. 41–66.

16. See testimony of Robert M. Ball in *Social Security,* Hearings before the Subcommittee on Retirement Income and Employment of the House Select Committee
on Aging, 94:1 (GPO, 1975), pp. 102–11.

17. *1976 Annual Report of the Board of Trustees,* p. 35.

its obligations, can continue to compel future generations of workers to pay social security taxes.

The Short-Run Problem

According to estimates in the 1976 Trustees' Report, scheduled benefits will exceed projected revenues in each year from 1976 through 1981.[18] At these rates of spending and income, the trust funds will be exhausted soon after 1981. The combined OASDI funds declined by $1.5 billion in 1975; it is estimated that the OASI trust fund will be dwindling at a $5 billion rate in 1981, while the DI trust fund will be exhausted by 1979 (table 5-4).

A major portion of the short-run revenue problems can be explained by the severity of the 1973–75 recession, which drained the trust funds in three ways. First, employment and real wages were lowered, which directly diminished payroll tax revenue. Second, the unpromising labor market prompted more workers to leave the labor force and seek retirement or disability payments. (The rising incidence of disability claims has been responsible for a large portion of the annual deficits in the OASDI trust funds.) Third, diminishing trust funds earn a diminishing amount of interest income. As the economy emerges from the recession, two of the adverse effects remain: (1) the smaller trust fund earning less interest and (2) the permanent loss of real wages caused by a downward shift in the trend growth—that is, while the *growth* of real wages returns to pre-recession rates, the *level* of real wages suffers a permanent reduction.

In view of the permanent loss in real wages, tax increases are now required to restore balance to the trust funds. Furthermore, it may be desirable to accumulate reserves equal to 60 percent of revenues so that the trust funds will be sufficient to withstand a recession similar to that in 1973–75 without requiring a payroll tax increase.[19] To meet those short-run financing requirements, there are three methods of increasing the revenues of the funds: (1) an increase in the wage base, (2) an increase in tax rates, and (3) transfers from other sources, such as general revenues.

18. Ibid.
19. Paul N. Van de Water and Lawrence H. Thompson, "The Social Security Trust Funds as Contingency Reserves," Technical Analysis Paper 9 (Department of Health, Education, and Welfare, Office of Assistant Secretary for Planning and Evaluation, Office of Income Security Policy, 1976; processed).

Table 5-4. Assets of Old Age and Survivors Insurance and Disability Insurance Trust Funds, Projected and Actual, Selected Years, 1940–81

Billions of dollars

End of year	Old age and survivors insurance						Disability insurance					
	Year of projection					Ac-tual	Year of projection					Ac-tual
	1972	1973	1974	1975	1976		1972	1973	1974	1975	1976	
1940	...	...	...	...	...	2.0	...	...	...	...	...	...
1945	...	...	...	...	...	7.1	...	...	...	...	...	...
1950	...	...	...	...	...	13.7	...	...	...	...	...	...
1955	...	...	...	...	...	21.7	...	...	...	...	...	...
1960	...	...	...	...	...	20.3	...	...	...	...	...	2.3
1965	...	...	...	...	...	18.2	...	...	...	...	...	1.6
1970	...	...	...	...	...	32.5	...	...	...	...	...	5.6
1971	...	...	...	...	...	33.8	...	...	...	...	...	6.6
1972	37.6	...	...	...	...	35.3	8.0	...	...	...	...	7.5
1973	46.8	36.6	...	...	...	36.5	9.5	7.7	...	...	...	7.9
1974	58.2	40.4	36.5	...	...	37.8	11.1	8.2	8.0	...	...	8.1
1975	71.0	43.4	37.0	35.6	...	37.0	12.9	8.4	8.0	7.3	...	7.4
1976	86.7	47.0	37.3	31.3	34.3	...	14.9	8.6	7.7	5.8	5.8	...
1977	...	49.8	37.6	27.3	32.3	...	...	8.5	7.2	4.0	3.8	...
1978	...	...	37.3	23.0	29.3	...	...	...	6.8	2.4	1.6	...
1979	...	...	...	18.2	26.3	...	...	...	...	0.4	−1.3ᵃ	...
1980	...	...	...	...	22.8	...	...	...	...	...	−5.0ᵃ	...
1981	...	...	...	...	17.9	...	...	...	...	...	−8.7ᵃ	...

Sources: *1976 Annual Report of the Board of Trustees of the Federal Old Age and Survivors Insurance and Disability Insurance Trust Funds*, H. Doc. 94-505, 94:2 (GPO, 1976), pp. 31, 33, and Trustees' Reports for 1972–75.

a. It is estimated that the disability insurance fund will be exhausted in 1979.

As discussed earlier, with an annual perspective and redistribution as the major goal, there are strong arguments for financing benefits through the most progressive source of revenue, general revenue. Entitlement to benefits could still be based on earnings histories with transfers considered an earned right. Several precedents exist for the use of general revenues within the social security system, such as the gratuitous wage credits granted to servicemen, transitional benefits for certain uninsured people, and general revenue financing of some hospital payments.[20] On the other

20. In his testimony before the Subcommittee on Retirement Income and Employment, Robert M. Ball recommends raising the payroll tax base to $24,000 in 1977 and shifting the scheduled 0.2 percent increase in the health insurance portion of the payroll tax to the OASDI portion (*Social Security*, p. 105). The 1975 Advisory Council on Social Security recommends that payroll tax support of the health

hand, a switch to general revenue financing means a break in the perceived link between individual contributions and benefits. Although the link in the current system is tenuous, it could be strengthened by moving toward a stricter earnings-replacement scheme.

If direct general revenue support of the cash benefits program is considered undesirable, another possibility is to transfer one of the other financial responsibilities of the payroll tax to general revenues. One proposal, which was advanced by the 1975 Advisory Council, is to shift all or some portion of the 1.8 percent tax for health insurance to general revenues and credit the scheduled increases in the health tax rate to the OASDI funds. Since health insurance benefits bear no direct relation to contributions or earnings in covered employment, none of the program's underlying philosophies would be violated by such a change. Employment history could still be maintained as an entitlement mechanism to ensure the earned-right principle of the social security system.

If the payroll tax is to provide all the necessary revenue, it must be increased by raising the tax rate or broadening the wage base, or a combination of the two. Raising the rate exacerbates the problem of regressivity of the overall tax system and might be politically unacceptable unless contributions were more closely allied to subsequent benefits.

An alternative is to broaden the earnings base to $24,000 (with automatic increases thereafter, calculated as under the current law). Increasing the wage base, however, also has drawbacks. Expansion of social security may have a negative effect on private saving, worsening the shortage of capital. Too, the higher social security benefits that would automatically be generated for the affected high-wage earners would encroach upon the role of the third tier of retirement income, the funded private pensions. In addition, the increased social security benefits in themselves would represent increased financial obligations for the system, since half the increased revenues accruing from the broadening of the wage base would eventually be paid out in benefits to the affected high-wage earners. At the same time, since these contributors would receive only part of the value of the increased tax bill in the form of higher benefits, such a negative

---

insurance program be phased out with financing coming from general revenues and income from the payroll tax previously allocated to the HI fund directed to the OASDI fund (*Reports of the Quadrennial Advisory Council on Social Security,* H. Doc. 94-75, 94:1 (GPO, 1975), p. xvii). In *Social Security: Perspectives for Reform,* Pechman and others recommend that the employer portion of the payroll tax be financed from general revenues, while the employee and self-employed portions be incorporated into personal income taxes (p. 222).

Table 5-5. Alternative Financing Arrangements[a] for OASI and DI Trust Funds and Effect on Long-run Deficits, Selected Years[b]

Year	Present law (A)	Rate increase only (B)	Wage base increase only (C)	Low base increase with rate increase (D)	High base increase with rate increase (E)	Eliminate employer's maximum (F)	Eliminate employer's maximum with rate increase (G)
			Contribution and benefit base (dollars)				
1975	14,100	14,100	14,100	14,100	14,100	14,100	14,100
1980	21,600	21,600	34,200	27,600	31,200	21,600	21,600
1985	29,400	29,400	46,200	37,200	42,300	29,400	29,400
			Contribution rate, employee–employer combined (percent of taxable payroll)				
1975	9.9	9.9	9.9	9.9	9.9	9.9	9.9
1980	9.9	10.6	9.9	10.1	9.9	9.9	10.0
1985	9.9	11.0	9.9	10.6	10.5	9.9	10.4
			Assets of OASI and DI trust funds, beginning of year (billions of dollars)				
1975	45.9	45.9	45.9	45.9	45.9	45.9	45.9
1980	20.5	48.1	52.2	47.2	46.3	46.5	50.6
1985	−40.0	67.3	62.8	67.4	70.0	47.0	66.8
			Change in long-run actuarial deficit (percent of taxable payroll)				
1975–85	0.0	−0.51	0.35	−0.27	−0.05	−1.07	−1.26
			Long-run actuarial deficit (percent of taxable payroll)				
1975–85	5.32	4.81	5.67	5.05	5.27	4.25	4.06

Source: *Examples of Methods of Increasing Income into the Social Security Trust Funds,* prepared by the Subcommittee on Social Security of the House Committee on Ways and Means, 94:1 (GPO, 1975), pp. 2, 6, 7.

a. Included in alternatives B–G is an increase in the contribution rate for the self-employed to 1.5 times the rate for employees. Each example assumes continuation of the 1985 contribution rate until 2011, when the contribution rate would increase to 11.9 percent, as under present law, and no change in the current automatic cost-of-living adjustment. Decoupling would reduce the long-run actuarial deficit under each example.

b. The following percentage increases between 1975 and 1980 are assumed for wages and prices, respectively: 1975, 6.2, 9.0; 1976, 9.0, 6.6; 1977, 11.0, 6.5; 1978, 8.8, 5.7; 1979, 7.7, 4.6; 1980, 7.0, 4.0. For 1981–85, wage increases of 6 percent and price increases of 4 percent a year are assumed.

rate of return can only be justified on the basis of income redistribution from high-wage to low-wage earners.

Two compromises combining wage base and tax rate increases are shown in table 5-5.[21] A low wage-base increase (to $18,000 in 1976, $21,000 in 1977, with automatic increases thereafter) would require

21. Estimates are based on 1975 projections. However, the relative impact of the alternatives would not be greatly altered if later projections were used.

moderate increases in the tax rate (9.9 to 10.1 percent in 1976, 10.4 percent in 1982, and 10.6 percent in 1984). In contrast, a higher increase in the wage base ($19,500 in 1976, $24,000 in 1977, with automatic increases thereafter) would require considerably smaller tax increases.

Another possibility is to eliminate the limit on the taxable earnings for the employer but maintain the scheduled tax base for the employee. This change, combined with a small tax rate increase (9.9 to 10.0 percent in 1976 and 10.4 percent in 1984), would generate revenues equivalent to those raised under the schemes mentioned above. Maintaining the limit on the employee's wage base can serve as a rationale for not paying higher benefits to those workers earning over the maximum. Advocates of a redistributional social security program might find this scheme an appealing way of financing the short-term deficit.

Though there are a number of alternative financing measures, there is less leeway in the need for additional financing and the timing of remedial action. The fact that by 1980 the problem of declining trust-fund balances will be permanent rather than cyclical makes an increase of revenues into the funds imperative. However, that goal is currently at odds with fiscal policy, because an increase in the tax rate or the earnings base, now, would retard economic recovery and should be postponed until unemployment has been substantially reduced. Though the short-term deficit need not be financed immediately, there is a time constraint on action set by predictions that the disability insurance fund will be exhausted by 1979. That limit could be extended by one to two years, however, if the trust funds were consolidated, because the OASI fund is projected to last until 1984. With this measure of flexibility in timing it should be possible to adequately finance the trust funds without adversely affecting the economy as a whole.

The Long-Run Problem

According to recent estimates, if nothing is done to change the current social security law the combined impact of the demographic shifts and the overindexing of the benefit formula will require the social security tax rate to almost triple by the year 2050. Table 5-6 summarizes the increasingly pessimistic long-run projections under the current overindexed system and also presents 1975 and 1976 official cost estimates, which were based on the assumption that the overindexing would be corrected

Table 5-6. Long-run Projections for the Combined OASDI Trust Fund, Selected Years, 1975–2050

	Expenditures as a percentage of taxable payroll							
	Projections under present overindexed system						*Projections under decoupled system*	
Year	*1975 law*	*1973 Trustees*	*1974 Trustees*	*1975 Trustees*	*1975 Senate Panel*	*1976 Trustees*	*1975 Trustees*	*1976 Trustees*
1975[a]	9.9	9.7[b]	10.2	10.9	10.2	10.6	10.9	10.6
1990	9.9	10.0	11.0	11.2	11.5	12.1	11.1	11.8
2010	9.9	10.3	12.7	14.1	14.6	16.0	12.6	13.7
2030	11.9	12.5	17.6	21.8	23.3	26.0	17.2	19.4
2050	11.9	12.6[c]	17.9[c]	22.4	23.9	28.6	16.3	19.2
Average	11.0	11.0[d]	13.9[e]	16.3	16.9	18.9	13.8	15.2
Average deficit[f]	...	...	3.0	5.3	6.0	8.0	2.9	4.3

Sources: *1976 Annual Report of the Board of Trustees of the Federal Old-Age and Survivors Insurance and Disability Insurance Trust Funds*, pp. 28, 48, 54, and Trustees' Reports for 1973–75; *Report of the Panel on Social Security Financing to the Committee on Finance, United States Senate*, 94:1 (GPO, 1975), p. 2.

a. Figures from the 1973, 1974, and 1975 Trustees' Reports and from the Senate Panel are estimates done before the actual experience; the figures from the 1976 Trustees' Report are based on actual experience but are preliminary.

b. Estimate for 1973.

c. Estimate for 2045.

d. Average for 1975–2045.

e. Average for 1974–2048.

f. Additional yearly tax required for funds sufficient to meet total benefit costs and administrative expenses during the seventy-five-year period.

and replacement rates stabilized at 1977 and 1978 levels, respectively. (These projections are taken from the last four annual reports of the board of trustees of the social security system and from the Report of the Panel on Social Security Financing, a group of outside actuaries and economists appointed by the Senate Committee on Finance to provide an independent analysis of the actuarial status of social security.)

Under the coupled (overindexed) system, the forecasts become progressively more pessimistic over the four-year period, with the 1976 Trustees' Report projecting tax rates close to 30 percent by the year 2050. The increasing pessimism came about because the economic situation remained unfavorable, the rate of inflation rose, the fertility rate continued to decline, and legislation provided for more generous benefits.

According to the assumptions in the 1976 Report (inflation of 4 percent and productivity growth of 1.75 percent), the average deficit over the seventy-five-year period 1975–2050 is 8 percent of taxable payrolls,

which can be interpreted as a need for an 8 percent higher tax rate—
4 percent for the employee and 4 percent for the employer—in every
year from 1975 on.[22] These projections contrast sharply with the relatively
sanguine actuarial valuation in the 1973 Trustees' Report, which indicated
that there would be only a slight long-run imbalance of 0.3 of 1 percent
over the forecast period.

According to the projection of the 1976 Trustees' Report, the average
deficit would be cut approximately in half if the overindexing error were
corrected and replacement rates were stabilized at 1978 levels. Once this
correction is made, the average deficit over the seventy-five years would
drop to 4.3 percent, a more manageable level, which could be dealt with
by a 2.15 percent increase in both employer and employee tax.

With a decoupled system, the payroll tax rate required to finance
benefits in the year 2050 is projected at 19.2 percent. This cost estimate is
considerably higher than the comparable 1975 projection, which required
a rate of 16.3 percent of taxable payrolls by the year 2050. The higher
1976 projection is derived primarily from the lower fertility rate assumption of 1.9, compared to 2.1 for the 1975 projections. In addition, the
assumed growth of real wages was reduced from 2 percent in the 1975
Report to 1.75 percent in the 1976 Report. Both of these assumptions
may be unduly pessimistic, but if they prove correct even the decoupled
system will require a significant increase over the current levy. The nature
of the new demographic assumptions is examined more closely in the
following section.

Demographic Changes

Changes in population are extraordinarily difficult to predict. Population growth depends on three factors—fertility rate, mortality rate, and
migration rate. The impact of the migration rate is very small and mortality rates are reasonably predictable, with a steady downward trend. In
contrast, the fertility rate[23] has been subject to wide swings and is very

22. This interpretation is not strictly correct, since the so-called long-run deficit
is merely a simple average of sixteen quinquennial deficit figures with no weighting
or discounting.
23. The fertility rate for a particular calendar year is the number of children
that a woman entering childbearing age can expect to have throughout her childbearing years if the birthrates then current apply to her and she survives those years.
Thus, a fertility rate slightly higher than 2.0 is necessary to maintain a mature
population—the so-called zero population growth.

difficult to forecast; at the same time, however, it has an enormous influence on the size of the population.

The hazards of forecasting population growth can be easily demonstrated by the following quotation from the report of the Senate panel: "In 1946 it was authoritatively estimated that the 1975 United States population would perhaps be as low as 147 million, or perhaps be as high as 191 million; in 1958 the corresponding low and high forecasts of the 1975 population were 216 million and 244 million; the event—a population of 213 million—has confounded both those prophecies."[24]

Since 1800 there has been a persistent decline in the fertility rate, although there was a transient deviation from this trend during the 1945–60 period (see figure 5-3). Since 1960 the fertility rate has been cut in half, from 3.65 to 1.82 in 1975. The 1976 official projection of the Social Security Administration assumes that the downward trend will be checked at a level of 1.75 in 1977, when a gradual upswing will begin. The projected rate will eventually reach 1.9 in the year 2005, remaining constant thereafter, and generating a slowly declining population.

Figure 5-3 presents the fertility rates underlying the 1976 social security cost estimates as well as earlier social security fertility assumptions, the projections of the Bureau of the Census and the assumptions incorporated in the report of the Panel on Social Security Financing. The differences in the various fertility rate assumptions have important implications for estimates of the size and age structure of the population. In contrast to the Social Security Administration's 1973 fertility assumptions, which resulted in estimates of population growth from 228 million in 1975 to 312 million in the year 2000 and finally 515 million in the year 2050, the comparable figures based on 1976 Social Security assumptions are 260 million in the year 2000, a peak of 279 million in 2030, and a decline to 274 million by 2050. The various population estimates under differing fertility assumptions are summarized in table 5-7.

The most significant implication of the alternative fertility assumptions for social security, however, is not the absolute size but the changing age composition of the population (see figure 5-4). The ratio of aged population to working age population has increased from 11.6 aged per 100 of working age in 1940 to 19.2 aged per 100 of working age in 1975 and is projected in the 1976 Trustees' Report to rise to 31.9 aged per 100 of working age by the middle of the next century (see figure 5-5).

24. *Report of the Panel on Social Security Financing to the Committee on Finance, United States Senate,* 94:1 (GPO, 1975), p. 5.

Figure 5-3. Actual and Projected Fertility Rates in the United States, 1800–2050[a]

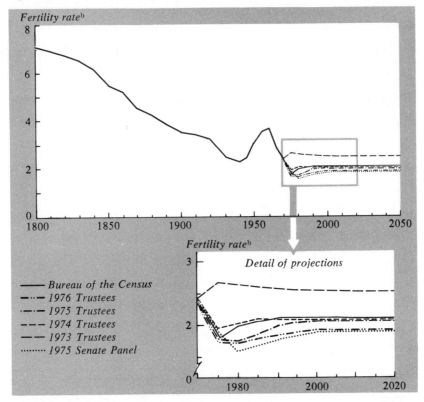

Fertility rate[b]

Detail of projections

Fertility rate[b]

—— Bureau of the Census
—··— 1976 Trustees
·—·— 1975 Trustees
——— 1974 Trustees
—— 1973 Trustees
········ 1975 Senate Panel

Sources: Actual rates, 1800–1910, Ansley J. Coale and Melvin Zelnik, *New Estimates of Fertility and Population in the United States* (Princeton University Press, 1963), p. 36; 1920–30, Public Health Service, *Natality Statistics Analysis, United States, 1965–1967*, series 21, no. 19 (GPO, 1970), p. 6; 1940–65, Public Health Service, *Vital Statistics of the United States, 1969*, vol. 1, *Natality* (GPO, 1974), p. 1–9; 1970, Bureau of the Census, *Current Population Reports*, series P-25, no. 601 (October 1975), p. 126. Projected rates, Bureau of the Census, *Current Population Reports*, series P-25, no. 601, "Projections of the Population of the United States, 1975 to 2050" (GPO, 1975), p. 126; Francisco Bayo, *United States Population Projections for OASDHI Cost Estimates*, Actuarial Study 62 (Social Security Administration, Office of the Actuary, 1966), p. 7, for figures used by 1973 trustees; SSA, unpublished data, for figures used by 1975 and 1976 trustees; *Report of the Panel on Social Security Financing to the Committee on Finance, United States Senate*, 94:1 (GPO, 1975), p. 8, for the 1975 panel and 1974 trustees' figures.
  a. Data for 1800–1910 are for the white population only; from 1920 on, for the total population. Data for 1940–55 are adjusted for underregistration of births.
  b. Births per woman during childbearing years.

From these projected ratios of aged to working age population, the Social Security Administration has made estimates of the ratio of beneficiaries to workers for a seventy-five-year period. There are now over 30 beneficiaries for every 100 workers. By the year 2050, with a fertility rate of 1.9 children per woman, there will be 51 beneficiaries for every 100 workers. Under the current method of pay-as-you-go financing, a 70

Table 5-7. Population Estimates under Alternative Fertility Assumptions, Selected Years, 1975–2050[a]
Millions

Study	1975	1980	1990	2000	2025	2050
			Total population			
1973 Trustees' Report	228	244	278	312	411	515
1974 Trustees' Report	223	233	254	271	305	320
1975 Trustees' Report	223	230	248	264	293	308
1975 Senate Panel	...	...	...	...	...	...
1976 Trustees' Report[b]	223	231	247	260	278	274
			Aged 20–64			
1973 Trustees' Report	121	132	149	173	225	282
1974 Trustees' Report	122	132	147	159	173	181
1975 Trustees' Report	122	132	147	157	166	174
1975 Senate Panel	122	132	147	156	154	154
1976 Trustees' Report[b]	122	132	148	158	161	156
			Over 65			
1973 Trustees' Report	22	24	29	31	49	63
1974 Trustees' Report	23	25	29	31	48	51
1975 Trustees' Report	23	25	29	30	47	49
1975 Senate Panel	23	25	29	31	49	50
1976 Trustees' Report[b]	23	25	29	30	48	50

Sources: *1976 Annual Report of the Board of Trustees of the Federal Old Age and Survivors Insurance and Disability Insurance Trust Funds*, and Trustees' Reports for 1973–75; *Report of the Panel on Social Security Financing to the Committee on Finance, United States Senate*; Francisco Bayo, *United States Population Projections for OASDHI Cost Estimates*, Actuarial Study 62 (Social Security Administration, Office of the Actuary, 1966), p. 25; Francisco Bayo and Steven F. McKay, *United States Population Projections for OASDHI Cost Estimates*, Actuarial Study 72 (SSA, Office of the Actuary, 1974), p. 27.
a. Different fertility assumptions were used in each study.
b. Assuming an ultimate fertility rate of 1.9.

percent increase in the relative number of beneficiaries will require a 70 percent increase in the OASDI tax rate to maintain benefit replacement rates. This 70 percent increase implies an OASDI tax rate in 2050 of approximately 18.5 percent, since the tax rate required to finance existing benefits is 10.7 percent.[25]

Given the past difficulties in predicting the fertility rate, it is important to try to assess the reliability of the most recent social security projections. Demographers generally agree that the recent decline in the fertility rate is the continuation of a long-run trend begun in 1800, and that the postwar baby boom was merely a temporary aberration.[26] These expectations are

25. The actual combined tax rate on employer and employees is currently 9.9 percent, but revenues fail to cover total costs.
26. See Lawrence A. Mayer, "It's a Bear Market for Babies, Too," *Fortune*, vol. 90 (December 1974), pp. 134–37.

Figure 5-4. Change in Age Composition of Population, 1900, 1975, 2050

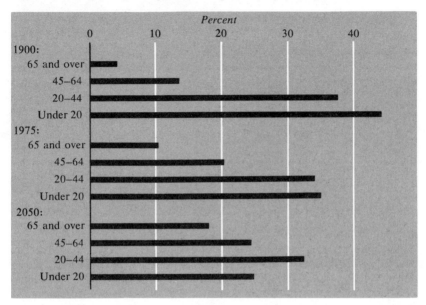

Source: Bureau of the Census and Social Security Administration, Office of the Actuary.

consistent with a series of major developments, all pointing toward smaller families. Birth control information and inexpensive methods of contraception have become more available and widespread. In addition, more people recognize that in an urbanized society a smaller family makes possible a higher standard of living, and people have come to prefer that standard of living. Furthermore, the changing role of women has led them to increase their participation in the labor force rather than spend long periods at home with children. Finally, zero population growth has become an accepted social goal.

While there is general agreement that fertility rates will remain low, there is less consensus on the level at which the rate will eventually stabilize. The 1976 social security intermediate cost estimates were based on a fertility rate of 1.9 (alternative cost estimates were also presented, based on fertility rates of 1.7 and 2.3), which is considerably below other recent estimates, including the Census Bureau's intermediate projection of a fertility rate of 2.1 beginning around the year 1990 (see figure 5-3). The higher Census Bureau estimate, which corresponds with previous social security projections, is buttressed by data from annual surveys of

Figure 5-5. The Aged as a Percentage of the Working Population, 1900–2050

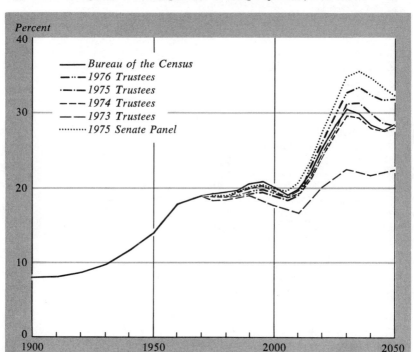

Sources: 1900–70, Bureau of the Census, *Census of Population, 1970,* vol. 1, *Characteristics of the Population,* pt. 1, *United States Summary,* sec. 1 (GPO, 1973), p. 276; Bureau of the Census estimates for 1975–2050, Bureau of the Census, *Current Population Reports,* series P-25, no. 601, tables 8, 11; other data, same as table 5-7.

young married women between the ages of eighteen and twenty-four, indicating an average number of expected births of 2.4 in 1971, 2.3 in 1972 and 1973, and 2.2 in 1974.[27] Even with a downward adjustment for those who will remain single, the fertility rate implied here is closer to the census figure of 2.1 than to the Social Security Administration's latest projection of 1.9. In short, the 1976 social security cost estimates may be too pessimistic because of an unrealistically low fertility rate forecast.

Long-Run Financing

Even if the Social Security Administration's recent fertility rate assumption is too low, the system faces cost increases resulting from demographic

27. Bureau of the Census, *Current Population Reports,* series P-25, no. 601, "Projections of the Population of the United States, 1975 to 2050" (GPO, 1975), p. 21.

changes. Furthermore, if uncorrected, the overindexing of the benefit formula would double that deficit. However, as discussed in chapter 3, overindexing should be eliminated as soon as possible to avoid capricious replacement rates and undesirable long-run costs and should not be allowed to cloud the issues involved in financing the true long-term deficit. Financing the cost increases arising from an aging population requires the resolution of two important issues. First, sole reliance on the payroll tax must be reevaluated for the long run. Second, the replacement of pay-as-you-go financing by a partially or fully funded system must be considered.

SOURCES OF REVENUE. The payroll tax rates required in the next century will not be excessively high once the system is decoupled, since a combined OASDI rate of 19.2 percent would be adequate to finance benefits in the year 2050.[28] Although this rate represents a 64 percent increase over the current levy, it is roughly equivalent to the present payroll tax rates of many European countries (see table 5-8). Furthermore, the cost projections are based on two key assumptions—one pertaining to the retirement age and one to the level of replacement rates—which, if altered, could reduce long-run financial requirements.

As long as social security is financed on a pay-as-you-go basis, future costs will be extremely sensitive to the ratio of retirees to working population, which in turn hinges on retirement age. Cost projections are based on the assumption that full benefits are awarded at sixty-five. However, the average life expectancy at sixty-five increased 23 percent between 1930 and 1970, rising from 12.2 to 15.0 years. Moreover, between 1958 and 1974, the number of days of restricted activity for people aged sixty-five and over declined 21 percent, dropping from 49.1 to 38.8 days. The large projected deficits and the evidence of the increased health and life expectancy of the aged raise the question of reversing the trend toward early retirement and extending the normal retirement age to sixty-eight. As noted in chapter 4, it is estimated that if the retirement age were increased gradually from sixty-five to sixty-eight by one month every six months beginning in 2005 and ending in 2023, the combined payroll tax rate could be reduced by 1.5 percentage points by 2050.[29]

Extending the retirement age would simultaneously ease the burden on future taxpayers and bolster the economic welfare of the elderly by

28. On the other hand, new demands may be placed on payroll tax revenues. For example, many of the national health insurance programs now under consideration include payroll tax financing.

29. *Reports of the Quadrennial Advisory Council,* p. 63.

Table 5-8. Employee-Employer Payroll Tax Rates by Type of Program, Selected Countries, 1973

Percent

Country	All social security programs			Old age, invalids, and survivors insurance[a]		
	Total	Employee	Employer	Total	Employee	Employer
Austria	34.80	13.40	21.40	17.50	8.75	8.75
Belgium	39.85	10.40	29.45	14.00	6.00	8.00
Canada	10.00	4.70	5.30	3.60	1.80	1.80
Federal Republic of Germany	31.20	14.35	16.85	18.00	9.00	9.00
France	39.15	6.64	32.51	8.75	3.00	5.75
Italy	54.16	7.05	47.11	20.65	6.90	13.75
Japan[b]	17.59	7.35	10.24	6.40	3.20	3.20
Netherlands	51.40	24.00	27.40	19.80	14.55	5.25
Norway[c]	25.90	9.20	16.70	25.90	9.20	16.70
Spain	70.82	10.05	60.77	19.00	5.00	14.00
Sweden[d]	23.70	9.65	14.05	16.18	5.68	10.50
Switzerland	24.32	6.75	17.57	8.60	4.30	4.30
United Kingdom[b]	13.46	6.57	6.89	12.47	6.00	6.47
United States	14.60	5.85	8.75	9.70	4.85	4.85

Sources: Social Security Administration, *Social Security Programs Throughout the World, 1973* (GPO, 1974); Martin B. Tracy, "Payroll Taxes Under Social Security Programs: Cross National Survey," *Social Security Bulletin*, vol. 38 (December 1975), p. 5.

a. Includes financing for some programs in addition to old age, invalids, and survivors insurance in the Netherlands, Norway, Spain, and the United Kingdom. Excludes financing for certain programs in Belgium and France that are covered by separate taxes under other programs.

b. Includes rates based on a percent of average earnings in manufacturing.

c. Includes 3.8 percent tax on income and 5.47 percent on pension-producing income.

d. Sweden has a dual universal pension and a social insurance system. Employees pay 5 percent tax on income toward the universal pension (the government contributes the remainder). Employers pay 10.5 percent of wages between a base amount and 7.5 times the base amount to the social insurance system.

shortening the period over which they must live on reduced retirement income. Recent evidence indicates that social security has contributed to the trend toward early retirement (see chapter 4) and therefore, if it is desirable to extend the retirement age, it would be appropriate to eliminate some of the social security provisions that discourage labor force participation of the elderly.

The second assumption embedded in the long-run cost projections is that overindexing will be corrected in a way that not only stabilizes replacement rates but in fact ensures constant replacement rates over time. As discussed in chapter 3, a reasonable alternative is a benefit formula that, while making replacement rates independent of wage and price increases, allows the ratio of benefits to preretirement earnings to decline gradually over time.

There is one interesting implication of the demographic shift beyond the inescapable increase in taxes that will be required to support the proportionately larger retired population. Lower fertility rates, resulting in fewer children per worker, will cause a stabilization or even a decline in the dependency ratio, a measure of total economic burden on active workers. (The ratio is the number of people under twenty and over sixty-four for every 100 people between those ages.)

The pros and cons of payroll tax financing for social security are discussed earlier in this chapter. The appropriateness of this source of revenue depends in large measure on the nature and distributional intent of the program. The payroll tax seems the most logical way to finance a wage-related benefit system, once the burden on low-income people is alleviated, as it is in part through the earned income credit. However, if social security is not viewed as wage-related but as an annual transfer program with a strong redistributional orientation, then the payroll tax should be eliminated and the system financed by the personal income tax.

Finally, if social security is a lifetime saving program with some redistributional elements, the financing could be a combination of payroll taxes and personal income tax revenues. One possibility is to retain the payroll tax to finance benefits paid to primary workers and rely on general revenues to finance benefits for dependents and survivors. This option (which might be accompanied by expansion of the earned income credit in order to ease the regressivity of the payroll tax) maintains the contributory principle, which has sustained public approval of the program, and transfers some of the redistributional role to the more appropriate general revenue financing mechanism.

Another possibility, also discussed by the 1975 Advisory Council as part of the short-run solution, is to transfer the financing of health insurance to general revenues. Health insurance benefits generally bear no relation to covered wages and therefore should be financed by a more general tax. Entitlement could still be based upon earnings in covered employment, ensuring that it be considered an earned right. Health insurance tax rates are scheduled to increase slowly to a combined rate of 3 percent by 1986. These revenues would finance most of the projected deficit under a decoupled system.

In sum, the long-term financial requirements of the social security program are relatively manageable once the double inflation adjustment (overindexing) is eliminated. Furthermore, the cost estimates for a decoupled system are based on the assumption of constant replacement rates

Table 5-9. Actual Past and Projected Future Dependency Ratios, Selected Years, 1930–2050[a]

Year	Under 20	65 and over	Total
1930	69.6	9.7	79.3
1940	58.5	11.7	70.2
1950	59.2	14.1	73.3
1960	74.1	17.4	91.5
1970	71.7	18.4	90.0
1975	64.1	19.2	83.3
1990	48.1	19.6	67.7
2000	45.9	19.3	65.2
2010	42.0	19.8	61.7
2020	42.4	25.8	68.2
2030	43.9	32.8	76.7
2040	43.2	32.6	75.8
2050	43.5	31.9	75.4

Sources: 1930–70, "Statement of Robert M. Ball," in *Social Security*, Hearings before the Subcommittee on Retirement Income and Employment of the House Select Committee on Aging, 94:1 (GPO, 1975), p. 111, 1990–2050, *1976 Annual Report of the Board of Trustees of the Federal Old Age and Survivors Insurance and Disability Insurance Trust Funds*, p. 63; 1975, Bureau of the Census, *Current Population Reports*, series P-25, no. 601, "Projections of the Population of the United States, 1975 to 2050" (GPO, 1975), p. 67. Figures are rounded.

a. The dependency ratio is the total number of people under twenty and over sixty-four per 100 people aged twenty to sixty-four.

over time and full benefits at sixty-five. Additional cost reductions are possible by lowering replacement rates or extending the retirement age, or both.

THE TIMING OF TAX INCREASES. Tax increases can be timed to coincide with or precede rising outlays. If the OASDI system is kept on a purely pay-as-you-go basis, payroll taxes, which amount to about 10 percent now, will increase to 13.7 percent by 2010, jump to 19.4 percent by 2030, and fall slightly to 19.2 percent in 2050 (see table 5-6). The sudden increase between 2010 and 2030 is because of the increasing proportion of elderly. The ratio of people aged sixty-five and over to those aged twenty to sixty-four will increase from 19.8 in 2010 to 32.8 in 2030 (see table 5-9).

If equity over time were an important criterion, it might be difficult to justify such low tax rates now and such high rates later. Financing on a pay-as-you-go basis means that current workers will receive significantly higher rates of return than workers who enter the labor force after the turn of the century. An alternative to pay-as-you-go is a rate raise within the next few years to about 14 percent, thereby spreading the required tax levy evenly over the period.

An immediate increase in rates would produce substantial surpluses, forming a moderate trust fund. If allowed to build up until about 2010, the fund would amount to three to five years' outgo, or about $400 billion (in 1975 dollars). After 2010, it would be drawn down to finance benefits. In short, the accumulation of a moderate trust fund could smooth out the demographic bulge and keep tax rates relatively constant until 2050. This move would violate the pay-as-you-go nature of the system, but it would serve to equalize rates of return over time. Chapter 6 focuses on some of the difficulties involved in accumulating reserves in the social security trust funds.

Summary

Determining the appropriate method of financing the social security program involves defining its role as either an annual redistributive transfer program or a lifetime compulsory saving mechanism. The progressive income tax is preferable to the payroll tax as a means of financing a program aimed at redistribution, since the regressivity of the payroll tax weakens the effectiveness of the transfer. Those who view social security as essentially a tax transfer system therefore advise scrapping the payroll tax and financing the program out of general revenues.

However, general revenue financing would not be appropriate for a program that based entitlement on earnings rather than need. If the more traditional lifetime perspective of social security as a system of compulsory saving is adopted, the payroll tax, which maintains the link between contributions and benefits, is an appropriate finance mechanism as long as special provision is made for low-income workers.

Eliminating the duality of goals within social security by assigning its transfer role to the means-tested supplemental security income program and strengthening the wage-related aspect of social security benefits would clarify the choice of financing method. In any event, the burden of the payroll tax on low-income people should be modified by extension of the earned income credit to all poor taxpayers.

Payroll taxes versus general revenues is just one of the major issues involved in the problem of social security financing. There remains the question of the adequacy of present financing schemes to meet both the short-run and long-run expenditure requirements.

The short-run problem of declining trust fund balances is attributable to the recent period of severe recession. Temporary declines in the trust funds, which are accumulated as contingency reserves, are the expected consequence of revenue shortfalls during economic downturns. However, the recession has resulted in a permanent loss in real wages and, therefore, a tax increase is required to restore balance to the trust funds. Several methods of supplementing revenues in the short run are available, including increasing the tax rate, raising the taxable earnings ceiling, transferring health insurance revenues to OASDI, and financing through general revenue. However, any method that is adopted should not raise taxes until recovery from the 1974–75 recession is assured. The need for coordination with fiscal policy requires the consolidation of the OASI and DI trust funds to allow the greater flexibility required for timing the additional financing.

The long-run deficit results from shifts in the demographic structure and the imbalance created by an overindexed benefit structure. Eliminating the overindexing would reduce long-run costs to a manageable level so that the deficit could be financed by either a moderate increase in the payroll tax rate or a combination of increased rate and the alternative short-run methods listed above. Furthermore, extension of the normal retirement age to sixty-eight years or adoption of a schedule of replacement rates that decline gradually over time would further reduce the long-term deficit.

The financial problems facing the social security system, then, are not insurmountable; in fact, there are so many avenues of relief that much of the difficulty lies in choosing among solutions. The choice will depend on the perceived distributional goals of the social security program.

chapter six **Saving and Capital Accumulation**

Recent evidence indicates that, contrary to earlier notions, social security may reduce the volume of saving in the economy. If social security thus curtails saving, it diminishes the supply of funds to the capital markets, reduces investment, and thereby lowers the rate of growth. The relation between social security, saving behavior, and capital accumulation is the subject of this chapter.

Social Security and Saving Behavior

The impact on saving of a simple pay-as-you-go tax transfer system, in which workers do not regard contributions as saving, depends on the spending habits of the taxed workers relative to those of the beneficiary population. For example, if workers consume 90 percent of their income and beneficiaries 100 percent of theirs, the transfer of $67 billion in 1975 through old age, survivors, and disability insurance from workers to beneficiaries would have reduced aggregate saving by $6.7 billion.

However, workers know they will receive benefits in exchange for their current OASDI taxes, and a guaranteed retirement income enters into their saving plans. To the extent that they think of their social security contributions as saving, they will tend to save less on their own, thus substituting public for private saving. But since their social security contributions are immediately paid out as benefits rather than accumulated in a fund, there is, in reality, no public saving; and the implied reduction in individual private saving implies a corresponding reduction in the nation's total capital accumulation. On the other hand, by encouraging early retirement (see chapter 4), social security has an offsetting positive effect on saving, as a person increases saving over a shorter working life to provide for a longer period of retirement.

An example may clarify how the offsetting benefit and retirement effects could alter a worker's saving behavior.[1] Suppose a typical worker begins working at the age of twenty-five, earns $12,000 a year, plans to retire at seventy, and expects to live until eighty. Assume further that he or she plans no bequests and wants to have an annual income of $6,000 during retirement. At an interest rate of 5 percent, this worker would have to put aside $281 or 2.34 percent of earnings each year to meet retirement income needs. If the worker were guaranteed annual retirement benefits of $3,000, he or she would cut private saving in half, to only 1.17 percent of income. This reduction in saving represents the benefit effect.

The retirement effect comes about in the following manner. Suppose that in order to receive these benefits the worker is forced to retire at sixty-five, five years earlier than planned. This reduction in working years and increase in retirement years requires a saving of 2.09 percent of earnings to attain the retirement income goal of $6,000 each year. The retirement effect thus increases the saving rate and acts to offset the decline in private saving brought about by the guarantee of benefits.

The view that social security benefits reduce saving is relatively new. Until recently, most experts have argued that participation in any pension plan encourages personal saving. The 1968 Brookings study by Pechman, Aaron, and Taussig concludes, "The available evidence suggests that, over the long run, individuals covered by government and industrial pension plans tend to save more than those who are not covered."[2] This argument was based on the historical performance of the saving rate and on cross-sectional studies of pension coverage and saving. As illustrated in figure 6-1, the ratio of personal saving to disposable income has not shown any downward trend since the introduction of social security; and in fact, if social security contributions are considered saving, the saving ratio has increased. The relative stability of the private saving rate in the face of rapid expansion of the social security program can now be explained by the offsetting impact of the retirement and benefit effects.

Two cross-sectional studies of the relation between private pension coverage and saving behavior have been cited in the past as indirect evidence that social security has increased personal saving. In a 1965 study, Phillip Cagan analyzed the saving behavior in 1958–59 of over 15,000

1. This example is based on a presentation of the retirement and benefit effects by Selig D. Lesnoy and John C. Hambor, "Social Security, Saving, and Capital Formation," *Social Security Bulletin,* vol. 38 (July 1975), pp. 3–15.

2. Joseph A. Pechman, Henry J. Aaron, and Michael K. Taussig, *Social Security: Perspectives for Reform* (Brookings Institution, 1968), p. 186.

Figure 6-1. Personal Saving as a Percentage of Disposable Income, with and without Social Security, 1929–75

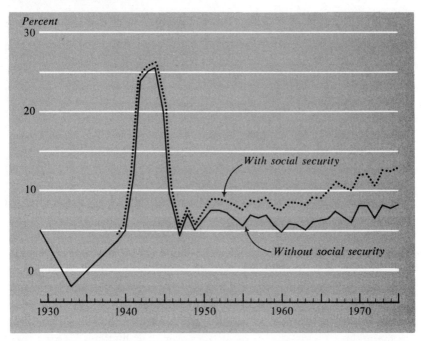

Sources: Personal saving and disposable personal income, Bureau of Economic Analysis; contributions to OASI trust fund, Social Security Administration.

members of Consumers Union and found that those covered by private pension plans saved more than those not covered.[3] Cagan's explanation of the surprising results is that pension coverage calls attention to retirement needs and prospects and thereby fosters a "recognition effect" that counteracts individuals' disinclinations to plan for the future.

A study reported by George Katona, based on personal interviews conducted by the Survey Research Center of the University of Michigan with representative samples of all American families in 1962–63, also concludes that pension plans stimulate voluntary saving.[4] Katona added a second explanation for his results, hypothesizing a "goal feasibility" effect, wherein people intensify their saving efforts the closer they get to their retirement

3. Phillip Cagan, *The Effect of Pension Plans on Aggregate Saving: Evidence from a Sample Survey,* Occasional Paper 95 (Columbia University Press for the National Bureau of Economic Research, 1965).

4. George Katona, *The Mass Consumption Society* (McGraw-Hill, 1964), chap. 19.

Figure 6-2. Saving and Consumption Related to Age

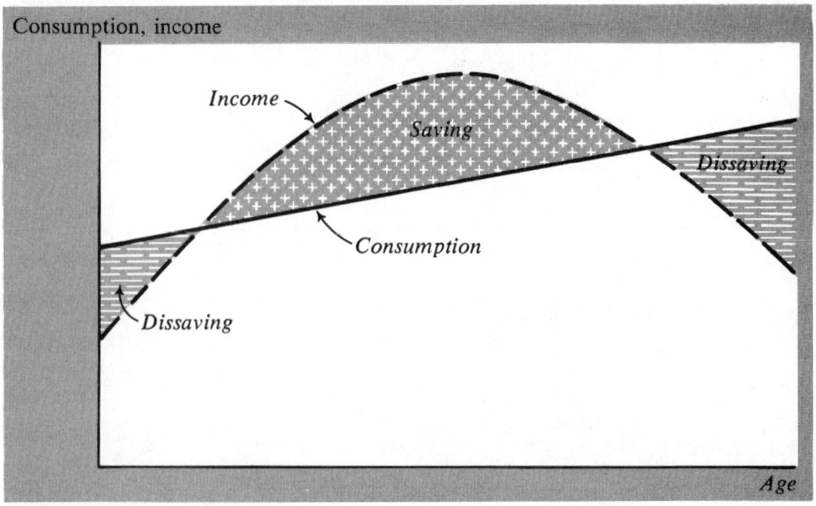

goal. Both the Cagan and Katona explanations imply that a person's preferences for present income over future income are modified by participation in a pension plan. This assumption differs fundamentally from that underlying the life-cycle model of consumer behavior.

In the life-cycle model, consumers try to allocate their resources so as to maintain a steady stream of income over their lifetimes. During their working years they do not consume all their income but set aside positive saving, which they later dissave in retirement. Figure 6-2 illustrates the pattern of saving and consumption implied by the model. The important difference between this generally accepted model of consumer behavior and that implied by Cagan's and Katona's hypotheses is that the life-cycle model states that consumers' preferences for current over future consumption are fixed—that is, they are unaffected by the particular income situation faced by the consumer or by his or her participation in a pension plan.

Empirical Evidence

Recent studies support the predictions of the life-cycle saving model—that guaranteed retirement benefits reduce individual saving and earlier retirement increases saving. The relation between private pension coverage and saving was examined using a sample of men in their preretirement years over the period 1966–71, in a study based on a series of surveys

Table 6-1. Effect of Social Security on Personal Saving in 1969: Results of Two Studies
Billions of dollars

Item	Munnell	Feldstein
Actual saving	38.2	38.2
Social security effect	−3.6	−36.8
Benefit effect	−14.0	...
Retirement effect	10.4	...
Effect of social security taxes	...	−14.4
Net effect of social security	−3.6	−51.2
Estimated saving in absence of social security	41.8	89.4

Sources: Derived from Alicia H. Munnell, *The Effect of Social Security on Personal Saving* (Ballinger, 1974), chap. 4; and Martin Feldstein, "Social Security, Induced Retirement, and Aggregate Capital Accumulation," *Journal of Political Economy*, vol. 82 (September–October 1974), pp. 919–21.

conducted by the Labor Department.[5] The results indicate that coverage by private pension plans discourages saving in other forms, at least for those older men for whom retirement is the primary saving motivation. A similar analysis was undertaken for a subsample of Cagan's Consumers Union data, for which more complete and consistent information was available than for the larger sample.[6] These results, too, indicate that pension coverage slightly discourages private saving, contradicting Cagan's finding. The negative impact on saving was particularly pronounced for older men, though discernible for younger groups.

Two larger studies have estimated the impact of the social security benefit and retirement using aggregate consumption and saving for the period 1929–71. Although both studies conclude that aggregate private saving has been reduced by the social security program, they differ on the magnitude of the impact on saving, a discrepancy that has important implications for an analysis of the future of the social security program.

The first study, by Martin Feldstein, concludes that without social security personal saving in 1969 would have been more than double the actual saving of $38.2 billion.[7] The second study, by Munnell, found that the reduction in saving for 1969 was only $3.6 billion.[8] Table 6-1 demonstrates how widely the estimates vary.

5. Alicia H. Munnell, "Private Pensions and Saving: New Evidence," *Journal of Political Economy*, vol. 84 (October 1976), pp. 1013–32.

6. Alicia H. Munnell, *The Effect of Social Security on Personal Saving* (Ballinger, 1974), chap. 5.

7. Martin Feldstein, "Social Security, Induced Retirement, and Aggregate Capital Accumulation," *Journal of Political Economy*, vol. 82 (September–October 1974), pp. 905–26.

8. Munnell, *Effect of Social Security on Personal Saving*; calculations used 1969 data and equations on p. 68.

Table 6-2. Social Security Wealth, Net Worth of Consumers, and Gross National Product, Selected Years, 1940–75

Amounts in billions of 1972 dollars

Year	Wealth			Social Security as percent of total	Gross national product
	Social security[a]	Net worth of consumers[a]	Total[a]		
1940	253	1,289	1,542	16.4	344
1945	431	1,583	2,014	21.4	559
1950	477	1,643	2,120	22.5	534
1955	744	1,976	2,720	27.4	655
1960	988	2,335	3,323	29.7	737
1965	1,507	2,645	4,152	36.3	926
1970	2,049	2,971	5,020	40.8	1,075
1975	3,238[a]	3,459	6,697	48.4	1,192

Sources: Social security wealth estimates are based on author's calculations except for 1975, which is from the Social Security Administration (see note a). For a description of the methodology see Munnell, *Effect of Social Security on Personal Saving*. Net worth of consumers is based on the Ando-Modigliani concept (see ibid., chap. 4), adopted by the Board of Governors of the Federal Reserve System for use in the FRB-MIT (Federal Reserve Board–Massachusetts Institute of Technology) model, which is the source of these data. GNP data are from Bureau of Economic Analysis.

a. The value of social security wealth for 1975 is not strictly comparable with earlier years. The 1975 value, prepared by the Social Security Administration, is an actuarial estimate that incorporates changes in the social security laws. The earlier figures represent the perceived wealth of individuals and assume a constant ratio of benefits to disposable income.

The two studies used the same measure of expected benefits. Social security benefits were treated as annuities that workers receive when they reach the age of sixty-five. In estimating the impact of social security on aggregate asset accumulation, one must find some measure of the assets represented by expected benefits. In both studies a wealth variable for each year between 1929 and 1971 was constructed by calculating the present value of the sum of all the individual annuities owed to the insured labor force in each year. To calculate such a variable, one must make many assumptions about the future growth in benefits, the number of workers collecting, their mortality rates, and the appropriate interest rate at which to discount benefits. As a result, the value of social security wealth cannot be estimated with precision. However, its relative size is large, especially compared to total private wealth of households, as shown in table 6-2[9] Further-

9. The data in table 6-2 may somewhat overstate the importance of social security wealth relative to total household wealth. First, the social security wealth values are gross wealth; net social security wealth, which involves subtracting the present discounted value of future tax payments, would be substantially lower. Whether or not to subtract future taxes depends on whether people perceive their contributions as compulsory saving for future benefits or simply as another tax. Second, the values of social security depend on the rate at which future benefits are discounted. A real discount rate of 3 percent was used in these calculations; if a higher discount rate were assumed, the value of social security wealth would be smaller.

more, the social security wealth estimates, which are based on the assumption of a constant ratio of benefits to disposable income, are consistent with the Social Security Administration's independent actuarial calculation for 1975, which includes changes in the law. The fact that the wealth figure increased by 58 percent between 1970 and 1975 can be explained by the large benefit increases in the early 1970s (15 percent effective January 1970, 10 percent January 1971, 20 percent September 1972, and 11 percent June 1974).

The difficulty in using this social security wealth variable in time-series statistical analyses is that it moves with the unemployment rate although in a reverse direction. The wealth variable was very small during the 1930s (zero until 1937) when the unemployment rate was extraordinary high. The similarity in the two variables, which are almost mirror images in these earlier years, means that when the unemployment rate is included in the consumption function, the coefficient of the social security wealth variable is no longer statistically significant. Therefore, Feldstein based his conclusions on equations that exclude the unemployment rate.

Munnell used an alternative approach to derive more detailed estimates of the benefit and retirement effects.[10] On the assumption that information about the trend in saving for retirement cannot be gained from looking only at aggregate saving, a saving for retirement series was constructed. Using this series as the dependent variable, it was possible to derive statistically significant results for both the retirement and benefit effects even when an unemployment variable was included in the equation. The coefficients of both the benefit and retirement variables were consistent over the two periods, 1929–69 and 1946–69. Furthermore, the impact on saving was exactly the same whether social security wealth or combined employer-employee social security taxes were used as the proxy for future benefits. Nevertheless, the arbitrariness introduced by the construction of the retirement saving series makes the results subject to criticism.

On the other hand, Feldstein's results seem to seriously overstate the impact of social security on saving. This overstatement can be attributed to four factors:

1. Unemployment rate. Because the unemployment rate, which is likely to influence saving and is highly correlated with social security, is not included in Feldstein's equations, part of the variation in saving that might be caused by fluctuations in unemployment is reflected in the coefficient of the social security wealth variable. The exclusion of the unemployment

10. Munnell, *Effect of Social Security on Personal Saving,* chap. 4.

rate thus results in an overstatement of the negative effect on saving of social security.

2. Saving rate. Feldstein's evidence is "consistent with the Keynesian view that the aggregate rate of saving would increase as income rose if there were no offsetting government policies."[11] This secular increase is difficult to explain, however, within the life cycle model used in his analysis. In fact, the increasing proportion of elderly dissavers in the United States between 1929 and 1971 implies a decline in the aggregate saving rate over time.[12]

3. Social Security taxes. Feldstein believes that there is an additional negative impact on saving from social security taxes: "In 1971, social security taxes and contributions reduced disposable income by $51 billion in 1971 prices. The corresponding reduction in personal saving is, therefore, $18 billion."[13] In fact, the social security program does not reduce disposable income in the aggregate. Since the program works on a pay-as-you-go basis, the taxes collected under the social security program, reducing disposable income for some, are returned immediately in the form of benefits, increasing disposable income for others. The transfer of income from workers to the retired therefore has no effect on total disposable income. There is a legitimate question, of course, of whether the saving habits of the beneficiaries differ from the saving habits of those who pay the tax. While it is true that the aged have a high propensity to consume, most of the tax comes from earners who also have high consumption propensities. Moreover, it has been estimated that the effect on saving from redistribution is small.[14] Therefore, the most plausible assumption is that the current impact of transferring income from the working population to the retired would only negligibly affect saving behavior.

4. Retirement effect. While Feldstein acknowledges the indirect impact of social security on saving through the retirement effect, no variable for this important phenomenon is included in his equations. In its absence, the coefficient of social security wealth is interpreted as the net impact of the

11. Feldstein, "Social Security, Induced Retirement, and Aggregate Capital Accumulation," p. 922.

12. In 1929 people aged sixty-five and over accounted for 5.3 percent of the population; by 1974 the ratio had increased to 10.3 percent. *Economic Report of the President, January 1976*, p. 195.

13. Feldstein, "Social Security, Induced Retirement, and Aggregate Capital Accumulation," p. 920.

14. See George F. Break, "The Incidence and Economic Effects of Taxation," in Alan S. Blinder and others, *The Economics of Public Finance* (Brookings Institution, 1974), pp. 193.

benefit and retirement effects. He estimates that in 1969, had there been no social security program, people would have saved an additional $36.8 billion—an amount considerably in excess of total OASDI taxes of $29.6 billion. These results imply a very small or nonexistent retirement effect, since there is no reason for people to dissave more than the net increase in their future benefits.

Although Feldstein's calculations overestimate the impact of the social security benefit effect, the combined evidence of the two studies indicates that in the future the influence of social security on private saving must be taken into account.

The importance of both retirement and benefit effects on the saving rate is confirmed in another study by Feldstein, which examined saving rates in a cross-section sample of fifteen developed countries.[15] The study consists of three parts. Estimates of saving functions and a model of retirement behavior were made, and then the two results were combined to assess the net impact of intercountry differences in social security on private saving. The results indicate that a 25 percent increase in the ratio of benefits to income implies a benefit effect that decreases the saving rate by about 2.7 percentage points, or about one-fifth of the sample average rate of saving (12.7 percent). At the same time, higher benefits induce a 6.2-percentage-point decline in the labor force participation of the aged and a consequent 1.5 percent increase in the saving rate. Therefore, Feldstein's international study confirms the importance of the retirement effect as well as the benefit effect on saving behavior.

Some additional information about the saving response of workers to social security over the past thirty-five years can be gained from the surveys of OASDI beneficiaries conducted periodically by the Social Security Administration. The survey data show that people retiring today have saved about the same proportion of their income as people who retired thirty years ago, which indicates that social security has not led to a drastic reduction in saving. First, the income and wealth of elderly beneficiaries has increased since the introduction of social security (see table 6-3). According to a 1968 social security survey, real median income of aged beneficiaries—both the grand total and the total excluding social security—had doubled since the early 1940s. Furthermore, a significantly smaller portion of the 1968 income was derived from public assistance and con-

15. Martin Feldstein, "Social Security and Private Savings: International Evidence in an Extended Life Cycle Model," Discussion Paper 361 (Harvard University, Institute of Economic Research, 1974; processed).

Table 6-3. Median Income and Net Worth of Aged Beneficiaries, Selected Years, 1941–68

Year of survey	Median income		Net worth	
	Current dollars	June 1966 dollars	Current dollars	June 1966 dollars
Married couples				
1941–42	743	1,598	1,685	3,648
1944	1,110	2,060	3,830	7,110
1946	1,090	1,850	3,000	5,080
1949	1,130	1,540	4,800	6,510
1951	1,550	1,930	5,830	7,270
1957	2,250	2,590	8,790	10,130
1963	2,710	2,900	10,840	11,600
1968	3,199	3,106	n.a.	n.a.
Unmarried men				
1941–42	458	998	138	305
1944	550	1,010	1,330	2,470
1946	710	1,200	710	1,200
1949	670	910	370	500
1951	850	1,060	340	420
1957	1,170	1,350	800	920
1963	1,380	1,480	2,780	2,970
1968	1,742	1,691	n.a.	n.a.
Widows				
1941–42	332	720	1,830	3,955
1944	470	870	3,240	6,020
1946	550	920	2,000	3,390
1951	620	780	2,700	3,430
1957	880	1,020	4,380	5,050
1963	1,100	1,180	4,780	5,110
1968	1,297	1,259	n.a.	n.a.

Sources: Survey data for 1941–63 are summarized in Edna C. Wentworth and Dena K. Motley, *Resources After Retirement*, Research Report 34 (GPO, 1970), tables 2 and 14; data for 1968 are from Lenore E. Bixby, "Income of People Aged 65 and Older; Overview from 1968 Survey of the Aged," *Social Security Bulletin*, vol. 33 (April 1970), p. 12.
n.a. Not available.

tributions of relatives; the higher median income comes from the retirees' own efforts (see table 6-4).

The real net worth of beneficiaries at retirement more than tripled over the same period because of the increase in home ownership, which represents the greater part of net worth. In early surveys, slightly over 50 percent of married couples owned their own homes; by the 1968 survey this percentage had increased to 77.

Table 6-4. Percentage of OASDHI Beneficiaries with Income from Other Sources, Selected Surveys, 1941–68

Year of survey	Type of survey	Earn-ings[a]	Retire-ment pension	Interest, divi-dends, rents	Public as-sistance	Contri-butions from relatives
			Married couples			
1941–42	Large cities, combined[b]	36	18	43	10	12
1944	Middle-sized Ohio cities	57	16	56	7	16
1946	Boston	27	22	70	16	17
1949	Philadelphia–Baltimore	24	24	55	6	22
1951	National Beneficiary Survey	36	23	50	12	6
1957	National Beneficiary Survey	38	25	59	7	5
1963	Survey of the Aged	33	27	65	6	3
1968	Survey of the Aged	43	30	62	5	2
			Unmarried men			
1941–42	Large cities, combined[b]	37	14	31	16	9
1944	Middle-sized Ohio cities	48	15	40	9	14
1946	Boston	20	22	61	22	9
1949	Philadelphia–Baltimore	23	25	43	17	14
1951	National Beneficiary Survey	28	16	34	22	5
1957	National Beneficiary Survey	29	19	38	14	5
1963	Survey of the Aged	24	18	50	10	2
1968	Survey of the Aged	19	22	46	11	*
			Widows			
1941–42	Large cities, combined[b]	20	...	54	5	16
1944	Middle-sized Ohio cities	35	...	58	5	34
1946	Boston	15	...	69	18	18
1951	National Beneficiary Survey	14	2	49	13	10
1957	National Beneficiary Survey	15	2	52	12	11
1963	Survey of the Aged	17	3	58	8	5
1968[c]	Survey of the Aged	15	12	52	10	5

Sources: Same as table 6-3.
* 0.5 percent or less.
a. For couples, the 1941–63 figures are earnings of married men; the comparable figure for 1968 to those in the earlier surveys is 50 percent.
b. Simple numerical average of surveys from Philadelphia–Baltimore, St. Louis, Birmingham–Memphis –Atlanta, and Los Angeles.
c. 1968 figures include retired nonmarried women.

The impression one gains from such income and asset data is that in-dividual saving for retirement (other than social security) has more than kept pace with the increase in real income. One problem in interpreting the data is that people retiring in the early 1940s had unusually low wealth and income because of the Great Depression, which may tend to exag-gerate the growth of wealth and income. Nevertheless, the doubling over the years of real retirement income, the tripling of real net worth, and the increased reliance on personal resources rather than aid, lend support to the hypothesis that in the past private saving for retirement has not been dramatically reduced by social security.

Past experience does not deny, however, the possibility that in the future social security may have a greater impact on saving. The apparent small influence to date has really been the net result of two strong but offsetting forces. Since the extraordinary decline in labor force participation seems to have slowed (and for reasons discussed in chapter 4 ought even to be reversed), and the pace of benefit increases seems to have accelerated, the net impact of social security in the future may be a reduction in the rate of saving.

Summary

Two recent studies overwhelmingly conclude that guaranteed retirement benefits discourage saving and that earlier retirement patterns can have an offsetting stimulating effect on personal saving. While there is no longer much question about the direction of the effect, there is still considerable uncertainty about its past magnitude. Estimates now range from virtually zero, with the benefit and retirement effects almost completely offsetting one another, to a halving of the individual saving rate, with people reducing their saving by more than total OASDI taxes. Such a dramatic change in saving behavior is not discernible in the Social Security Surveys of New Beneficiaries, and the estimates probably overstate the negative impact of social security on saving. Nevertheless, considering the leveling off in labor force participation of the aged and the enormous benefit increases of the early 1970s, the net impact of social security on saving in the future will probably be negative. Much depends on future capital needs and the desirability of offsetting any negative impact on saving by accumulating reserves in the trust funds.

Future Capital Needs

Several widely publicized studies forecast a chronic shortage of funds for the next five to ten years. A study by the New York Stock Exchange projected a "capital gap" of $650 billion out of total projected investments of $4.7 trillion in the 1974–85 period.[16] These predictions assume a sharp increase in future private investment and a sharp decline in the saving rate. The ratio of personal saving to gross national product was projected to decline smoothly over the 1973–85 period, from 4.25 percent to 3.9 percent. In fact, saving as a percentage of GNP was 5.1 percent in 1974, declined to 4.8 percent for 1976, and is forecast to rise to about 5.2 percent in 1978.[17] Even when measured as the ratio of personal saving to full-employment GNP (to correct for any cyclical component), no long-term decline in the saving rate is evident. Furthermore the NYSE projections make no allowance for the inflow of any foreign capital.

Another projection, presented by the chairman of the General Electric Company before the Joint Economic Committee, forecast similar investment needs but a slightly higher saving rate, which results in a saving deficiency of $200 billion over the same period.[18]

In contrast to these alarmist predictions, a recent study by the Brookings Institution concluded that future needs for investment capital in this country can be met provided the federal government runs budgetary surpluses offset by easier monetary policy.[19] The authors of this study base their conclusion on more realistic saving rates and more conservative estimates of capital needs. The study does project a steep rise in business' need for investment capital, which cannot be met by profits or other internally generated funds, and foresees rising capital needs for housing and for state and local governments. To some extent, rising investments in those areas will be offset by a decline in school construction and the completion of the interstate highway system. Nevertheless, there will be a net upsurge in demand for capital by business, which can be offset by a decline in the demand for funds by the federal government. The study's balance sheet projects a required budget surplus of about 0.5 percent of full-employment GNP for 1980. The Brookings study indicates clearly that there is currently no reason for alarm about long-term projections of a capital short-

16. New York Stock Exchange, "The Capital Needs and Savings Potential of the U.S. Economy: Projections through 1985" (NYSE, 1974; processed).

17. The 1978 forecast is from Data Resources, Inc., *The Data Resources Review*, vol. 5 (August 1976), pp. II.13, II.24.

18. See testimony of Reginald H. Jones in *Long-term Economic Growth*, Hearings before the Subcommittee on Economic Growth of the Joint Economic Committee, 93:2 (GPO, 1974), pp. 66–77.

19. Barry Bosworth, James S. Duesenberry, and Andrew S. Carron, *Capital Needs in the Seventies* (Brookings Institution, 1975).

Figure 6-3. Genuine and Nominal Rates of Return on Nonfinancial Corporate Capital, 1948-73[a]

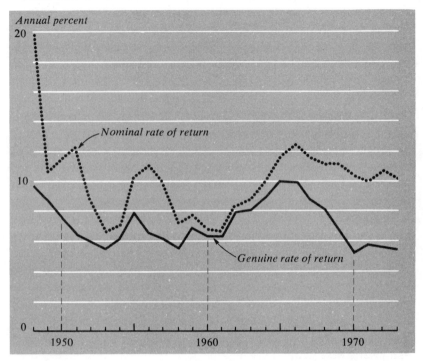

Source: William D. Nordhaus, "The Falling Share of Profits," *Brookings Papers on Economic Activity*, *1:1974*, p. 180.
a. The genuine rate of return after taxes is the genuine capital income divided by the net stock of capital, while the nominal rate of return after taxes is the nominal capital income divided by the net stock of capital. All values are undeflated. The denominator for all calculations is the net stocks of all nonfinancial corporate capital, including an adjustment for valuation of government surplus assets in current prices.

age. This sanguine conclusion is supported by a Joint Economic Committee report.[20]

The current returns on capital investment lend further support to the Brookings conclusion. If shortage implies that investment demand is rising faster than the supply of saving, the return on capital both before and after taxes should be rising. In fact, William Nordhaus of Yale University concluded that both the nominal and real rate of return on nonfinancial corporate capital has been falling in recent years.[21] The after-tax real rate of

20. *Achieving Price Stability Through Economic Growth*, Report of the Joint Economic Committee, 93:2 (GPO, 1974), pp. 93–99.
21. William D. Nordhaus, "The Falling Share of Profits," *Brookings Papers on Economic Activity, 1: 1974*, pp. 169–208.

return has declined from about 9 percent in the mid-1960s to 5–6 percent in the 1970s (see figure 6-3).

Is a Large Social Security Trust Fund Desirable?

Although the evidence of a widespread capital shortage is unpersuasive and the link between the alleged capital shortage and social security is tenuous, it is interesting to speculate whether there are conditions under which the social security trust fund would be the appropriate mechanism to increase the supply of capital: the advantages of funding versus pay-as-you-go if the social security program were started de novo today; the desirability of moving from the current pay-as-you-go to a funded pension system in order to increase the supply of saving.[22]

The Initial Decision

According to economic theory, a funded system is preferable to a pay-as-you-go system if the real rate of return on capital exceeds the implicit rate of return in a currently financed program. In fact, deciding whether or not to have a funded system is really equivalent to deciding whether or not there is an optimal supply of capital in the economy. If the real rate of return on capital exceeds the implicit return for a pay-as-you-go program, the capital supply is suboptimal and society would gain by accumulating reserves in a trust fund.

The implicit rate of return in a currently financed social security system is equal to the rate of growth of population plus the rate of growth of real earnings per capita.[23] An example will help clarify the implicit return calculation. If the first generation pays t percent of earnings, Y_1, to finance benefits for the retired population, its tax burden is tY_1. The second generation, in turn, pays t percent of its earnings, Y_2, that is, tY_2, to finance the retirement benefits for generation 1. If the rate of growth of population and labor force is equal to n and the growth of per capita earnings is de-

22. For an excellent discussion of the feasibility of moving to a funded system, see Lesnoy and Hambor, "Social Security, Saving, and Capital Formation."

23. See Henry J. Aaron, "The Social Insurance Paradox," *Canadian Journal of Economics and Political Science,* vol. 32 (August 1966), pp. 371–74; Paul A. Samuelson, "An Exact Consumption-Loan Model of Interest with or without the Social Contrivance of Money," and "Reply," *Journal of Political Economy,* vol. 66 (December 1958), pp. 467–82, and vol. 67 (October 1959), pp. 518–22.

noted by m, then $Y_2 = Y_1 (1 + n)(1 + m)$. Therefore, generation 1 pays taxes of tY_1 and receives benefits equal to $tY_1 (1 + n)(1 + m)$, gaining implicit interest of approximately $(n + m)$. Each future generation will receive the same implicit rate of return as long as population and per capita earnings maintain their growth rates.

From 1956 to 1976, both the labor force and the total population grew at an average annual rate of 1.6 percent, and real wage per worker increased by 1.6 percent, so that total real wages increased by 3.2 percent.[24] During approximately the same period, the after-tax real rate of return on capital investment ranged between 5 and 10 percent, while the more relevant before-tax return rate fluctuated between 9 and 16 percent.[25] While the return to capital has been steadily declining, the implicit return to a pay-as-you-go system is also scheduled to decline. With zero population growth, the implicit return will equal the rate of growth of the real wage, or about 2 percent.

Given the magnitudes of the two rates of return, the conclusion might be that if the system were established de novo, it would be better to fund it than to finance it on a pay-as-you-go basis. In fact, the original social security legislation of 1935 provided for the creation of a substantial trust fund. Four years later, however, in the first, critical, 1939 amendments to the original legislation, Congress decided to pay benefits in excess of contributions to the entire first generation of retirees. This transfer was, in fact, a decision to give away the trust fund that would have accumulated if current workers' contributions had been stockpiled for their retirement. However, it was felt at the time of the Great Depression that the need of current retirees warranted the transfer and the shift to a pay-as-you-go system.

Second Thoughts

A few years ago, Feldstein proposed moving the social security system to a funded basis.[26] He suggested the creation of an extremely large trust fund financed by more than doubling the OASDI payroll tax rates. All future benefits could be paid out of the interest on this fund, and the payroll tax could then be abolished. This would be accomplished by having the fund's investment earn the social rate of return of about 13 percent,

24. *Economic Report of the President, January 1976,* pp. 174, 184, 196.
25. Nordhaus, "Falling Share of Profits," p. 180.
26. Martin Feldstein, "The Optimal Financing of Social Security," Discussion Paper 388 (Harvard University, Institute of Economic Research, 1974; processed).

Feldstein's estimate of the average pretax return on investments of business corporations.[27] Feldstein sees a large trust fund as a means of increasing the rate of saving in the economy, which he believes has been adversely affected by the growth of the social security program. The resulting higher rate of national saving could greatly increase the growth rate of the economy, which in turn would mean higher levels of national output in the future.

There are two assumptions underlying this argument. One is that private saving is inadequate and the second is that the social security fund is the logical place to accumulate the needed reserves.

Feldstein's advocacy of increased saving is not for the reasons of projected capital shortages discussed earlier in this chapter, for he believes that any gap between available saving and desired investment will be closed by rising interest rates, which will "force firms to tailor their aggregate investment demands to the available supply."[28] Rather, Feldstein argues that the national rate of capital accumulation is too low because the additional future consumption that would be generated by more saving and investment now "would more than compensate for the current sacrifices." He estimates that a dollar invested today would yield $2 (measured in 1976 prices) in five or six years and that this high real yield is the reason to increase the national saving rate. Feldstein argues, however, that people are saturated with saving through the social security program and furthermore that corporation and personal income taxes place a wedge between the rates of return yielded by investments and the rates of return realized by savers. Therefore, since people are unwilling to increase their saving at available rates and since no market exists where they can invest and receive the social rate of return, he advocates increased saving by the government through the social security system.

There are no indications, however, that Americans collectively have any desire to save more so that the economy could grow faster. The current saving pattern may reflect their rational belief that the country is rich enough now and need not save for the benefit of future generations, who will be materially better off than the present generation even without additional capital accumulation.

27. Feldstein assumes that the trust funds are invested in government securities and that general revenues are appropriated to make up the difference between their rate of return and the pretax corporate rate. No mention is made of who pays the costs of the taxes required to finance the additional general revenues.

28. Martin Feldstein, "Social Security, Tax Reform and Capital Accumulation," Tax Foundation, *Tax Review*, vol. 37 (February 1976), p. 6.

Suppose, however, that it were decided that saving was too low and that remedial action should be undertaken by the federal government. Are there any advantages to using the social security program rather than some other fiscal measure? The distributional implications of the payroll tax make it a completely inappropriate mechanism for increasing the supply of saving. It makes little sense to ask the current generation of low and median income workers to contribute not only for their own retirement but also, in effect, for that first generation of retirees who received gratis benefits. Doubling the payroll tax on these workers increases the required saving of families who, in the absence of social security, would have saved nothing. If it is decided to take collective action to promote saving by running a budget surplus, it would be more reasonable to use a tax that will not collect saving from people whose current consumption needs are relatively urgent and who would not have saved even at rates of return considerably higher than those offered through social security.

There are difficulties with accumulating a large trust fund even if it is not financed by the payroll tax. First, while a higher rate of saving at full employment leads to higher rates of investment and growth, running budgetary surpluses at less than full employment can reduce the level of output and actually lead to lower total investment. Feldstein dismisses this important Keynesian argument by saying, "the past 25 years have seen a relatively low average unemployment rate of 4.8 percent. The early fear of excessive savings has now changed to a serious concern about a capital shortage in the years ahead."[29] Unfortunately, the average postwar unemployment rate does not provide an accurate picture of the economic problems of the 1970s. The unemployment rate in the first half of this decade averaged almost 6 percent and for the year 1976 averaged 7.7 percent.[30] Moreover, even official estimates set unemployment rates in excess of 5 percent for the rest of this decade.[31]

The stated policy of both the Ford administration and the Federal Reserve Board was to bring the rate of inflation down to normal levels over a period of several years. In this situation, increased government saving would not lead automatically to higher levels of investment and faster growth. In fact, increased government saving could lead to lower output

29. Martin Feldstein, "Toward a Reform of Social Security," *The Public Interest,* no. 40 (Summer 1975), p. 76.

30. The national unemployment rate was 4.9 in 1970, 5.9 in 1971, 5.6 in 1972, 4.9 in 1973, 5.6 in 1974, and 8.5 in 1975. (*Economic Indicators,* July 1974 and September 1976.)

31. *The Budget of the United States Government, Fiscal Year 1977,* p. 26.

and less saving unless monetary policy were sufficiently expansive to offset the contractionary fiscal effect of a payroll tax increase. Given the 1975–76 performance of the monetary authorities and their concern about inflation, it is not clear that monetary policy would be sufficiently expansionary to offset the deflationary effect of higher government saving.

A second difficulty would be investing the accumulated reserves, and this problem increases directly with the size of the required fund. Feldstein advocates the establishment of a $600 billion trust fund yielding interest at a rate of 13.4 percent.[32] The size of the eventual required trust fund may be understated for two reasons. First, a 13.4 percent interest rate is high; it may not be possible to earn such a return. Second, even at such a high interest rate, a $600 billion trust fund yields only $80.4 billion annually. This yield falls short of the $83.6 billion OASI disbursements projected in the 1976 Trustees' Report for calendar year 1978 and will definitely be insufficient for all subsequent years.

The social security trust fund is currently restricted to U.S. government securities. Total U.S. securities outstanding at the end of 1975 amounted to $577 billion.[33] Even if the OASDI trust fund held all outstanding U.S. securities in 1976, it would not be sufficient to finance it under Feldstein's funding scheme. Therefore, social security would be required to participate in the private capital market. Table 6-5 shows the types and outstanding amounts of private and public debt that the fund could acquire. It is obvious from the magnitudes involved that fully funding the system is a proposal of mammoth and unrealistic proportions. Partial funding might be possible and need not involve any direct government control over private business. For instance, a fund of $400 billion could be invested in $100 billion of state and local debt and $300 billion of U.S. government securities.

Complete ownership of government securities by the social security fund would make the Federal Reserve System's open-market operations impossible. For the constant purchase and sale of U.S. securities to be effective in altering the money supply, commercial banks, the Federal Reserve, and individuals must hold these securities. Unless new financial instruments are found, monetary policy will be limited as a means of stabilization and growth. One tool that would remain unhampered is changes in the reserve ratio, but this can only be used for short-run stabilization purposes.

32. "Optimal Financing of Social Security," p. 27.
33. *Economic Report of the President, January 1976*, p. 253.

Table 6-5. Market Debt Owed by Nonfinancial Sectors, 1975
Billions of dollars

Sector and type of security	Debt
Government	**816.0**
U.S. public debt	576.6
Agency issues and mortgages	8.9
State and local government debt	230.5
Other nonfinancial	**1,610.4**
Debt capital instruments	1,073.6
Corporate and foreign bonds	280.1
Mortgages	793.5
Home	488.0
Other residential	97.7
Commercial and farm	207.8
Other private credit	536.8
Bank loans n.e.c.	215.0
Consumer credit	197.3
Open-market paper	17.8
Other	106.8
Total	**2,426.4**
Corporate equities[a]	**858.6**

Sources: U.S. public debt, *Economic Report of the President, January 1976*, p. 253; other data, Board of Governors of the Federal Reserve System, "Flow of Funds Accounts, 2nd Quarter 1976" (Board of Governors, 1976; processed), pp. 64–65.
n.e.c. Not elsewhere classified.
a. Includes financial issues.

There is a third problem with a funded system, more political than economic in nature. The accumulation of a large reserve might create its own pressure for expanding the social security program and increasing benefits. This danger, however, seems less likely now than in the past, since benefits currently replace a substantial percentage of earnings and are adjusted automatically for increases in wages and prices. Nevertheless, political pressure to spend accumulated funds might arise, and consideration would have to be given to steps that would guard against such a contingency.

Although the difficulties involved in creating a large trust fund appear substantial, nations such as Canada and Sweden have used social security reserves to augment their supply of saving.

Sweden, in particular, has accumulated large reserves, which it uses to finance residential mortgages and purchase local government securities, thereby freeing private saving for industrial investment.[34] Sweden's pen-

34. Assar Lindbeck, *Swedish Economic Policy* (University of California Press, 1974), p. 9.

sion fund (known as the AP-fund) holds a significant share of credit market liabilities and each year supplies more than one-third of the flow of credit to the market. Assar Lindbeck concludes that, while the fund has increased the supply of money to the long-term capital market, short-term credit and the allocation of long-term credit have been unaffected. He traces the lack of allocational changes to the fact that the fund has generally maintained the same portfolio as would private pension funds and insurance companies. Predictably, the most dramatic impact of the fund has been a decline in the share of private insurance company holdings in the total credit market.

In Canada, the public pension plan surplus accounted for approximately 14 percent of net private saving in 1973. The funds were invested in provincial government bonds, the counterpart to state and local bonds in the United States.[35]

Summary

Recent evidence indicates that social security benefits tend to reduce private saving. In the past, this benefit effect may have been offset substantially by a retirement effect, in which workers increase saving rates to save over a shorter working life for a longer retirement. In the future, as the decline in retirement age abates, the benefit effect will dominate and the social security program will cause a lower level of saving.

If social security does reduce saving, should this effect be offset by shifting from a pay-as-you-go to a funded pension system? In other words, should the federal government attempt to increase the rate of saving through an increase in the payroll tax? The answer depends on attitudes toward the distribution of the tax burden. If it were decided that the capital supply is inadequate due to saving behavior caused by the social security program and that it is incumbent upon the federal government to increase saving, only those who believe that the federal tax system should be made more regressive would approve of using the payroll tax to increase the national saving rate.

35. Feldstein, "Optimal Financing of Social Security," p. 6.

chapter seven **The Future of Social Security**

Social security is at the most crucial juncture of its more than forty-year life. The financial difficulties created by overindexing and recent demographic shifts have startled the public and generated concern that the system is not capable of meeting its commitments. Although the overindexing is simply a technical flaw and easy to rectify, devising an overall solution requires a thorough reexamination of the program—its goals and the adequacy of its design to meet present and future needs in the context of a changed social milieu.

Decoupling

Approximately half the projected long-run deficit is avoidable, being merely the result of the error in the automatic inflation adjustment introduced in 1972. The procedure simultaneously adjusts present benefits and projected benefits by raising the factors in the benefit formula in line with increases in the consumer price index. For retired workers, this process maintains the purchasing power of their benefits at their original levels. Future retirees, however, receive double compensation for inflation, since their earnings as well as the benefit formula increase with inflation. Over-indexing introduces instability in replacement rates, distorts the benefit structure, and makes future costs highly dependent on the increases in wages and prices. Adjusting present retirees' benefits separately from those of future beneficiaries would correct the distortion. However, since decoupling involves choosing another inflation adjustment procedure for the benefits of those who are still working, it raises complex issues of equity—vertical, horizontal, and intertemporal.

134

Vertical Equity

The issue in vertical equity is how to relate benefits to covered earnings. The decision is complicated by the conflicting goals within the social security program. A progressive benefit structure and the provision of minimum and dependents' benefits represent the sacrifice of individual equity to the goal of social adequacy. The present structure is based on the assumption that social security is an appropriate mechanism for redistribution, although transferring income to the poor in the absence of a means test is inefficient. Increased incidence of dual beneficiaries and the superior income ranking of married couples indicate that considerable funds are being directed to the nonpoor through the minimum benefit, dependents' benefits, and a steeply progressive benefit formula. The provision of dependents' benefits, in particular, has come into question because of the inequities it creates between single and married workers and between one- and two-earner families. This problem has become more serious as the dual earner family is now the typical economic unit.

The advent of the supplemental security income program raises the question whether social security is the best of available tools to meet the welfare needs of the elderly. The SSI is a means-tested program financed by the progressive income tax, and is thereby both a more efficient and more effective income transfer than social security. If SSI were expanded it could adequately achieve redistribution, leaving social security to focus on the goal of individual equity. The possibility would then exist of streamlining social security to a more effective compulsory saving system characterized by a proportional benefit structure, with no minimum and dependents' benefits. Within such a system the problems of equity inherent in the design of the present program would not occur.

On the other hand, if the national goal of social adequacy is to be reached by means of the social security program, then a series of adjustments could be made to alleviate the problems mentioned above. Possible reforms include a length-of-service adjustment, to prevent dual beneficiaries from profiting from the progressive benefit structure; dependents' benefits that reflect actual support costs, to equalize the living standards of single and married retirees; and adoption of the family as the unit of taxation and benefit computation, to correct the inequity between benefits for single and dual earner families.

Horizontal Equity

The problem in horizontal equity is the choice of a method to convert wage histories into realistic averages on which to base the benefit calculation. In a dynamic economy, some form of indexing is required to compare dollars earned in one year with those earned in another. Furthermore, indexing either by wages or prices would ensure that workers would have an inflation-adjusted base on which to calculate their benefits. Choosing between wage and price indexing, however, involves both distributional and philosophical considerations.

Since wages rise more rapidly than prices, wage indexing gives greater weight to earnings in the distant past, favoring workers with high earnings early in life and slow wage growth thereafter. As this pattern is more typical of low-income people, wage indexing is preferable on distributional grounds.

Intertemporal Equity

The pattern of replacement rates is the central issue of intertemporal equity and the key to the decoupling controversy. Over time, that pattern will be determined by whether wages or prices are chosen to index the break points in the benefit formula to adjust for inflation. If the Consultant Panel's recommendations were adopted, and cost-of-living increases were introduced by price indexing the break points in a progressive benefit formula, the ratio of benefits to preretirement earnings would decline as real wages grew. On the other hand, wage indexing the break points in the benefit formula, as suggested by the 1975 Advisory Council and proposed by the Ford administration, would lead to constant replacement rates. A pattern of constant replacement rates would also emerge if the present progressive structure were replaced by a proportional benefit formula.

Generally, stability is assumed to be the appropriate criterion for an equitable system, but there are arguments for allowing replacement rates to decline. If the current level of benefits provides adequate support for the aged, they could be kept at that purchasing power level through adjustments for price increases. Maintaining a real benefit level in an economy with rising real wages would result in declining replacement rates, alleviating some of the financial burden.

Demographic Changes

The portion of the long-term deficit resulting from demographic changes cannot be solved by a technical correction. The ratio of aged to working population is rising as a result of the declining fertility rate and increasing life expectancy. This means that the increased cost of the social security system will be borne by a smaller work force, with the result that the payroll tax will increase 64 percent by the year 2050.

Both considerations of cost and the increased health of the aged raise the question of the desirability of reversing the trend toward early retirement, extending the normal retirement age to sixty-eight. This would simultaneously ease the burden on future taxpayers and bolster the economic welfare of the elderly by shortening the period over which they must live on reduced income. It has been shown that social security contributes to changing retirement behavior through its influence on corporations' choice of a compulsory retirement age and through its policy of making receipt of benefits contingent on satisfying an earnings test. Therefore, if it is desirable to push the retirement age forward, it may be appropriate to eliminate social security provisions that discourage labor force participation by the elderly, by either reducing the earnings test or increasing the delayed retirement credit. Completely eliminating the earnings test, however, would violate the wage-replacement principle of the program and could be done only if the decision were made to award benefits as annuities.

The need for a tax increase to pay the equivalence of present-day benefits to tomorrow's large retired population raises further questions of intertemporal equity. If future taxpayers bear the entire burden, they will face lower returns on their contributions than today's taxpayers. Alternatively, the burden could be spread by raising the payroll tax now, thus accumulating reserves for the future. However, in line with the ability-to-pay criterion, decisions on how to spread the burden should take into consideration the fact that the overall dependency ratio may decline in the future, since a lower fertility rate means that the population under twenty will be smaller than today.

An equitable spreading of the tax burden also raises the issue of the appropriateness of financing social security through the payroll tax instead of from general revenues. The regressivity of the payroll tax makes it an inefficient and unfair means of financing an annual redistribution program.

Those who view social security as essentially a welfare program, therefore, advise paying benefits out of general revenues, which are generated through the progressive income tax. On the other hand, since in the payroll tax there is a perceived link between contributions and benefits, it is preferable to the income tax as a mechanism for financing a compulsory saving program. Thus, those who maintain the more traditional lifetime perspective of social security favor using the payroll tax modified by an extended earned income credit to assist low-income workers.

Summary

As long as there exists an ambivalence of goals within social security, the program's design will be prone to inefficiencies and inequities, because it will contain aspects that are irrational for the attainment of either goal. Resolution of the complex issues facing social security requires that the system be defined as either an annual redistribution program or a compulsory saving mechanism. Clarification of social security's goals and role would dictate the method of financing and the magnitude and nature of adjustments necessary to cope with the projected deficit and yet meet the commitment to future retirees.

chapter eight Summary of Conference Discussion

The preceding chapters provided the background for a two-day conference on social security held at the Brookings Institution in June 1976. One speaker characterized the conference participants as the proverbial blind men feeling the elephant, all holding their own views of what the social security program is. However, the participants had a more difficult problem than the blind men, because they were asked not only to define the social security system as it is today but to propose what it should be in the future. The introductory analogy was indeed prophetic, for participants displayed substantial disagreement on the role for social security, the appropriate benefit structure, and how the program should be financed. The differing recommendations were derived directly from the participants' differing perceptions about the nature of the beast.

The Role of Social Security

Two issues addressed in the manuscript and debated at the conference were (1) to what extent should the social adequacy function of social security be reduced or transferred to the supplemental security income program and (2) where should social security stop and private pensions pick up. The differences expressed about the appropriate role for social security hinged on the participants' view of the adequacy of other programs to do the job—namely, SSI for low-income workers and private pensions for high earners.

Social Security and SSI

The following quotations highlight the concern of those who opposed transferring the social adequacy role to SSI.

"If we were starting all over . . . I have absolutely no objection to a flat general pension not income-tested and a more closely wage-related system on top. But that is not where we are and I would be very much afraid that the lower deck of such an approach would be income tested, and there are lots of problems with that."

"A wage-related system . . . might be very reasonable as long as we can devise some means of protecting [low-income] people against the indignity of the means test."

"It is crucial that we not have a large proportion of our population, of an aged population, or any part of our population, that is subject to a means test."

The concern over a large means-tested program for the low-income elderly centered on two factors. First, a means test is thought demeaning partly because of the way it is generally administered and partly because of the inherent nature of such a test. "Self-declaration is accepted, by and large, for the income tax," said one critic, "but for the means test we have a whole corps of people investigating every aspect of their private lives." Another argued that there is something inherently demeaning about a means test no matter how well it is administered because it implies that "you can't make it on your own."

Second, there are political advantages in financing benefits to the poor through earmarked payroll taxes as opposed to general revenue. Under social security, there is the assurance that the funds will be available, since payroll tax revenues are earmarked for retirement benefits. With a means-tested program financed by general revenues, there would be year-to-year uncertainty about appropriations.

Those who supported an expanded SSI program recognized these arguments but felt that there would be significant advantages (although serious implementation problems) in moving social security toward a wage-related system and using an expanded SSI program for income support for the elderly poor. It was argued that social security is a poor vehicle for income redistribution, since it is financed by the regressive payroll tax. Furthermore, many of the disproportionately high benefits go to workers with short periods of covered employment rather than to those truly in need. Providing for the low-income elderly through an expanded SSI program would shift the burden of their support from the payroll tax to the more progressive income tax.

Another argument in favor of a more strictly wage-related social security program was couched in terms of worker's perceptions of the nature of their social security contributions. If they perceived a link between payroll tax contributions and future benefits, they would view their contributions as saving rather than a tax. Distortions in labor supply could result from the opposite view, since contributions would be seen as a reduction in net wages. (However, several participants believed the link existed without further changes in the structure of the program.)

Responding to the specific objections to a large income-tested program, supporters of an expanded SSI argued that a program would lose its stigma if it applied to a majority of the aged. There was also the feeling that more money could be channeled to the elderly poor through such a program than through social security.

Even the supporters of expanding SSI to include the social adequacy components of social security recognized serious difficulties in implementation. Some modifications needed before SSI could assume the major role in providing low- and moderate-income people with retirement income include (1) revision of the asset test, (2) federal regulation of state supplements, and (3) reconsideration of the SSI earnings test.

First, the SSI asset test is now unreasonably stringent; it would require a complete overhaul before SSI could take on a larger role. Not only is it too stringent, but it is poorly conceived. Various categories of assets are set out and limits are applied to each category. Particularly troubling is the break that homeowners get relative to renters, which penalizes those who divest themselves of their home in their old age.

Second, the existence of state supplementary programs complicates any attempt to lower the SSI tax on retirement benefits. Under the current program, the SSI payment is reduced by a dollar for each dollar of social security benefits after a $20 a month disregard. Reducing the SSI payment by only 50 cents for each dollar of social security income would be essential to insulate low-wage workers from a decline in retirement income as a result of the introduction of a proportional social security benefit formula. Furthermore, it would ensure that workers received some payoff for a lifetime of contributions.

Less than half the SSI beneficiaries receive state supplements (and this fraction is falling as the number of people grandfathered-in declines), which raises the questions whether and how the federal government should attempt to ensure uniformity of state and federal welfare programs in the event of large-scale change in social security and SSI. Supplement guarantees for a couple are very high in many states. (In 1976 in California it was $522; Massachusetts, $430; Wisconsin, $351; and New York, $328;

the 1976 maximum social security benefit was $581 for a couple.) Therefore, simply changing the federal SSI tax rate on social security would not in itself be sufficient; the state tax rates on social security would have to be changed as well, which brings up the problem of increased cost to the states and the question whether the federal government has the power to require the states to make such changes. Controlling state tax rates would be particularly difficult in those states where the supplement is not federally administered, although these states do not include the high benefit states. On the cost side, if states were compelled to reduce their tax rate on social security benefits to 50 percent, state costs for supplemental payments would increase significantly, perhaps forcing a reduction in benefit levels.

The third problem with an expanded SSI program is that an increasing proportion of the aged would be bound by the SSI earnings test rather than the social security retirement test. The current tax rate on earnings under SSI, as under social security, is 50 percent, but the SSI program disregards only $65 a month whereas social security disregards $230. Therefore, any attempt to encourage labor force participation of the elderly must take into account that with an expanded SSI program over 50 percent of the aged would be subject to the more stringent SSI test. In addition, many would be subject to both the social security and SSI earnings test; the pyramiding of these two taxes would raise the combined tax on earnings to 75 percent.

Social Security and Private Pensions

The 1977 social security wage base is $16,500 and is increased annually in line with the growth of average wages. Some conference participants felt there was no reason to extend coverage beyond the base level, since replacing earnings up to this maximum guarantees a modest level of retirement income. Beyond that, workers should rely either on private pensions or individual saving. Any gain from higher guaranteed retirement benefits for those who earn above the maximum has to be weighed against the overall loss in saving and labor supply. There was also the philosophical argument on the right of government to infringe upon individual freedom beyond assuring a basic retirement benefit.

In contrast, others argued in favor of expansion of social security at the upper level of the earnings scale on the ground that private pension plans fail to meet the needs of retired workers. This group felt that the description of private pensions in chapter 2 is too optimistic, and they could not see why private pension coverage would be in any way superior to social security. They emphasized that less than half of all workers are covered by such plans, that many receive very low benefits, and that high-salaried executives often get larger relative benefits than low-wage employees. They argued that private pension plans tend to be an automatic accompaniment of the job, just like social security, and therefore individual freedom is not an issue. Furthermore, private pension benefits are no more related to lifetime earnings than social security benefits, being generally based on five years of highest earnings. Therefore, the issue is which does the job the best, social security, which provides an inflation-adjusted benefit after retirement and low administrative expenses, or private pension plans, which are funded and provide private capital accumulation.

Opponents of extending social security benefits argued that private pensions are voluntary and can be viewed as part of a total compensation package, which workers select when they choose jobs, and are often the subject of labor union negotiation. Furthermore, the welfare of high-income workers is not served best by the social security program, since it is heavily weighted with redistribution toward the lower end. When the present system matures, upper-income retirees will receive substantially less in benefits than the additional combined employer-employee contribution. Even with social security's low administrative costs, high-income retirees might do better with private pensions or individual saving.

There was no resolution of this issue. While some participants favored no extension of social security at the upper end, others remained convinced that social security is a superior vehicle to private pensions for providing retirement benefits to those with earnings above the present maximum taxable level. The possible negative impact of social security on saving was their only concession to private pensions.

Decoupling and the Benefit Structure

Differing perceptions about the appropriate role of social security were reflected, also, in the discussions of the decoupling issue and the benefit structure. The decoupling controversy, which centered on whether the break points used in the benefit formula should be indexed by prices or wages, in fact hinged on whether participants wanted constant or declining replacement rates over time. The discussion of the benefit structure involved the basic question of how much income distribution should be attempted through social security.

Decoupling

It was agreed that the overadjustment of social security benefits for inflation should be corrected promptly. Benefits for retirees should continue to be indexed on the basis of the consumer price index, although it was acknowledged that the present procedure presents a problem for the very elderly, whose relative position declines as their benefits fall behind the growth in productivity. The issue was raised whether to index retirees' benefits by wages rather than prices. In view of the high cost of indexing benefits on the basis of wages, a suggestion that gained support was to recompute retirees' benefits to partially or fully adjust for productivity increases either periodically or at a certain age, such as eighty years. There was unanimous support for increasing retirees' benefits at least in line with prices, as under the current law, combined with a separate inflation adjustment for those future beneficiaries still in the labor force.

For those still in the work force, the two indexing schemes considered were (1) the proposal of the Ford administration to index by wages both workers' earnings records and the break points in the benefit formula, and (2) the proposal of the Senate Consultant Panel on Social Security to index by prices both the earnings records and benefit formula. These proposals seemed the logical alternatives, since it was noted that combining two types of indexes created serious administrative problems. While some attempt was made to focus on the equity considerations of the two schemes given a certain level of expenditures over time, most of the discussion centered on the fact that wage indexing guarantees constant replacement rates, whereas price indexing results in gradually declining replacement rates.

Supporters of price indexing argued that it would allow greater flexibility and would leave the discretion of raising benefits up to Congress. Constructing a system that preserved the real value of today's benefits would allow Congress to finance future benefit increases out of surpluses as it had done in the past, an option that might be precluded by wage indexing in view of the large projected cost increases. Eliminating ad hoc increases woud mean that once a person retired his real benefits from social security would remain stable, in which case retirees who live for a long time would fall further and further behind. While Congress could spend as much on social security under either method of indexing, price indexing offers greater flexibility in dividing the funds between new and old retirees and making other structural reforms in the social security system.

Adamant rejection of the price indexing proposal came from those who opposed any reduction in the relative size of the system. They argued that price indexing, which results in declining replacement rates, represents a tremendous deliberalization of the well-established concept that social security benefits would keep up with a rising level of wages. It would be unjust to ask workers just entering the system to risk a ratio of benefits to earnings "substantially lower than that being paid right now in what is an inadequate system." Furthermore, their political judgment was that Congress would continue to improve the program regardless of whether there was wage or price indexing.

Benefits

The discussion of the benefits focused on four issues: (1) how to translate a worker's earnings history into a single number—the calculation of average monthly earnings, (2) how the benefits of low-wage workers should relate to those of high-wage workers, (3) how the benefits of single workers versus married workers and one-earner versus two-earner families should compare, and (4) how social security benefits should be treated under the personal income tax.

AVERAGE MONTHLY EARNINGS. It was generally agreed that any benefit computation that calculates preretirement earnings as an average over a period of years requires some adjustment to ensure a true comparison of dollars earned in one year with those earned in other years. However, different groups in society will fare relatively better or worse depending upon whether the adjustment is made on the basis of wages or prices. Therefore, the choice of indexing method inevitably requires a value judgment.

One of the discussants clarified the relative impact of each indexing scheme with an example. Consider two women: the first has her children at an early age and enters the labor force later; the second woman postpones having children and is in the labor force for the early part of her life. Both women work the same number of years and at the same wage rate in relation to the wage structure that prevailed at the time. The question is whether to treat these women differently simply because one woman was in the labor market later and could benefit from the productivity increases that occurred throughout the early part of her life when she was not working, or to treat the women equally, recognizing that they were at the same place in wage distribution when they were working. Price indexing would treat the women differently while wage indexing would treat them the same. (Some preference was indicated for the latter, but little attention was really paid to these interpersonal equity issues, since most of the discussion went back to indexing the break points in the benefit formula and its impact on replacement rates and the size of the system over time.)

Whether earnings are indexed by wages or prices, a decision must be made on the period over which average wages are to be calculated. Without indexing, there would be some argument for using the last five years or the highest five years in order to derive a more current basis on which to base benefits. A short averaging period would work to the disadvantage of many workers (low-wage workers who enter the labor force at an early age and workers who experience a decline in earnings after fifty-five) and would create an incentive for workers and employers to collude to raise wages just before retirement. In general, it was agreed that short averaging periods induce windfalls, manipulations, and disincentives. Almost all conference participants preferred a long averaging period with indexed earnings. Under the current law the averaging period is thirty-five years out of a likely working life of forty years (from the age of twenty-one to sixty-two). The exclusion of five years from the average working life is considered desirable in a social insurance system, providing some insurance against temporary reductions in earnings at very little loss in horizontal equity.

REDISTRIBUTION. Redistribution in social security is achieved primarily through the minimum benefit and the progressive benefit formula. In the discussion on redistribution, conference participants divided (as in the earlier dialogue on the role of social security) into those who favored a proportional social security benefit formula with an expanded SSI program for the elderly poor and those who preferred to retain both earnings replacement and social adequacy within the social security program. However, even among those who favored retaining the progressive benefit formula, there was little support for continuing the minimum benefit.

The consensus was that the minimum benefit had outlived its usefulness and that this provision went "too far in a group insurance system in breaking down the relationship between benefit protection and contributions." Since the minimum benefit was designed to alleviate poverty, its function would be more efficiently performed by the SSI program.

Those who supported some progressivity in the benefit formula argued that the required replacement of earnings declines as income increases and that a progressive formula is consistent with the goals of a social insurance system. One rationale offered was that social security could be considered as replacing 100 percent of the earnings required for necessities and, say, 50 percent required for luxuries. Even those who supported a flat rate system in the long run did not advocate an immediate elimination of all the tilt in the benefit formula, but saw a flat rate as the goal toward which social security should move.

BENEFICIARY UNIT. There was considerable criticism of the current structure of dependents' benefits, largely because of the 50 percent spouse's benefit awarded to couples. This additional benefit gives married workers considerably more benefits per dollar of contribution than single workers, and couples with a nonworking spouse are treated more favorably than two-earner couples.

One suggestion for alleviating this inequity is to eliminate the spouse's benefit, average the earnings records for the couple, and award a benefit to each spouse on half of the combined earnings record. The averaging could be done either annually or at retirement. It was argued that annual averaging suffers from a disadvantage if there is a significant difference in the age of the spouses because the benefit for the older spouse would probably be inadequate to allow him or her to retire. On the other hand, annual averaging would provide an individual earnings record that would ensure each spouse a benefit in the case of divorce. An alternative suggestion was to average the earnings records at the retirement of the second spouse. A couple would then still receive a higher benefit than a single worker with the same earnings because of the impact of the progressive benefit formula. However, averaging at retirement would not solve the problem of benefits in the case of divorce.

Another alternative suggested in the report of the Consultant Panel is to build individual earnings records with additional individual contributions. A nonworking spouse would be assumed to earn 50 percent of the earnings of the working spouse. Any gap between 50 percent and the actual earnings of the working spouse would be taxed as self-employment income. Naturally, this added tax would require an expansion of the earned income credit to avoid overburdening low-income workers. This approach would ensure each spouse an adequate benefit in the case of divorce or if an older spouse wanted to retire. The long-run solution could be combined with averaging at retirement, which could be implemented immediately.

Another suggestion is to reduce but not eliminate the spouse's benefit. This suggestion was based on the assumptions that (1) setting the couple's benefit at 150 percent of the single worker's benefit is excessive and (2) it is not feasible to reduce replacement rates for present couples. The proposal would reduce the spouse's benefit from 50 to 33.3 percent and increase the primary benefit by 12.5 percent. Several advantages were claimed for this proposal. It would reduce the importance of the dependents' benefit by increasing the proportion of women who would take benefits based on their own earnings record rather than the spouse's benefit. In addition, raising the primary benefit would increase the money going to single workers and to widows and thereby improve their position relative to couples.

Although all expressed dissatisfaction with the current structure of social security's dependents' benefits, the conference participants did not agree on a solution.

TAXATION OF BENEFITS. There was considerable support for revising the tax treatment of social security benefits under the personal income tax. Social security benefits have been exempt from the personal income tax since the beginning of the program for two reasons: first, contributions are subject to the income tax when earned, and second, the aged are presumed to be needy. The participants felt that neither of these rationales was a compelling reason for exempting the entire benefit from taxation. The suggestion was made to tax approximately half the benefit, reflecting the fact that the employer's contribution was not subject to the income tax; but this would forgive any tax on the earnings of the fund. An alternative, not subject to this criticism, would eliminate the tax on employees' contributions but tax the entire benefit. On the other hand, if social security were regarded as a tax transfer system, full taxation of social security benefits would be appropriate without any adjustment to the tax status of employee contributions.

The advantages of taxing social security benefits are numerous. First, there would be consistency in the treatment of social security benefits and other pension income, which is subject to tax to the extent that it exceeds employee contributions. Second, if a progressive benefit structure is retained, taxing social security benefits will help to ensure that the progressive benefits aid the needy and not those for whom they are second pensions. Third, taxing social security benefits would reduce the discrimination against those who choose to work beyond the age of sixty-five. Finally, if social security benefits were taxed, the revenues could be used to relieve the financial problems of the OASDI trust funds or to finance higher benefits and other structural changes in the system.

Financing

The discussion of financing centered on the implications of the various views regarding the objective and the role of social security. More specifically, the argument focused on the desirability of introducing general revenues to finance the long-term deficit. Those who favored some general revenue financing envisioned a system that combined wage replacement with social adequacy. Those who opposed the use of general revenues favored a strictly wage-related retirement program.

General revenue financing was considered appropriate on the ground that the existing program is a compromise. If social security were a strictly wage-related benefit program and all assistance to the poor were provided through SSI, a flat payroll tax on earnings would be the appropriate method of financing, provided special provisions were made for low-income workers. On the other hand, if social security were a tax transfer scheme similar to many other major government programs, it should be financed entirely by the most progressive source of revenue. Since the program contains elements of both extremes, financing should borrow from both rationales. The element of wage relatedness in the present system justifies a payroll tax component and the nonwage-related benefits justify the introduction of other revenues into the system.

Many participants who had felt that general revenue financing would undermine the earned-right aspect of the social security program came to feel that the system is mature enough to withstand an infusion of general revenues without undermining its basic principles. However, they felt that it was important to base entitlement on past earnings in order to avoid pressure for a means-tested program.

Other arguments in favor of general revenue financing included the danger that the payroll tax would be used to finance national health insurance. The destabilizing macroeconomic effects of the payroll tax were also mentioned, since under the current system there is pressure to raise rates in recessions as the trust funds face shortfalls. Finally, a participant who wanted to see the system expanded felt that this goal would meet less resistance if financed with general revenues rather than with the payroll tax.

Those opposing the use of general revenues agreed that there would be more of a tendency to expand the program without the "countervailing constituency" created by the payroll tax. However, they felt that further increases in social security benefits should have a low priority and saw more pressing needs for general revenues. Furthermore, they were not persuaded by the argument for the use of general revenues to finance the social adequacy components of the program, since they felt that the program should be divested of its welfare function and be based on individual equity.

Several opponents of general revenue financing for the retirement and disability portions of social security did, however, support the 1975 Advisory Council's proposal to finance the health insurance component of OASDHI out of general revenues. Since health insurance benefits are in no way related to previous earnings, there is little rationale to finance them through a payroll tax on labor income. Some participants expressed concern that general revenue financing might lead to means testing for health insurance benefits and suggested combining medicare Part A and Part B and financing 50 percent of the combined expenditure out of the general fund.

Regardless of whether participants preferred general revenues or payroll tax financing, many agreed that the poor should not be burdened with high taxes. There was considerable support for the earned income credit as a method of alleviating the current payroll tax burden on low-income workers. The earned income credit included in the personal income tax has the advantage of maintaining the principle that the poor contribute toward their retirement benefits.

Many participants felt that the credit should be expanded by including childless families, by raising the rate to reflect the full payroll tax of 11.7 percent, and by differentiating on the basis of family size the level at which the credit is phased out. It was noted that the existing earned income credit was not fully effective in its first year, since only 50 percent of the estimated refundable amount was claimed. For those who filed an income tax return, this failure to take advantage of the credit could be remedied by an audit. The more difficult problem is to reach low-income workers who do not file.

As with earlier discussions there was no resolution of how social security should be financed. However, the controversy on general revenue highlighted how the participants' views about the nature of the program directly influenced their policy recommendations for financing and income redistribution. In contrast, the rest of the discussion focused on the more empirical questions of the effect of social security on labor force participation and on saving.

Labor Force Participation

Social security can affect the labor force participation of the elderly through (1) the income effect of the benefits, (2) the wage rate effect of the earnings test, and (3) its effect on retirement provisions in the private sector. The ideas under consideration included changing the replacement rates, altering the earnings test, increasing the delayed retirement credit, and changing the actuarial reduction for early retirement. Almost all the participants agreed that the social security program influences the retirement decisions of older workers but that substantial change would be premature until more is known about the probable response of the elderly.

There is little direct evidence on the effect of the earnings test on the work effort of the aged. With regard to early retirement, there is some crude evidence about changes in the law and declines in participation rates, but there are no systematic studies. There are also no systematic studies on the impact of social security legislation on private pension plan provisions. The role of employment opportunities, the effects of the business cycle, the role of health on the retirement decision, and of retirement on health are unresolved and perplexing.

Conference participants disagreed on whether it is desirable to keep the elderly in the labor force. One view was that health does not decline because of retirement, people adjust well to it, and the work ethic held by researchers is not shared by the retired elderly themselves. The debate revealed how little is known about the sociological and psychological factors that accompany withdrawal from the labor force.

When the conference considered how retirement provisions should be designed if the system were established today, there was agreement that they should be more flexible. One proposal included more liberal retirement provisions between the ages of fifty-five and sixty-two, perhaps extending the disability program with occupational tests, actuarially reduced benefits at sixty-two as under the current system, full benefits at sixty-five with increases of 2 or 3 percent a year between sixty-five and sixty-eight, and repeal of the earnings test beginning at sixty-eight.

Many of the participants favored liberalizing the earnings test, although they found it impossible to agree on a specific suggestion given the lack of information on how much the earnings test affects the labor supply. If the effect is significant, it might be worth $2 billion to $3 billion a year to eliminate the test completely at sixty-five. There was little support for eliminating it at sixty-two because it would encourage workers to elect permanently reduced benefits while continuing to work. In addition, it would be very expensive, costing between $6 billion and $7 billion annually.

Saving and Capital Accumulation

Although the discussion of social security and saving was also limited by lack of precise data, many believed that social security has a negative effect on the saving rate, but there was little support for increasing the saving rate by accumulating a substantial trust fund through payroll tax revenues.

Social security can affect saving in two opposing ways. First, a substitution effect reduces saving, since the guarantee of social security benefits supplants the need to save for retirement. Second, social security induces workers to retire earlier and this increases the need for retirement income and the rate of saving. The conference discussion centered on the studies of social security and saving summarized in chapter 6. The results range from a net reduction of 50 percent in household saving to a net of zero.

In an attempt to reconcile these two results, it was noted that the lower estimate attributed all the increased retirement during the sample period (1929–69) to the social security program, though it may be more realistic to ascribe a large portion of early retirement to industrialization, urbanization, and rising incomes. If one made the extreme assumption that none of the increased retirement was caused by social security but rather reflected a continuation of historical trends, the two estimates would be slightly closer. However, even then the $38.2 billion of saving in 1969 would have been $14.0 billion higher without social security in the zero-effect estimate and $51.2 billion higher under the 50 percent reduction estimate (all numbers in 1969 dollars).

The discrepancy indicates that more research is needed in this area. In spite of the imperfect information, however, more is known now than was known two or three years ago. Although there is no agreement on magnitude, social security probably has had some negative impact on capital accumulation and will have a greater effect in the future in view of the large increases in benefits and the slowing of the decline in the retirement age.

The rest of the discussion focused on the policy implications for the federal government, assuming that the rate of national saving is too low and that the social security program depresses the saving rate. One participant suggested increasing the saving rate by accumulating revenues in the social security trust fund, basing his reasoning on political considerations. "It is hard to imagine raising taxes for the valiant national purpose of accumulating capital or reducing the size of the government debt. I don't think those are very appealing. I do think protecting the future of social security has an aura of goodness about it which may allow us to accumulate a surplus." Another argued that social security should be fully funded on an individual basis as well as in the aggregate, in order to remove what he regarded as the "intertemporal saving distortion" of social security at the individual level.

There was little support for these proposals. Opponents argued that the payroll tax falls largely on people who by their own behavior reveal that they do not want to save anything at all and who may be forced to borrow at injurious interest rates; therefore, the distributional implications of raising the payroll tax to accumulate a surplus were completely unacceptable to almost all the participants. Alternative suggestions to increase saving included integrating corporation and personal income taxes or shifting from an income tax to a consumption tax. There was some support for these proposals, but there was also considerable opposition.

Conclusions

While the conference participants disagreed on many issues, there were important exceptions. First, the social security system performs very important functions and is not in danger of going bankrupt. Second, in a universal system mandatory coverage of federal, state, and local government workers is necessary. Third, the benefit calculation should be decoupled (although some participants opposed decoupling if benefits were to be calculated on the basis of price indexing). Fourth, the treatment of the nonworking spouse should be improved. Fifth, the minimum benefit should be eliminated. Sixth, some portion of social security benefits should be included in the personal income-tax base.

However, participants left the conference with the same divergence of opinion on the broad role that social security should play in the future. These opinions ranged from a preference for a strictly wage-related system financed by the payroll tax and supplemented by an expanded SSI program to advocacy of an enlarged social security program with substantial income redistribution financed in part by general revenues.

A major conclusion of the conference was that considerably more research is needed to determine the effect on costs of reducing the tax on social security benefits, the distributional implications of alternative means of integrating SSI and social security, and the effect of social security on labor force participation and saving. For the latter two, research in the last few years has established the direction of the impact, but the results lack precision and robustness.

Social security is now an enormous and complex program of increasing interest to economists and increasingly important to the economy. The conference clarified many issues, but the program remains a fertile area for further research.

appendix **History of Social Security Legislation**

Programs established in accordance with the Social Security Act have expanded enormously and undergone considerable change in coverage, benefits, and tax rates since the 1935 act was passed. Coverage has been broadened to include virtually all employees, the self-employed, and professionals, including doctors and lawyers. Though only retirement benefits were contemplated in 1935, benefits for dependents and survivors of retired workers were added in 1939, disability benefits in 1956, and benefits for dependents and survivors of disabled workers in 1958. In 1965, health and medical benefits for people sixty-five or older were added, along with special benefits for certain of those seventy-two or over. The program was further enlarged in 1972 to include supplemental income benefits for the aged, with entitlement based solely on need. The size of benefits has been increased several times, and the level of earnings permitted after retirement without a reduction in benefits has been gradually increased. In addition, requirements for attaining insured status and thus qualifying for various benefits have been gradually relaxed.

To finance the program, it has been necessary to increase the payroll tax from a combined employer-employee rate of 2 percent in 1937 to 11.7 percent in 1977 (with scheduled increases bringing it to 14.9 percent by 2011). The maximum taxable earnings level has also been increased several times, from $3,000 in 1937 to $16,500 in 1977. In accordance with the 1972 and 1973 amendments to the Social Security Act, benefit amounts and the maximum taxable earnings level are now automatically adjusted, with adjustments triggered by changes in the consumer price index (CPI) and in average taxable earnings.

Coverage

There are five ways in which employment may be covered under social security legislation: (1) compulsory, (2) elective by the employer, (3) elective by the employer and the employee, (4) elective by the individual, or (5) gratuitous. The 1935 Social Security Act provided for compulsory coverage for all workers under sixty-five engaged in commerce or industry (except the railroad industry, which was exempted by the Railroad Retirement Act of 1935) in the continental United States, Alaska, Hawaii, and on American vessels. In 1939, coverage was extended to all such employees by elimination of the under-sixty-five age restriction. Under legislation enacted in 1946, railroad workers were, in essence, included in the survivors benefits portion of the old age and survivors insurance program, and World War II veterans who died within three years of discharge were given fully insured status. (See table A-1.)

A major expansion in coverage was effected by legislation in 1950. Compulsory coverage was extended to regularly employed farm and domestic workers, nonfarm self-employed (except professionals), and federal civilian employees not then under a retirement plan. Moreover, the geographical area for which compulsory coverage applied was extended to include Puerto Rico, the Virgin Islands, and Americans employed anywhere outside the United States by American employers. Under the same legislation, state and local government employees not under a retirement system could be covered if their employer elected coverage, and employees of nonprofit organizations could be covered if both they and their employer elected coverage. In the same act, members of the armed forces were granted gratuitous coverage.

Legislation in 1954 further expanded coverage to self-employed farmers and self-employed professionals except those in medicine or law. Also, Americans employed outside the United States by a foreign subsidiary of an American employer could be covered if their employer elected to do so. Additional coverage for state and local government employees already covered by a retirement plan, except firemen and policemen, could be granted if both the employees and the employers requested it. For the first time, ministers could be covered if they so chose. The 1956 legislation changed the gratuitous status of the armed forces, set forth in the 1950 legislation, to regular compulsory coverage and extended coverage of the self-employed to include all professionals except physicians.

Thus, by 1956, coverage had been extended to practically all gainfully employed people other than federal government employees (who are covered by the federal civil service retirement system) and railroad workers (who are covered by the Railroad Retirement Act). Legislation in 1958, 1960, and 1961 resulted in small increases in coverage for state and local government employees. The 1960 act also extended coverage to the inhabitants of Guam and American Samoa and to Americans employed in the United States by foreign governments or international organizations. The inclusion of self-employed physicians and interns in 1965 made coverage of the working population by old age survivors, disability, and health insurance or some other government retirement program virtually complete. In addition to providing minor extensions of coverage for state and local government employees, legislation in 1967 made coverage for ministers compulsory unless they opted out on grounds of conscience or religious principles. In the 1972 legislation, changes in coverage were again minor; compulsory coverage was extended to the self-employed temporarily living abroad and to members of religious orders subject to vows of poverty if their employer elected coverage.

Benefits

There have been three major trends in legislation affecting OASDHI benefits since the original 1935 act. First, new types of benefits have been added, making the simple retirement program of 1935 much more extensive. Second, eligibility requirements have been gradually liberalized by easing the requirements for becoming fully insured and creating several less rigorous categories of insured status, to permit people with limited coverage to receive benefits. Third, the method of calculation of benefits has been changed to provide larger average benefits.

Types of Benefits

The 1935 Social Security Act provided primarily for monthly retirement benefits for insured workers aged sixty-five or over (table A-2). Benefits were based on a worker's cumulative wages, and those who retired before becoming fully insured received a lump-sum refund of their contributions plus an interest payment. (This provision was eliminated in 1939.) The 1935 legislation also provided for a lump-sum death payment.

In 1939, the scope of the old age insurance program broadened greatly with the addition of monthly benefits for dependents and survivors of insured workers. Benefits were provided (subject to a family maximum) for wives sixty-five or over or children under eighteen. Monthly survivors' benefits were provided for insured workers' wives sixty-five or over, dependent parents sixty-five or over, children under eighteen, or widows caring for eligible children.

Table A-1. Employment Coverage by Social Security Legislation, 1935 to Date (1976)

Year of legislation[a]	Type of coverage	Group and geographical area covered[b]
1935[c]	Compulsory	All workers under 65 in commerce and industry (except railroad), in United States, including Alaska, Hawaii, and American vessels
1939	Compulsory	Workers over 65 in commerce and industry (except railroad)
1946	Compulsory	Eligibility for and amount of survivors' benefits for railroad workers determined from combined railroad and social security earnings
1946	Gratuitous	World War II veterans who died within 3 years of discharge given fully insured status and average monthly earnings of $160
1950	Compulsory	Regularly employed farm workers, regularly employed domestic workers, nonfarm self-employed (except professionals), federal civilian employees not under a retirement system, and Americans employed outside the United States by American employers; workers in Puerto Rico and Virgin Islands included
1950	Elective by employer	State and local government employees not under a retirement system
1950	Elective by employer and employee	Employees (other than ministers) of nonprofit organizations
1950	Gratuitous	Members of the armed forces given wage credits of $160 per month of service during World War II
1951	Compulsory	Railroad workers with less than 10 years of service
1952	Gratuitous	Wage credits for members of the armed forces extended to December 31, 1953
1953	Gratuitous	Wage credits for members of the armed forces extended to June 30, 1955
1954	Compulsory	Farm self-employed, additional regularly employed farm and domestic workers, homeworkers, and professional self-employed (except those in medicine or law)
1954	Elective by employer	Americans employed outside United States by foreign subsidiary of American employer
1954	Elective by employer and employee	State and local government employees (except firemen and policemen) under retirement systems
1954	Elective by individual	Ministers and members of religious orders not under vow of poverty
1955	Gratuitous	Wage credits for members of the armed forces extended to March 31, 1956
1956[d]	Compulsory	Members of the armed forces, professional self-employed except physicians, and farm landlords who participate materially in farm operations

Table A-1. (*Continued*)

Year of legislation[a]	Type of coverage	Group and geographical area covered[b]
1956	Elective by employer and employee	Firemen and policemen in designated states
1956	Gratuitous	Wage credits for members of the armed forces extended to December 31, 1956
1960	Compulsory	Americans employed in the United States by foreign governments or international organizations and parents working for a child (except domestic or casual labor); workers in Guam and American Samoa included
1965[e]	Compulsory	Self-employed physicians, medical interns, recipients of tips (subject to employee tax only)
1965	Elective by individual	Members of certain religious sects may obtain exemption from self-employment coverage (retroactive to 1951)
1967	Compulsory	Ministers and members of religious orders not under vow of poverty (unless exemption is claimed on grounds of conscience or religious principles)
1967	Gratuitous	Members of the armed forces given wage credits of $100 for each $100 (or fraction thereof) of basic pay not in excess of $300 per quarter
1972	Compulsory	Self-employed temporarily living abroad
1972	Elective by employer	Members of religious orders subject to a vow of poverty
1972	Gratuitous	Members of the armed services receive wage credits of $300 per quarter after 1956
1972	Gratuitous	Those of Japanese descent interned during World War II receive wage credits for period of internment

Sources: Social Security Act of 1935 and amendments.
a. For all tables in this appendix except A-12 most of the provisions are effective as of the calendar year after the year of the passage of the act, or, for the self-employed, at the beginning of the taxable year after the year of legislation.
b. Subsequent legislation assumes continuation of coverage specified in earlier legislation.
c. Effective as of 1937.
d. Effective with taxable year beginning after January 1, 1955, for armed forces and professionals.
e. Effective as of taxable year beginning January 1, 1965, for physicians and interns.

Legislation in 1950 expanded coverage for dependents' benefits to include dependent husbands sixty-five and over and wives of any age caring for children under eighteen. Survivors' benefits were also expanded to dependent husbands and to divorced dependent wives caring for an eligible child.

The 1956 act provided for alterations in coverage for the various types of benefits. Women could retire at sixty-two and receive permanently re-

Table A-2. Benefits Provided by Social Security Legislation, 1935 to Date (1976)[a]

Year of legislation	Recipient	Age of recipient	Insured status of worker[b]
	RETIREMENT BENEFITS		
1935	Retired worker, male or female	65 and over	Fully
1956	Retired female	62 and over[c]	Fully
1961	Retired male	62 and over[c]	Fully
	TRANSITIONAL BENEFITS		
1965	Retired worker, wife	72 and over	Transitionally[d]
1966	Retired worker, wife	72 and over	Uninsured[e]
	DISABILITY BENEFITS		
1956	Disabled worker	50–64	Disability and currently
1958	Disabled worker	50–64	Disability
1960	Disabled worker	Under 65	Disability
	DEPENDENTS' BENEFITS		
1939	Wife	65 and over	Fully
1956	Wife	62 and over[f]	Fully
1950	Wife with eligible child[g]	Under 65	Fully
1965	Wife, divorced, dependent[h]	62 and over[f]	Fully
1972	Wife, divorced[h]	62 and over[f]	Fully
1939	Child	Under 18	Fully
1956	Child disabled before 18	18 and over	Fully
1965	Child, full-time student	18–21	Fully
1972	Child disabled before 22	18 and over	Fully
1972	Grandchild, under certain circumstances	Under 18	Fully
1972	Grandchildren disabled before 22	18 and over	Fully
1972	Grandchild, full-time student	18–21	Fully
1950	Dependent husband	65 and over	Fully and currently
1961	Dependent husband	62 and over[f]	Fully and currently
1967	Dependent husband	62 and over[f]	Fully
1958[i]	Dependents of disabled workers	Same as for dependents of retired workers	Same as for dependents of retired workers plus disability insured
	SURVIVORS' BENEFITS		
1939	Wife	65 and over	Fully
1956	Wife	62 and over	Fully
1965	Wife	60 and over[c]	Fully
1965	Wife	72 and over	Transitionally
1972	Wife	60 and over[j]	Fully
1967	Wife, disabled	50–59[k]	Fully
1972	Wife, disabled	50–59[m]	Fully
1965	Wife, divorced, dependent[h]	60 and over[c]	Fully
1972	Wife, divorced[h]	60 and over[j]	Fully
1967	Wife, disabled, divorced, dependent[h]	50–59[k]	Fully
1972	Wife, disabled, divorced[h]	50–59[m]	Fully

Table A-2 (*Continued*)

Year of legislation	Recipient	Age of recipient	Insured status of worker[b]
	SURVIVORS' BENEFITS (*Continued*)		
1939	Wife, with eligible child[g]	All	Fully or currently
1950	Wife, divorced, dependent, with eligible child[g,h]	All	Fully or currently
1972	Wife, divorced, with eligible child[g]	All	Fully or currently
1939	Child	Under 18 (must be student at 16–17)	Fully or currently
1946	Child	Under 18	Fully or currently
1956	Child disabled before 18	18 and over	Fully or currently
1965	Child, full-time student	18–21	Fully or currently
1972	Child disabled before 22	18 and over	Fully or currently
1972	Grandchild, under certain circumstances	Same as for child	Same as for child
1939	Dependent parent	65 and over	Fully
1956	Dependent mother	62 and over	Fully
1961	Dependent father	62 and over	Fully
1950	Dependent husband	65 and over	Fully and currently
1961	Dependent husband	62 and over	Fully and currently
1967	Dependent husband	62 and over	Fully
1972	Dependent husband	60 and over[j]	Fully
1967	Dependent husband, disabled	50–61[n]	Fully
1972	Dependent husband, disabled	50–59[m]	Fully

Sources: Same as table A-1.

a. Subsequent legislation assumes continuation of coverage of earlier legislation.

b. See pp. 163–68 for explanation of types of insured status.

c. Benefits permanently reduced 5/9 percent for each month before sixty-five for a retired worker and before sixty-two for a widow, or a divorced dependent wife.

d. Man must be seventy-two before 1964, woman must be seventy-two before 1967. With the provision of transitional benefits for uninsured people (see note e), the age restriction became, in effect, seventy-two before 1969.

e. Transitional benefits provided to uninsured if they (1) reached seventy-two before 1968, or (2) had three quarters of coverage for every year after 1966 and before seventy-two.

f. Benefits permanently reduced 25/36 percent for each month under sixty-five.

g. 1965 legislation excludes students over eighteen.

h. If marriage lasted twenty years or more.

i. After 1958, follows history of benefits for dependents of retired workers.

j. Benefits permanently reduced 19/40 percent per month under sixty-five. For sixty-five and over, benefits limited to amount spouse or former spouse would receive if still living but not less than 82.5 percent of PIA. For sixty-two to sixty-four whose husband retired before sixty-five, benefits limited to the larger amount.

k. Benefits permanently reduced 13-1/3 percent plus 43/198 percent per month under sixty.

m. Benefits permanently reduced 28.5 percent plus 43/240 percent per month under sixty.

n. Benefits permanently reduced 5/9 percent per month between the ages of sixty to sixty-two plus 43/198 percent per month under sixty.

duced benefits. Wives of retired workers became eligible for dependents' and survivors' benefits at sixty-two, permanently reduced if claimed before sixty-five. Dependent mothers become eligible for survivors' benefits at sixty-two. Children over eighteen became eligible for dependents' and survivors' benefits if they became disabled before eighteen.

The major provision of the 1956 act, however, was the institution of monthly payments (after a six-month waiting period) to workers between the ages of fifty and sixty-four who had been permanently or totally disabled. These monthly benefits were established at 100 percent of the worker's primary insurance amount (the amount payable to a retired worker who begins receiving benefits at 65). In 1958, dependents of disabled workers became eligible for dependents' benefits under the same conditions, age restrictions, and benefit levels as dependents of retired workers. In 1960, the fifty-year age restriction was eliminated, so that all workers under sixty-five and their dependents were eligible for disability and dependents' benefits.

The age limitations for males were liberalized in 1961 as they had been for females in 1956. Men aged sixty-two to sixty-four could retire with permanently reduced benefits (reduced $5/9$ percent per month under sixty-five). Dependent husbands and dependent male parents were eligible for benefits at sixty-two; however, benefits for dependent husbands were permanently reduced if claimed before sixty-five. Further age reductions in 1965 allowed widows to claim reduced benefits at sixty.

The 1965 legislation extended coverage to children aged eighteen to twenty-one who were full-time students and to divorced dependent wives if the marriage had lasted at least twenty years. It also added health insurance—known as medicare—to the existing old age, survivors, and disability insurance. Insured sixty-five-year-olds and certain other aged people became eligible for health and related benefits provided by the program. These benefits included the following: (1) inpatient hospital care for 90 days for each illness, with $40 deductible and $10 coinsurance for each day after 60 days; (2) a maximum of 100 posthospital days in an extended-care institution, with $5 coinsurance for each day after 20 days; (3) outpatient diagnostic services, with a $20 deductible and 20 percent coinsurance; (4) up to 100 posthospital home visits; and (5) a lifetime maximum of 190 days of psychiatric hospital care. Enrollment in the supplementary medical insurance program was available on an elective basis (with no insured status required) at a charge of $3 a month. This program covered 80 percent of physician and related expenditures, with a $50 deductible per year (raised to $60 in 1972). Amendments in 1967 provided each medicare beneficiary with a lifetime reserve of 60 days of hospital care, which could be used when the 90 days per illness were exhausted. There was a $20 coinsurance for each such reserve day of coverage.

The 1967 legislation expanded coverage for survivors' benefits to disabled widows and widowers fifty or over (including divorced dependent wives if the marriage had lasted twenty years) if they become totally disabled not more than seven years after the spouse's death.

Most of the changes made in 1972 were relatively minor. Children of any age were eligible if they were disabled before twenty-two. (Previously, children must have been disabled before eighteen.) Grandchildren became eligible in certain circumstances for benefits under the same conditions, age restrictions, and benefit levels as children. Divorced wives no longer had to meet a dependency requirement. Husbands became eligible for reduced survivors' benefits at sixty (an option available to wives since 1965).

Legislation in October 1972 instituted supplemental security income. The SSI program, which is financed entirely from general revenues, replaces state welfare programs for the aged, blind, and disabled (although states can supplement SSI benefits with their own funds if they so choose). All SSI eligibility rules, such as limits on assets and definitions of blindness and disability, are uniform nationwide, as is the basic minimum income guarantee—$167.80 per month for an individual and $251.80 for a couple as of July 1976. Benefits are reduced in accordance with income; however, the first $20 of earned income or unearned income (such as social security benefits) plus the next $65 plus half the remainder of earnings above $65 are excluded each month in deducting income from the monthly benefit.

Qualifications for Insured Status

Eligibility for social security benefits, though not SSI benefits, is based on the attainment of insured status. There are five classifications of insured. The term "fully insured" was introduced in 1935 to identify those people entitled to monthly retirement benefits at sixty-five. With the institution of survivors' benefits in 1939, the less vigorous classification "currently insured" relaxed the minimum requirements so that the family of a young deceased worker could receive survivors' benefits without the worker being fully insured. In 1954, the classification "disability insured" was included in the legislation in line with the introduction of the disability freeze (omission of periods of extended total disability in computing average monthly earnings). Two additional classifications were added in 1965, "transitionally insured" and "health insured." The details of these various types of insured status, which are summarized in table A-3, are discussed more fully below.

Table A-3. Requirements for Coverage Specified by Social Security Legislation, 1935 to Date (1976)

Year of legislation	Basis[a]	Amount	Time period	Minimum	Maximum
		FULLY INSURED			
1935	Wage credits	$2,000	Employment in each of 5 years after 1936 and before 65	$2,000	...
1939	Quarters of coverage	1/2	After 1936 (or the age of 21) to 65 (or death)	6	40
1950	Quarters of coverage	1/2	After 1950 (or the age of 21) to 65 (or death)	6	40
1954	Quarters of coverage	1/2	Period of disability excluded from elapsed period[b]	6	40
1956	Quarters of coverage	1/2	Elapsed period measured to the age of 62 for women	6	40
1960	Quarters of coverage	1/3	No change	6	40
1961	Quarters of coverage	1/4	No change	6	40
1972	Quarters of coverage	1/4	Elapsed period for men measured to the age of 62	6	40
		CURRENTLY INSURED			
1939	Quarters of coverage	6 of 12	12 quarters preceding quarter of death	6	...
1946	Quarters of coverage	6 of 13	Includes quarter of death	6	...
1950	Quarters of coverage	6 of 13	Includes quarter of death or retirement	6	...
1954	Quarters of coverage	6 of 13	Includes quarter of death, retirement, or disability	6	...
		DISABILITY INSURED[b]			
1954	Quarters of coverage	20 of 40	Last 40 quarters, including quarter of disablement; currently insured	20	...
1956	Quarters of coverage	20 of 40	Last 40 quarters, including quarter of disablement; currently and fully insured	20	...
1958	Quarters of coverage	20 of 40	Last 40 quarters, including quarter of disablement; fully insured	20	...
1960	Quarters of coverage[c]	20 + minimum of 6	20 quarters of coverage and quarters of coverage earned in all quarters after 1950 with a minimum of 6 such quarters	20	...

Table A-3 (*Continued*)

Year of legis-lation	Basis[a]	Amount	Time period	Mini-mum	Maxi-mum
		DISABILITY INSURED (*Continued*)			
1965	For blind under age 31, quarters of coverage	1/2	From the age of 21 to disablement	6	...
1967	For disabled under age 31, quarters of coverage	1/2	From the age of 21 to disablement	6	...
		TRANSITIONALLY INSURED			
1965	Quarters of coverage	At least 3	None[d]	3	...
1966	Quarters of coverage	3 per year	Between 1967 and year reaching 72[e]	3	...
		HEALTH INSURED			
1965	Fully insured	...	...	None	...
1965	Railroad retirement beneficiary	...	...	None	...
1965	Quarters of coverage	3 per year	1966 to the age of 65	None	...
1965	Age	65 years	Before 1968	None	...
1967	Quarters of coverage	3 per year	1967 to the age of 65	None	...
1972	Enrollment in SMI program, over 65[f]	...	None	None	...
1972	Disabled before 65	...	None	None	...

Sources: Same as table A-1.

a. A quarter of coverage is a calendar quarter in which a worker received $50 or more in wages, $100 or more in self-employment income, or $100 or more in agricultural wages.

b. Disability is inability to engage in any substantial gainful work existing in the national economy. For surviving spouse, inability to engage in any gainful activity.

c. Alternative to 1958 method.

d. Must be seventy-two before 1969; widow must be seventy-two before 1967.

e. No coverage required if seventy-two or older before 1968.

f. Supplementary medical insurance pays part of the costs of physicians' services, outpatient hospital services, and other related medical and health services for the voluntarily insured aged and disabled.

FULLY INSURED. According to the 1935 act, a worker had to accumulate $2,000 in wage credits and have been employed in each of five years after 1936 and before sixty-five to be eligible for retirement benefits. In 1939, the basis for coverage was changed from wage credits to quarters of coverage, which is defined as a calendar quarter in which $50 in wages, $100 in self-employment income, or $100 in agricultural income is earned. To be fully insured, a worker had to be covered in half of the quarters after

1936 (or the age of twenty-one) to retirement age or death. The minimum number of covered quarters required was six; the maximum was forty.

In 1950, the starting year for the applicable period was changed from 1936 to 1950. The number of earned quarters required for coverage remained at half the quarters after 1950 (or the age of twenty-one) to retirement age or death, and quarters earned before 1951 could also be counted. With the institution of the disability freeze in 1954, periods of extended total disability were excluded from the period on which the number of covered quarters required is based.

In 1960, the number of quarters of coverage required for fully insured status was reduced from half to a third of the quarters after 1950 (or the age of twenty-one) to retirement age, disability, or death. In 1961, the requirement was again reduced, to a fourth of the quarters during the same period. As before, quarters of coverage earned before 1951 could be counted, and the minimum and maximum number of covered quarters required remained at six and forty, respectively.

With the 1956 legislation, calculations pertaining to insured status for women were based on the period after 1950 (or the age of twenty-one) to sixty-two, disability, or death. In 1972, an identical change was made for men.

CURRENTLY INSURED. Currently insured status was introduced in 1939 to allow dependents of young deceased workers to receive survivors' benefits. In 1939, six quarters of coverage in the twelve quarters preceding death were required for a worker to be currently insured. By 1954, the requirement was changed to six quarters of coverage in the thirteen quarters immediately preceding death, disability, or retirement, including the quarter of such event.

DISABILITY INSURED. When disability insured status was established in 1954, the requirement was twenty quarters of coverage in the last forty quarters, including the quarter of disability. In 1956, fully insured status was added to the requirements for disability insured status. The 1965 legislation contained alternative formulas for the blind under the age of thirty-one (quarters of coverage equaling half the quarters elapsed after the age of twenty-one, with a minimum of six covered quarters) and under the age of twenty-four (six quarters of coverage in the preceding three years). Amendments in 1967 extended these alternatives to all disabled workers under thirty-one, and in 1972 the requirement for insured status for the blind was reduced to fully insured status.

Table A-4. Amount of Benefits Provided to Transitionally Insured Workers by Social Security Legislation, 1965–76

Dollars

	Monthly benefit	
Year of legislation	Individual	Couple
1965	35.00	52.50
1966[a]	35.00	52.50
1967	40.00	60.00
1969	46.00	69.00
1971	48.30	72.50
1972	58.00	87.00
1973[b]	64.40	96.60
1975[b,c]	69.60	104.40
1976[b,c]	74.10	111.10

Sources: Amendments to the Social Security Act of 1935.

a. For those eligible under 1966 legislation, benefit reduced by amount of other government pensions. Benefits not available to those on public assistance.

b. For the noninsured, benefits suspended if eligible for supplemental security income.

c. Result of automatic revision based on the consumer price index. Amounts shown effective in June of year.

TRANSITIONALLY INSURED AND UNINSURED. The classification "transitionally insured" was added in 1965 to provide small retirement and survivors' benefits for certain workers, spouses, and surviving spouses aged seventy-two or older (see table A-4). To be transitionally insured, a worker must fulfill the requirements for fully insured status, with the exception that the minimum number of quarters of coverage needed is three. (The fully insured minimum is six.) In addition, the worker must have reached seventy-two before 1969.

Legislation in 1966 provided special monthly cash benefits to certain of the uninsured who (1) had reached seventy-two before 1968 or (2) had three quarters of coverage for each year after 1966 and before seventy-two. These benefit levels are the same as those for the transitionally insured.

HEALTH INSURED. When hospital and related benefits were instituted in 1965, the requirements for insured status were lenient, allowing almost all who were sixty-five or over to qualify. Insured status was achieved in any of four ways: (1) as a fully insured worker, dependent, or survivor, (2) as a railroad retirement beneficiary, (3) by working in covered employment in three-fourths of the quarters after 1965 to sixty-five, or (4) by reaching sixty-five before 1968. In 1967, the third alternative was changed to three quarters of coverage for each year after 1966 to sixty-five. The 1972 legislation granted benefits to certain insured persons with chronic kidney disease and to disabled workers under sixty-five who are entitled to monthly cash benefits for twenty-four months or longer.

Calculation of Benefits

When the social security program began in 1935, calculation of benefits was based on cumulative wages. However, before any benefits were paid, the 1939 legislation changed the method of determination to one based on the worker's average monthly earnings (AME). The AME is found by summing earnings per year, up to the maximum taxable amount, for all years in covered employment and dividing by the appropriate number of months in the period. A formula specified in the law is then applied to the worker's AME to determine the primary insurance amount (PIA). The PIA is the amount a worker's retirement benefit would be if claimed at sixty-five and is the amount upon which all other benefits are based. According to the 1939 law, the primary insurance amount was calculated by taking 40 percent of the first $50 of the AME plus 10 percent of the next $200, plus 1 percent of the total for each year the worker was employed in covered employment and received at least $200 in wages (see table A-5). The average monthly wage was based on the period after 1936 (or after the age of twenty-one) to sixty-five (or death). A minimum retirement benefit of $10 and a maximum family benefit of $85 were also established. Table A-6 gives the formulas used since 1939 to determine the maximum family benefit.

Benefit levels have been increased frequently since 1939. This has been done through three types of modifications: (1) increases in the formula rates applied to the AME (see table A-7), (2) increases in the maximum taxable earnings base resulting in a larger AME (see table A-12), and (3) modifications to allow years of low earnings to be excluded from the period upon which the average monthly wage is based.

In 1950, legislation changed the period for calculating the AME to include only earnings after 1950 (or the age of twenty-one). Legislation in 1954 allowed periods of extended total disability to be excluded in computing the AME and also permitted the omission of four years of lowest earnings from the computation period (five years could be omitted if there were at least twenty quarters of coverage). In 1956, this was changed so that the five years of lowest earnings were omitted in all cases. A special shortening adjustment for women was also incorporated, allowing the computation period for the AME to end at sixty-two (or death). (A similar change for men was included in 1972 legislation.) After 1960, those who worked after the minimum retirement age were permitted to substitute those years for years of lower earnings, thus further boosting their AMEs.

The benefit formula has been changed twelve times between 1950 and 1976. The 1950 law provided for an average increase in benefits of 77 percent. Other increases were between 7 and 20 percent (see table A-7).

In 1972, legislation provided for automatic increases in benefits according to changes in the cost of living and average earnings in covered employment. This provision was modified in 1973 to the form discussed below. Beginning in 1975 and every calendar year thereafter (except those years after a year in which Congress enacts a general benefit increase or in which such an increase becomes effective), benefits are adjusted in line with increases in the consumer price index of the Bureau of Labor Statistics. If the CPI for the first quarter of the year of determination is at least 3 percent greater than its level in the first quarter of the year that last triggered a cost-of-living increase in benefits, each percentage rate of the benefit formula is increased by the increase in the CPI, effective June of the year of determination. While changes in the CPI trigger changes in the benefit formula rates, changes in the average taxable wage trigger changes in the maximum taxable earnings base. The earnings base is automatically adjusted each year in which the rate formula is adjusted. Before 1976, the base in effect in the year of determination was multiplied by the ratio of average wages in covered employment in the first quarter of the year of determination to such wages in the first quarter of the year that last triggered a cost-of-living adjustment. This product was rounded to the nearest multiple of $300 and became effective for the taxable year beginning after the year of determination. In no case could benefits be reduced by either of these two mechanisms. In 1976 this procedure was changed so that changes in average wages are calculated on an annual basis instead of by comparing first quarters.

Survivors' and dependents' benefits are affected only indirectly by the automatic inflation adjustment. Since all secondary benefits are expressed as percentages of the worker's PIA, they increase in line with legislative and automatic increases in the PIA. (See tables A-8 and A-9 for secondary benefits as percentages of PIA.) However, over the years, nearly all survivors' benefits have risen more rapidly than PIAs, since legislative action has made them a larger percentage of the worker's PIA.

Table A-5. Formulas for Primary Insurance Amounts[a] Provided by Social Security Legislation, 1935–76

Year of legislation	Basis	Formula[b]
1935	Cumulative wages	1/2% of first $3,000 +1/12% of next $42,000 +1/24% of next $84,000
1939	Average monthly earnings after 1936	40% of first $50 +10% of next $200 +increase of total by 1% for each year of coverage
1950	Average monthly earnings after 1950	50% of first $100 +15% of next $200
1952	Same as 1950	55% of first $100 +15% of next $200
1954	Average monthly earnings after 1950 excluding 4 years (5 in some cases) of lowest earnings	55% of first $110 +20% of next $240
1956	Average monthly earnings after 1950 (excluding 5 years of lowest earnings), computation period ends at 62 for women	55% of first $110 +20% of next $240
1958	Same as 1956	58.85% of first $110 +21.4% of next $290
1965	Same as 1956	62.97% of first $110 +22.9% of next $290 +21.4% of next $150
1967	Same as 1956	71.16% of first $110 +25.88% of next $290 +24.18% of next $150 +28.43% of next $100
1969	Same as 1956	81.83% of first $110 +29.76% of next $290 +27.81% of next $150 +32.69% of next $100
1971	Same as 1956	90.01% of first $110 +32.74% of next $290 +30.59% of next $150 +35.96% of next $100 +20.00% of next $100
1972	Same as 1956, except for men computation period measured to 62 or to 1975, if later	108.01% of first $110 +39.29% of next $290 +36.71% of next $150 +43.15% of next $100 +24.00% of next $100 +20.00% of next $250
1973	Same as 1972	119.89% of first $110 +43.61% of next $290 +40.75% of next $150

Table A-5. (*Continued*)

Year of legislation	Basis	Formula[b]
		+47.90% of next $100
		+26.64% of next $100
		+22.20% of next $250
		+20.00% of next $100
1975[c]	Same as 1972	129.48% of first $110
		+47.10% of next $290
		+44.01% of next $150
		+51.73% of next $100
		+28.77% of next $100
		+23.98% of next $250
		+21.60% of next $175
1976[d]	Same as 1972	137.77% of first $110
		+50.11% of next $290
		+46.83% of next $150
		+55.04% of next $100
		+30.61% of next $100
		+25.51% of next $250
		+22.98% of next $175
		+21.28% of next $100

Source: Social Security Administration.

a. Primary insurance amount is amount payable to fully insured retired worker on which benefits of dependents and survivors are based (or the basis for benefits for survivors of worker who dies before retirement).

b. Formulas approximate benefit amounts. For exact amounts for 1959–75 see Albert Rettig, *A Precise Formula for Primary Insurance Amounts*, Social Security Administration, Office of Research and Statistics, Staff Paper 22 (GPO, 1975).

c. Change in earnings base (from $13,200 a year to $14,100 a year) effective January 1975; changes in percentages effective June 1975.

d. Change in earnings base (from $14,100 a year to $15,300 a year) effective January 1976; changes in percentages effective June 1976.

The 1935 Social Security Act also provided for a lump-sum death benefit equal to 3.5 percent of the worker's cumulative wage credits less any benefits already paid. In 1939, this was changed to six times the worker's PIA. It remained unchanged until 1950, when it was reduced to three times the worker's PIA. In 1954 a maximum of $255 was established, and in 1973 the lump-sum death benefit was set at a flat $255 (see table A-10).

The Earnings Test

The Social Security Act of 1935 required complete retirement from all covered employment as a condition for receipt of benefits. Legislators felt that this requirement would encourage aged workers to retire, making more jobs available for younger workers. Thus, if a retiree engaged in any

Table A-6. Maximum Family Benefit Formulas Stipulated by Social Security Legislation, 1939–76

Year of legislation	Formula	
	Average monthly earnings	But not less than
1939	80%	2 × PIA[a]
1950	80% of first $187.50	$40
1952	80% of first $210.93	$45
1954	80% of first $250.00	Greater of $50 or 150% of PIA
1958	80% of first $317.50	Greater of PIA + $20 or 150% of PIA
1961	80% of first $317.50	150% of PIA
1965	80% of first $370.00 +40% of next $180.00	No change
1967	80% of first $436.00 +40% of next $214.00	No change
1971[b]	88% of first $436.00 +44% of next $191.00	No change
1972[b]	105.6% of first $436.00 +52.8% of next $191.00	No change
1973[b]	117.2% of first $436.00 +58.6% of next $191.00	No change
1975[b,c]	126.6% of first $436.00 +63.3% of next $191.00	No change
1976[b,c]	134.7% of first $436.00 +67.3% of next $191.00	No change

Sources: Same as table A-4.

a. Primary insurance amount, or amount payable to fully insured retired worker on which benefits of dependents and survivors are based (or the basis for benefits to survivors of a worker who dies before retirement).

b. For average monthly earnings of $628 or more, maximum family benefit is 175 percent of PIA.

c. Result of automatic revision based on the consumer price index.

covered employment during the month, he or she forfeited an entire month's benefit.

Since 1939 this restriction has been gradually liberalized to allow higher earnings. In 1939, a retired worker was permitted to earn up to $14.99 per month in covered employment without loss of benefits. This amount was increased to $50 per month in 1950 and to $75 per month in 1952. Self-employed income fell under a different test, however; in 1935, it was defined as substantial gainful services. Though this definition has not changed, in 1950 a test for self-employment was established with an annual exempt amount of $600, which was increased to $900 in 1952.

The earnings test caused inequities because only earnings from covered employment fell under the restriction and because workers who earned slightly more than $75 (in covered employment) in some months—but well below the limit in others—suffered a substantial loss of benefits. In response to this, 1954 legislation placed the wage test on an annual basis for all earnings, covered and uncovered. The annual limit was $1,200, and for each $80 or fraction over $1,200, one month's benefit was lost. However, a worker could be paid for any month in which he or she earned less than $80 and did not engage in substantial self-employment. This permitted a worker retiring in the middle of the year to receive benefits as soon as monthly income fell below $80, regardless of annual earnings. In 1958, the monthly limit was increased to $100.

In 1960, the earnings test was again revised to provide a more equitable means of reducing benefits. Under the 1954 act, a worker who earned $1,201 and one who earned $1,280 received the same reduction in benefits. Under the 1960 act, a dollar of benefits was withheld for every $2 of earnings in excess of $1,200 up through $1,500; above $1,500, a dollar of benefits was withheld for each dollar of earnings. The annual and monthly exempt amounts were not changed. In 1961, the upper limit of the one-for-two bracket was extended to $1,700, with the one-for-one bracket beginning at $1,701. In 1965, the annual exempt amount was changed to $1,500 and the monthly limit was changed again to $125. The one-for-two bracket became $1,501–$2,700, and the one-for-one bracket became $2,701 and over. Legislation in 1967 again raised each of these figures. (See table A-11.)

In 1972, the annual and monthly limits were changed to $2,100 and $175, respectively, with provisions for automatic increases based on increases in average wages in covered employment. Furthermore, the benefit reduction formula was liberalized by eliminating the one-for-one bracket so that benefits were reduced a dollar for each $2 of earnings over $2,100. Exempt amounts were increased again in 1973, 1975, 1976, and 1977, the annual limit becoming $3,000 and the monthly limit becoming $250.

A hypothetical case illustrates the results of the present earnings test. Assume a worker is eligible for a benefit of $100 a month. If annual earnings are $3,000 or less, income can vary between $1,200 (twelve months of benefits and no earnings) and $4,200 (twelve months of benefits plus $3,000 in earnings). If earnings are more than $3,000, income will be $4,200 plus half the amount by which earnings exceed $3,000. Thus, if the worker earns $3,100, earnings in excess of $3,000 are $100; and since benefits are reduced $1 for every $2 of earnings above $3,000, they are reduced by $50. The resulting income is $3,100 plus $1,150 or $4,250.

This test, however, does not apply universally. Legislation in 1950

Table A-7. Primary Insurance Amounts,[a] Social Security Legislation, 1939–75

Dollars

Average monthly earnings	Year of legislation												
	1939[b]	1950	1952	1954	1958	1961	1965	1967	1969	1971	1972	1973	1975[e]
25	10.00	20.00	25.00	30.00	33.00	40.00	44.00	55.00	64.00	70.40	84.50	93.80	101.40
50	20.00	25.00	27.50	30.00	33.00	40.00	44.00	55.00	64.00	70.40	84.50	93.80	101.40
100	25.00	50.00	55.00	55.00	59.00	59.00	63.20	71.50	81.83	90.01	108.01	119.89	129.48
150	30.00	57.50	62.50	68.50	73.00	73.00	78.20	88.40	101.92	112.11	134.53	149.32	161.27
200	35.00	65.00	70.00	78.50	84.00	84.00	89.90	101.60	116.80	128.48	154.17	171.13	184.82
250	40.00	72.50	77.50	88.50	95.00	95.00	101.70	115.00	131.68	144.85	173.82	192.93	208.37
300	...	80.00[d]	85.00[d]	98.50	105.00	105.00	112.40	127.10	146.56	161.22	193.46	214.74	231.92
350	...	...	...	108.50[d]	116.00	116.00	124.20	140.40	161.44	177.59	213.11	236.54	255.47
400	...	...	...	...	127.00[d]	127.00[d]	135.90[d]	153.60	176.32	193.96	232.75	258.35	279.02
450	...	...	...	...	...	...	146.00	165.00[d]	190.22[d]	209.25	251.11	278.72	301.02
500	...	...	...	...	...	...	157.00	177.50	204.13	224.55[d]	269.46[d]	299.10[d]	323.03
550	...	...	...	...	...	...	168.00	189.90	218.03	239.84	287.82	319.47	345.03[d]
600	...	...	...	...	...	...	...	204.00	234.38	257.82	309.39	343.42	370.90
650	...	...	...	...	...	...	...	218.00	250.72	275.80	330.97	367.37	396.76
700	...	...	...	...	...	...	...	...	...	285.80	342.97	380.69	411.15
750	...	...	...	...	...	...	...	...	...	295.80	354.97	394.01	425.53
800	...	...	...	...	...	...	...	...	...	...	364.97	405.11	437.52
850	...	...	...	...	...	...	...	...	...	...	374.97	416.21	449.51

900											384.97	427.31	461.50
950											394.97	438.41	473.49
1,000											404.97	449.51	485.48
1,050												459.51	496.28
1,100												469.51	507.08
1,175													523.28
Addendum													
Minimum benefit	10.00	20.00	25.00	30.00	33.00	40.00	44.00	55.00	64.00	70.40	84.50[e]	93.80[f]	101.40
Maximum benefit													
Individual	60.00	80.00	85.00	108.50	127.00	127.00	168.00	218.00	250.72	295.80	404.97	469.51	523.28
Family	85.00	150.00	168.75	200.00	254.00	254.00	368.00	434.40	434.40	517.65	708.70	821.64	915.74
Maximum possible average monthly earnings for calculation of benefit	...	250.00	300.00	300.00	350.00	370.00	383.33	400.00	430.77	460.00	471.88	488.24	542.11

Sources: Social Security Administration and calculations from provisions in the Social Security Act of 1935 and amendments.

a. The primary insurance amount is the amount payable to a fully insured retired worker on which benefits of dependents and survivors are based (or the basis for benefits for survivors of a worker who dies before retirement).

b. Previous to 1939 legislation, benefit amounts were based on cumulative wages. Under the 1939 legislation, after computation by a formula based on average monthly earnings, all benefits were increased by 1 percent for each year of coverage. This provision was discontinued by the 1950 legislation.

c. As of June 1975: result of 1972–73 legislation providing for automatic cost-of-living increases.

d. Since average monthly earnings is based on earnings in amounts up to contribution and benefit base, it is impossible to have an AME that would result in benefits of this amount or greater.

e. A special minimum monthly benefit of $8.50 times years of coverage in excess of 10 and up to 30 years (that is, not in excess of $170) is payable to workers with the required years of coverage whose regular benefits are less than the minimum.

f. The special minimum monthly benefit was raised to $9 times years of coverage in excess of 10, up to $180.

Table A-8. Dependents' Benefits as Percent of Primary Insurance Amount,[a] **Social Security Legislation, 1939 to Date (1976)**

Year of legislation	Wife	Child	Dependent husband
1939	50[b]	50[c]	...
1950	50[d]	50	50[b]
1956	50[e]	50[f]	50
1961	50	50	50[e]
1965	50[g]	50[h]	50
1967	50[i]	50	50[i]
1969	50[j]	50	50[j]
1971	50	50	50
1972	50[k]	50[m]	50

Sources: Same as table A-4.

a. Primary insurance amount, payable to fully insured worker, on which benefit of dependents and survivors is based.

b. Aged sixty-five and over.

c. Under eighteen.

d. Under sixty-five and caring for eligible child.

e. Eligible at sixty-two; benefits permanently reduced by 25/36 percent per month younger than sixty-five.

f. Over eighteen if disabled before eighteen.

g. Divorced, aged sixty-two with reduced benefits (see note e), dependent, if marriage lasted twenty years. Eligible children aged eighteen–twenty-one attending school excluded.

h. Aged eighteen–twenty-one if attending school.

i. Maximum of $105.

j. Maximum eliminated.

k. Dependency requirement eliminated.

m. Disabled before age twenty-two; benefits extended to end of quarter or semester in which twenty-second birthday occurs while working on undergraduate degree; dependent grandchild eligible under certain circumstances.

exempted workers over seventy-five from the earnings restriction, and in 1954 this exemption was extended to include workers over seventy-two.

Financing

According to the 1935 legislation, contributions from the employer-employee payroll taxes were to exceed benefits in early years and result in the accumulation of a large trust fund. However, this plan was scrapped almost immediately and in 1939 emphasis was shifted to a pay-as-you-go plan, with excess revenues held in a trust fund. In 1950, legislation provided for a larger reserve and an increased tax schedule designed to produce contributions that, combined with interest earned on trust-fund moneys, would be sufficient to finance all future obligations of the program. However, funding did not replace current financing, and the social security trust fund, which now holds approximately enough money to

Table A-9. Survivors' Benefits as Percent of Primary Insurance Amount,[a] Social, Security Legislation, 1939 to Date (1976)

Year of legislation	Aged widow	Widow caring for eligible child	Widower	Child	Dependent parent	Lump-sum death benefit
1939	75[b]	75	...	50[c]	50[d]	600
1950	75	75[e]	75[f]	75[g]	75	300
1956	75	75	75	75[h]	75	300[i]
1960	75	75	75	75	75	300
1961	82.5	75	82.5	75	82.5[j]	300
1965	82.5[k]	75[m]	82.5	75[n]	82.5	300
1967	82.5[o]	75	82.5[p]	75	82.5	300
1969	82.5	75	82.5	75	82.5	300
1971	82.5	75	82.5	75	82.5	300
1972	100.0[q,r,s]	75[r]	100[q,s,t]	75[u]	82.5	300[v]

Sources: Same as table A-4.

a. Primary insurance amount, amount payable to fully insured retired worker, on which benefits of dependents and survivors are based (or the basis for benefit of survivors of worker who dies before retirement).

b. 1939–55, aged sixty-five; 1956–61, aged sixty-two; 1965, aged sixty.

c. Under eighteen.

d. Males, 1939, aged sixty-five; 1961, aged sixty-two. Females, 1939, aged sixty-five; 1956, aged sixty-two.

e. Divorced, dependent.

f. 1950, aged sixty-five; 1961, aged sixty-two; 1972, aged sixty.

g. 75 percent for oldest child, 50 percent for other children.

h. Disabled before eighteen.

i. Maximum of $255 enacted in 1954 legislation.

j. 75 percent each if two parents.

k. Divorced, dependent, marriage lasted 20 years; at sixty eligible for benefits permanently reduced by 5/9 percent per month under sixty-two.

m. Excludes child eighteen and over attending school.

n. Aged eighteen–twenty-one if attending school.

o. Disabled, aged fifty–fifty-nine; regular benefit reduced 13-1/3 percent plus 43/198 percent per month under sixty; includes divorced wife, dependent, married twenty years.

p. Disabled, dependent, aged fifty–sixty-one; regular benefit reduced 5/9 percent per month between the ages of sixty and sixty-two plus a maximum of 43/198 percent per month under sixty.

q. For those aged sixty-five and over, benefit limited to amount spouse or former spouse would be receiving if still living but not less than 82.5 percent of PIA. For those aged sixty-two–sixty-four, benefit reduced by 19/40 percent per month under sixty-five with a maximum of the larger of 82.5 percent of PIA or amount spouse or former spouse would be receiving if still living. For those aged sixty–sixty-one, benefits further reduced 19/40 percent per month under sixty-two.

r. No dependency requirement for disabled divorced wife and divorced wife caring for eligible child.

s. Benefits for disabled reduced 28.5 percent plus 43/240 percent per month under sixty.

t. Age requirements reduced to fifty–fifty-nine (disability requirements eliminated for sixty–sixty-one).

u. Benefits extended to end of quarter or semester in which twenty-second birthday occurs while working on undergraduate degree; surviving dependent grandchild eligible under certain circumstances.

v. Payment set at $255 in 1973 legislation.

finance one year of benefit payments, has been recognized simply as a contingency fund.

Since 1950, Congress has repeatedly asserted its intention to maintain the OASDI program as a self-supporting program. Thus, aside from small appropriations from general revenues to reimburse the OASI and DI trust funds in certain instances, benefits have been paid primarily from current

Table A-10. Lump-Sum Benefits, Social Security Legislation, 1935 to Date (1976)

Year of legislation	Type of lump-sum benefit	Amount[a]	Conditions
1935	At 65[b]	3.5 percent wage credits	Not insured
	Death benefit	3.5 percent wage credits less benefits received	Aged 65 or over, fully insured
1939	Death benefit	6 × PIA if no eligible survivor	Any age, fully or currently insured
1950	Death benefit	3 × PIA	Same
1954	Death benefit	3 × PIA (maximum $255)	Same
1972	Death benefit	3 × PIA (maximum $255; minimum $253.50)	Same
1973	Death benefit	$255	Same

Source: Same as table A-1.
a. PIA is primary insurance amount. See table A-9, note a.
b. Eliminated in 1939.

contributions. Therefore, benefits essentially represent a transfer of income from the working, taxpaying population to those eligible for old age, disability, and survivors' benefits.

As benefits and the number of beneficiaries have increased, so have the tax rate and the taxable earnings base. In 1935, the employer-employee tax schedule was established at 1 percent each for the employer and employee, levied on the first $3,000 of a worker's annual earnings. The schedule provided for four increases of 0.5 percent each, bringing the tax to 3 percent each in 1949. However, legislation in the 1940s extended the combined rate of 2 percent through 1949. The rate was increased by 1947 legislation to 1.5 percent each for employer and employee, effective in 1950. The 1950 act extended this rate through 1953 and increased it to 2 percent each for 1954, while also increasing the taxable earnings ceiling to $3,600. The taxable earnings base was raised to $4,200 and the 2 percent rate was again extended under the 1954 act, with the rate scheduled to reach a maximum of 8 percent each in 1975.

With the establishment of disability insurance in 1956, the tax rate was increased by 0.25 percent to 2.25 percent each, with the additional 0.25 percent going into the disability insurance trust fund.

In 1959, the taxable earnings base was increased to $4,800 and the OASI tax rate was increased from 2 percent to 2.25 percent (the DI rate remaining at 0.25 percent). Thus, the total tax rate was 2.5 percent each for employer and employee. In accordance with subsequent legislation, the OASI tax rate was increased to 3.375 percent by 1963, with the DI tax rate remaining at 0.25 percent.

Table A-11. Earnings Test, Social Security Legislation, 1935–77

Year of legislation	Earnings permitted without reduction in benefits (dollars)[a]		Benefit reduction	Age at which restriction ends
	Annual	Monthly		
1935	None	None	One month's	None
1939	...	14.99	One month's	None
1950	600[b]	50.00	One month's	75
1952	900[b]	75.00	One month's	75
1954	1,200	80.00	One month's[c]	72
1958	1,200	100.00	One month's[d]	72
1960	1,200	100.00	$1 for each $2 of earnings $1,201–$1,500; $1 for each $1 of earnings over $1,500	72
1961	1,200	100.00	$1 for each $2 of earnings $1,201–$1,700; $1 for each $1 of earnings over $1,700	72
1965	1,500	125.00	$1 for each $2 of earnings $1,501–$2,700; $1 for each $1 of earnings over $2,700	72
1967	1,680	140.00	$1 for each $2 of earnings $1,681–$2,880; $1 for each $1 of earnings over $2,880	72
1972	2,100	175.00	$1 for each $2 of earnings over $2,100	72
1973	2,400	200.00	$1 for each $2 of earnings over $2,400	72
1975[e]	2,520	210.00	$1 for each $2 of earnings over $2,520	72
1976[e]	2,760	230.00	$1 for each $2 of earnings over $2,760	72
1977[e]	3,000	250.00	$1 for each $2 of earnings over $3,000	72

Sources: Same as table A-1.

a. 1935–52, covered earnings only; 1954 on, all earnings (with special provisions for noncovered employment outside the United States).

b. Self-employment income only.

c. For every $80 or fraction over $1,200; benefit paid for any month when wages are $80 or less and worker does not engage in substantial self-employment.

d. For every $100 or fraction over $1,200; benefit paid for any month when wages are $100 or less and worker does not engage in substantial self-employment.

e. Exempt amount determined under the automatic revision formulas by the Secretary of Health, Education, and Welfare.

Introduction of health insurance resulted in a revised schedule in 1966, with the OASI tax at 3.5 percent, the DI tax at 0.35 percent, and the hospital insurance (HI) tax at 0.35 percent each for employer and employee. Revenues from the hospital insurance tax were deposited in the newly established hospital insurance trust fund. Thus, the total combined tax rate for employers and employees was 8.4 percent of taxable earnings. Contribution schedules were subsequently revised in 1967, 1969, 1971, and 1973. The 1973 act established the OASI tax at 4.375 percent, the DI tax at 0.575 percent, and the HI tax at 0.9 percent for 1974–77. Under that law, the OASDI tax rate is scheduled to remain at 4.95 percent each for employer and employee through the year 2010 (table A-12). However, the distribution between OASI and DI will change, with the OASI tax rate dropping to 4.25 percent and the DI rate increasing to 0.7 percent by 1986. In 2011, the OASI tax rate will increase to 5.1 percent and the DI tax rate to 0.85 percent. The HI tax rate is set to increase to 1.1 percent in 1978, 1.35 percent in 1981, and 1.5 percent in 1986. Thus, under the 1973 legislation the OASI tax rate remains constant from 1974–77, decreases from 1978 to 2010, and then increases substantially, while the DI and HI tax rates will increase throughout.

Since the 1965 legislation, maximum taxable earnings have increased from $6,600 in 1966 to $16,500 in 1977, with increases occurring in 1968, 1972, 1973, 1974, 1975, 1976, and 1977. The July 1972 act established a provision for automatic adjustment of the earnings base in accordance with changes in wage levels unless adjustment is made by an act of Congress.

Expansion of programs, increases in tax rates, and larger maximum taxable earnings have, together, resulted in growth of the maximum combined OASDHI taxes paid by employers and employees from $60 in 1937 to $1,930.50 in 1977.

When the self-employed were first brought into the social security program in 1950, their tax rate was established at 75 percent of the combined employer-employee rate (rounded to the nearest 0.1 percent after 1960). In the 1965 act, OASDI tax rates for the self-employed were scheduled to reach a maximum of 7 percent in 1973. The 7 percent maximum has been maintained, but the distribution between OASI and DI has changed from 6.205 percent for OASI and 0.795 percent for DI in 1973 to 6.185 percent for OASI and 0.815 percent for DI in 1977 (see table A-12). The health insurance tax rate for the self-employed was established at the same rate as for employers or employees (0.35 percent in 1966, 0.9 percent in 1977). Thus, the total tax rate for the self-employed in 1966 was 6.15 percent, while the combined tax rate for employers and employees was 8.4 percent. The figures for 1977 are 7.9 percent and 11.7 percent, respectively.

Although the primary method of financing benefits has been the payroll tax, appropriations from general revenues have been used on certain occasions. In the 1946 legislation, general revenues were appropriated to reimburse the OASI fund for noncontributory survivor insurance for certain World War II veterans, and since 1947, costs for gratuitous military service wage credits have also been covered by general revenues. Though legislation passed in 1950 stipulated that these costs be paid from the trust fund instead of general revenues, the 1950 law was reversed in 1956. Similar benefits paid from the disability insurance trust fund could also be reimbursed. However, no further reimbursements were made until 1966, when the OASI fund received $78 million and the DI fund received $16 million. In 1966, the costs of hospital benefits for those not entitled to benefits under either social security or the railroad retirement program were reimbursed, and contributions from general revenues equal to participant premiums for supplementary medical insurance were made. Legislation in 1966 also provided for reimbursement for benefits to the transitionally uninsured. In 1968 the various reimbursements amounted to $188 million for military service wage credits, $226 million for the transitionally uninsured, $54 million for hospital insurance costs, and $858 million for the SMI trust fund. Legislation in 1972 provided for reimbursement for the cost of gratuitous wage credits for those of Japanese descent interned during World War II and extended funding for supplementary medical insurance by providing funds from general revenues to cover all costs not met by participant premiums.

Summary

Legislative action over the past forty years has increased the scope and importance of the social security program. Coverage has been broadened to include virtually all employees, and eligibility requirements have been liberalized, thereby further enlarging the number of people with drawing rights in the system. In addition, the range of benefits has expanded and the amount has become more generous. Social security now provides income replacement for disabled workers as well as retired workers, secondary benefits for dependents and survivors of disabled and retired workers, hospital and medical benefits for the aged sick and certain disabled workers under sixty-five. A new program, supplemental security income for the destitute elderly, blind, and disabled, now overlaps some of social security's welfare roles.

Table A-12. Tax Schedule, Social Security Legislation, Actual 1937-77, and Scheduled, 1978-2011[a]

Applicable years	Maximum taxable earnings (dollars)	Tax rate (percent of taxable earnings)[a]							
		Employer and employee, each				Self-employed			
		OASI[b]	DI[c]	HI[d]	Total	OASI[b]	DI[c]	HI[d]	Total
1937–49	3,000	1.0	...	...	1.0	...	...	...	...
1950	3,000	1.5	...	...	1.5	...	...	...	...
1951–53	3,600	1.5	...	...	1.5	2.25	...	...	2.25
1954	3,600	2.0	...	...	2.0	3.00	...	...	3.0
1955–56	4,200	2.0	...	...	2.0	3.00	...	...	3.0
1957–58	4,200	2.0	0.25	...	2.25	3.00	0.375	...	3.375
1959	4,800	2.25	0.25	...	2.5	3.375	0.375	...	3.75
1960–61	4,800	2.75	0.25	...	3.0	4.125	0.375	...	4.5
1962	4,800	2.875	0.25	...	3.125	4.325	0.375	...	4.7
1963–65	4,800	3.375	0.25	...	3.625	5.025	0.375	...	5.4
1966	6,600	3.5	0.35	0.35	4.2	5.275	0.525	0.35	6.15
1967	6,600	3.55	0.35	0.5	4.4	5.375	0.525	0.5	6.4
1968	7,800	3.325	0.475	0.6	4.4	5.0875	0.7125	0.6	6.4
1969	7,800	3.725	0.475	0.6	4.8	5.5875	0.7125	0.6	6.9
1970	7,800	3.65	0.55	0.6	4.8	5.475	0.825	0.6	6.9

1971	7,800	4.05	0.55	0.6	5.2	6.075	0.825	0.6	7.5
1972	9,000	4.05	0.55	0.6	5.2	6.075	0.825	0.6	7.5
1973	10,800	4.3	0.55	1.0	5.85	6.205	0.795	1.0	8.0
1974	13,200	4.375	0.575	0.9	5.85	6.185	0.815	0.9	7.9
1975	14,100[e]	4.375	0.575	0.9	5.85	6.185	0.815	0.9	7.9
1976	15,300[e]	4.375	0.575	0.9	5.85	6.185	0.815	0.9	7.9
1977	16,500[e]	4.375	0.575	0.9	5.85	6.185	0.815	0.9	7.9
1978–80	...[e]	4.35	0.6	1.1	6.05	6.15	0.85	1.1	8.1
1981–85	...[e]	4.3	0.65	1.35	6.3	6.08	0.92	1.35	8.35
1986–2010	...[e]	4.25	0.7	1.5	6.45	6.01	0.99	1.5	8.5
2011 and later	...[e]	5.1	0.85	...[f]	...	6.0	1.0	...[f]	...

Sources: Same as table A-1.
a. Contribution rates provided by law but superseded before they became effective not shown.
b. Old-age and survivors insurance.
c. Disability insurance.
d. Health insurance.
e. Automatically determined by changes in the level of wages in covered employment.
f. Cost estimates for health insurance are limited to a twenty-five year period.

To finance the increased cost of this expansion, both the tax rate and the maximum taxable earnings base have been raised repeatedly. A comparison of the present maximum combined employer-employee social security taxes with the maximum under the original act indicates the magnitude of the increase—$1,930.50 in 1977 versus $60.00 in 1937.

Gradual evolution has produced a social security program far more complex than the simple retirement insurance program initiated in 1935. The result is an extensive system covering over 90 percent of employees and their families, and which in 1975 dispensed $70 billion in benefits and accounted for 25 percent of all federal revenues that year. An enormous program, it has and will continue to have great impact on all parts of the economy.

Index

Aaron, Henry J., 5n, 43n, 48n, 77n, 85n, 114, 127n
Abzug, Bella, 49n
Aged: health of, 69, 72–73, 137, 151; income transfer from working population to, 7; increasing proportion of, 110; labor force participation by, 69–71, 151; life expectancy, 78; welfare programs for, 3, 5, 9. *See also* Benefits, retirement; Benefits, social security; Earnings test; Retirement
Age requirements for benefits: arguments for extending, 78, 137; arguments for lowering, 76; cost of changing, 73, 78, 79
AME. *See* Average monthly earnings
AMIE. *See* Average monthly indexed earnings
Asset limitation, for SSI program, 9, 10, 141
Assets, effect of social security on accumulation of, 118
Average monthly earnings (AME): averaging of couples', 50; calculation of, 27–28; effect of overindexing on, 32; in PIA computation, 28–29
Average monthly indexed earnings (AMIE), 36–37

Ball, Robert M., 10n, 80, 81n, 94n, 96n
Bankers Trust Company study, 22
Barfield, Richard E., 72
Beneficiaries: compared with number of workers, 3, 103; dual, 15–16, 52, 135; net worth of, 122; percent of income consumed by, 113; Social Security Administration surveys of, 68–69, 121, 124; state supplements for SSI, 9, 141–42. *See also* Earnings test
Beneficiary unit, 135, 147
Benefits, retirement: civil service, 14;

private pension plans, 19–20, 23; railroad retirement system, 17; SSI, 10. *See also* Benefits, social security
Benefits, social security, 1, 6–7, 13; computation of, 26–30; criticism of spouses', 44–47; dependents', 7, 135; early retirement and reduced, 75–76; earnings test and, 29, 65–67; effect on saving, 114, 119, 121, 124; income redistribution from, 39–40, 84, 146–47; for late retirees, 78–79, 80, 83; methods for equalizing, 48–51; minimum, 38, 51–52, 135, 146–47; progressivity of structure for, 7, 29, 34, 39–40, 146, 147; proportional structure for, 40–42; taxation of, 29–30, 145, 148–49. *See also* Age requirements for benefits; Beneficiaries; Indexing; Overindexing
Bixby, Lenore E., 69n
Blind, SSI benefits for, 9
Blinder, Alan S., 120n
Boskin, Michael, 72
Bosworth, Barry, 125n
Bowen, William G., 71, 72
Break, George F., 120n
Break points, in benefit formula, 58, 59, 60, 61, 146
Brittain, John A., 88
Brody, Wendyce H., 49n
Buchanan, James M., 42n, 43n
Bureau of Labor Statistics, 63

Cagan, Phillip, 114, 115, 116, 117
California, SSI supplements, 141
Canada, social security trust fund, 132, 133
Capital: effect of social security on, 4, 97, 113, 153; projections, 125–26; rate of return on, 127, 128; social security trust fund to increase, 127
Carron, Andrew S., 125n